Special issue

The "Medieval" Undone:

Imagining a New Global Past

Edited by

Sierra Lomuto

boundary 2

an international journal

of literature and culture

Volume 50, Number 3

August 2023

Duke University Press

boundary 2

boundary 2
an international journal of literature and culture

Founding Editors   Robert Kroetsch and William V. Spanos

Editor   Paul A. Bové
Victoria Glavin, Assistant to the Editor

Managing Editor   Casey A. Williams

Editorial Collective
Jonathan Arac, University of Pittsburgh
Anthony Bogues, Brown University and University of Johannesburg
Paul A. Bové, University of Pittsburgh
Arne De Boever, California Institute of the Arts
Nergis Ertürk, Pennsylvania State University
Leah Feldman, University of Chicago
David Golumbia, Virginia Commonwealth University
Stathis Gourgouris, Columbia University
R. A. Judy, University of Pittsburgh
Kara Keeling, University of Southern California
Aamir R. Mufti, University of California, Los Angeles
Donald E. Pease, Dartmouth College
Bruce Robbins, Columbia University
Hortense Spillers, Vanderbilt University
Christian Thorne, Williams College

Editorial Board
Charles Bernstein, University of Pennsylvania
John Beverley, University of Pittsburgh
Rey Chow, Duke University
Colin Dayan, Vanderbilt University
Nuruddin Farah, Bard College
Margaret Ferguson, University of California, Davis
Anthony Grafton, Princeton University
Fredric Jameson, Duke University
Marcia Landy, University of Pittsburgh
Gayatri Spivak, Columbia University
Wang Hui, Tsinghua University, Beijing
Cornel West, Union Theological Seminary
Rob Wilson, University of California, Santa Cruz

Advisory Editors
Nancy Condee, University of Pittsburgh
Christopher L. Connery, University of California, Santa Cruz
Harris Feinsod, Northwestern University
Ruth Y. Y. Hung, Hong Kong Baptist University
Daniel Morgan, University of Chicago
Bécquer Seguín, Johns Hopkins University
Gavin Steingo, Princeton University
Henry Veggian, University of North Carolina, Chapel Hill
Lindsay Waters, Independent Scholar, Belmont, Massachusetts

Assistant Editors
Jason Fitzgerald, University of Michigan
Sierra Lomuto, Rowan University
Chris Taylor, University of Chicago

Contents

Belle da Costa Greene and the Undoing of "Medieval" Studies

Sierra Lomuto

Medieval studies is undergoing a disciplinary crisis. A field whose conventional purview is Europe's historical, literary, and cultural past from 500 to 1500 CE, its content of study predates the formation of the nation-state, racial capitalism, and European global imperialism, yet the ideological investments of modernity have nonetheless defined and shaped our access to this past. As the larger umbrella of the humanities confronts its exclusionary practices and structures within the university, from nationalizing linguistic departments to siloed curricular training, scholars must contend with a disciplinary formation that cultivates the hegemonic norms of

I am immensely grateful to the contributors of this volume for thinking with me about these issues; the privilege of reading and discussing their essays throughout the writing process helped sharpen my own perspective. I am also grateful to the librarians at the Morgan Library for their invaluable guidance on my research on Belle da Costa Greene, especially María Isabel Molestina. I am also grateful to Paul Bové for encouraging the project, Casey Williams for immense editorial support and compassion, Casey Wang for vital editing assistance, and the Rowan English department for generous feedback.

boundary 2 50:3 (2023)   DOI 10.1215/01903659-10472317   ©2023 by Duke University Press

European modernity. Medieval studies has not only propagated European history as white, cis-heteronormative, and Christian but also fostered an elite inaccessibility on the basis of esoteric specialization. Within the crisis of the humanities, medieval studies becomes a battleground: it is either a last priority because its inaccessibility masks its relevance to pressing concerns of the present, or it becomes a priority because it symbolizes tradition for those who want to hold onto Eurocentric narratives about the past.

Scholars have long recognized the colonial structures of medieval studies, but its consanguinity with white supremacist medievalism outside the ivory tower remained a peripheral topic in scholarly discourse until the August 2017 "Unite the Right Rally" in Charlottesville made it mainstream.[1] The visual display of Old Norse runes, "Celtic" crosses, and crusader flags at the white supremacist rally threw medievalists into a public relations crisis. It called them to task for not only their academic field's apolitical apathy but also its reification of the "Middle Ages" as a source for white heritage (Lomuto 2016; Kim 2017). In its aftermath, Jo Livingstone (2017), a journalist with a doctorate in medieval studies, wrote in the *New Republic* that the rally exposed the field's minimal awareness about the "history of medieval appropriation in the race discourse of the United States." However, since Charlottesville, discussions about white supremacist medievalisms have become so central to the field that the Medieval Academy of America addressed the issue while restructuring its bylaws (L. Davis 2021).

Medievalists now widely accept the complicity of the field in the popular understanding of the Middle Ages as a racially homogenous and isolated white space. In the first week of class, I often ask my students to find an image that reflects their vision of the Middle Ages and they *always without exception* share images of Europe and white people. They often share fantasy depictions, such as stills from *Game of Thrones* or a King Arthur adaptation, and sometimes dragons and elves, but I have not yet had a student share an image of a person of color. This whitewashed understanding of the Middle Ages has led the field to rebrand itself with the nomenclature of the global. An umbrella that aims to reach across the premodern world within and beyond Europe, it inevitably destabilizes the notion of what—and where—*medieval* signifies. The conceptual framework of a global Middle Ages stakes the claim that the Middle Ages happened not only in Europe

---

1. Kathleen Biddick (1998) argues that this separation between medieval studies as academic discipline and medievalism as external popular culture was the deliberate design of nineteenth-century scholars who created the discipline.

but everywhere around the world; thus, the framework opens up medieval studies, transforming it into a disciplinary space for research and knowledge production about any place between 500 and 1500 CE. This shift in the structural parameters of medieval studies has served institutional commitments to diversity, equity, and inclusion (DEI). But the Middle Ages is a category that exceeds that which it names in content; that is, it is not merely a time period that spans a thousand years of the past. As a historiographic category, *medieval* limits the interdisciplinary scope of the "medievalist" to European and premodern time.[2] Scholars have accepted the epistemological dissonance of "global medieval" and moved ahead anyway, citing the necessity for inclusion; however, an important question remains: can, or *should*, *medieval* continue to signify when discussing places outside of Europe?

Aamir R. Mufti's (2016: 11) excavation of world literature's entwined genealogy with Orientalism necessities an important query that elucidates the totalizing moves of medieval studies' global turn: "If 'Orientalism' is the cultural logic of the modern, bourgeois West in its outward orientation, what precisely is its relation to world literature, the concept of a single literary system or ensemble that, at least in theory, encompasses all the societies of the world?" His analysis of the imperial continuities of world literature resonates with how narratives of Western exceptionalism and Eurocentrism can remain housed within the global Middle Ages. *Medieval* ultimately points back to Europe and thus secures Europe's continuing presence even as it appears to recede within a global framework.

But the global Middle Ages can also offer a process of undoing rather than a destination. As Mufti (2016: 12) has asked, "Under what conditions exactly—methodological, conceptual, and institutional—can the practices of world literature be revalued and refunctionalized for a radical critique of our world?" The contradiction of making the "medieval" global exposes its walls, to use Sara Ahmed's metaphor for the phenomenological practice of diversity work. This exposure undoes the "medieval," and this undoing can help produce new ways of knowing. Undoing the "medieval" is not a rejection of the term or a call for its replacement, but a process of reformulating epistemologies and recalibrating perspectives on the past and its relation to the present. Geraldine Heng (2022: 29–31) has persuasively made the point that, particularly for global medieval literature, the concepts of world litera-

---

2. For a genealogy of this construction, see Davis and Altschul 2009; Ingham and Warren 2003.

ture and global literature differ. Whereas world literature, Heng argues, can merely amalgamate disparate texts under a hegemonic lens, global literatures necessarily capture interconnectivities across cultures that open themselves to the work of uncentering the world. The use of "medieval" serves the important role of a shared vocabulary that can facilitate interdisciplinary exchange, a concession on our way to progress and change within existing institutional structures. Heng's foundational work in the global Middle Ages demonstrates a path toward the undoing of the "medieval," for its impetus is the undoing of Eurocentric historiographies and temporalities.[3] However, if the global Middle Ages moves forward as a DEI rebrand and not a mode of undoing, far from transforming the field, it may in fact make anew the Orientalist frameworks that have accompanied the field all along. Medievalists can learn from what Mufti has shown about the concept of world literature, how "the cultural and social logics which . . . we have called Orientalism, continue to structure [its practices], even when in transformed and updated forms that do not allow the continuities to be perceived immediately as such" (19).

To offer context for the debates about the "medieval" that this special issue presents, in the introductory essay that follows I examine the link between medieval studies and white supremacist medievalism, and then explore two meeting points that illustrate both the field's current crisis and the necessity of interdisciplinary dialogue. I argue that as the field confronts white supremacist medievalism and pushes for a global turn, it exposes the unsustainability of the epistemologies, methodologies, and discourses that have buttressed the formation of the "medieval." The first meeting point concerns the obvious incompatibility of the global medieval turn within the English department, which creates a fissure that cracks open the colonial logic that still lays claim to both English literature and medieval studies. This collision invites the medievalist to reorient the function of medieval literature in the English canon from one of nationalist origin to one that introduces multilingual genealogies. The second meeting point turns to how the field's recuperation of Belle da Costa Greene, the founding librarian of the Pierpont Morgan Library and the first Black fellow of the Medieval Academy of America, inadvertently exposes the Orientalism that still lurks within the global Middle Ages. The business of undoing is varied, and the essays collected here reflect a range of approaches and perspectives on this process.

---

3. See also Young and Finn 2022, who develop the concept of "global medievalism," storytelling practices in popular culture that resist the colonialist systems and racist logic embedded within the construct of the Middle Ages.

Collectively, they demonstrate the necessity for not only speaking across disciplinary boundaries and periodization but also taking stock, reflecting, and imagining possibilities that may not ever be possible but offer progress in their imagining.

Whose Appropriation?

In 2019, Fordham University Press published a collection, *Whose Middle Ages?*, as a corrective to the field's glaring lack of scholarly discourse on white supremacist medievalism (Albin et al. 2019). Books by Helen Young (2016), Andrew B. R. Elliott (2017), and Daniel Wollenberg (2018) had already shown the necessity of this conversation, but Charlottesville created a wave of interest that drew the attention of scholars who had previously overlooked the topic. Social media and news outlets erupted in discussion about what scholars should do about white nationalists' appropriation of the Middle Ages. Public historians of the period agreed that they could intervene by delivering a more diverse picture of the medieval past, and *Whose Middle Ages?* emerged with the aim to do just that. The collection introduces the period to students and other nonexperts while also foregrounding how white supremacist movements throughout various points in history, such as the Nazi regime, used the Middle Ages to corroborate their fantasies about white purity and superiority. The editors invited David Perry, a journalist and former professor of medieval history, to write the introduction because he had used his considerable social media presence to fashion himself the leader of this discourse. However, I have argued elsewhere that Perry's public writing reflected public relations concerns—an investment in the public perception of white medievalists more than the experience of those targeted by white supremacy (Lomuto 2019, 2020).[4] His introduction and the structure of the collection itself captures a similar ethos. In my blurb for the book, I wrote that the collection is "a valuable teaching resource [that] will inspire necessary discussions about the politics of engaging the past in the present." But what the collection does not offer is an overt recognition that the reason the Middle Ages has resonated so easily within these racist ideologies is because of its significance as a historiographical category that is, in fact, inextricably bound with white supremacy,

4. Mary Rambaran-Olm 2022 shows how these investments underscore Perry's own book, *The Bright Ages*, co-authored with Matthew Gabriele, in a review that became the center of a highly publicized social media discussion (Schuessler 2022).

anti-Semitism, and Islamophobia. The perspective of *Whose Middle Ages?* regenerates the age-old myth that racism is borne of ignorance instead of a strategic product of the educated elite.

Certainly, sinister ideologies in the modern era have used specific aspects of the medieval past that have nothing to do with white supremacy, such as Norse mythology or the "Celtic" cross; and the notion that medieval Europe was racially homogenous and can emblematize modern fantasies of white ethnonationalism is just that: a fantasy. However, to speak of the "appropriation of the Middle Ages" raises an important question with serious implications for the future of the field tasked with studying it. What does it mean to appropriate a *time period*? And from *whom* is it being appropriated? The meaning of the Middle Ages resides within a specifically Eurocentric timescale that cannot be understood in isolation from its inherent ideologies of white supremacy: it is a modern historiographical category irrevocably bound to "rise of the West" narratives and their concomitant investments in modernity and white heritage production. The Middle Ages is both the barbaric past of a civilized modern Europe and the cradle that ushered Europe's exceptionalism into being.

The Middle Ages has belonged to white supremacists throughout its development; and thus it is not *their* appropriation of the Middle Ages we are currently witnessing, because you cannot appropriate what already belongs to you. Kathleen Davis and Nadia Altschul (2009: 1–2) have called out the iterative construction of the category of the medieval, explaining that it "came as a function of European colonization. . . . The Middle Ages, like many other periodizations, acquired its defining characteristics and apparent solidity over the course of several centuries, in concert with political, economic, nationalistic, and territorial efforts that included those of colonialism." And in her monograph *Periodization and Sovereignty*, Davis (2008) details the colonial violence of periodization that the "medieval" wields. With the display of Old Norse runes by the neo-Nazis at Charlottesville, we are witnessing the natural evolution of this construct's deployment within white supremacist ideology, and at the same time we are experiencing a disciplinary transformation in which it is the medievalist scholar who aims to appropriate "the medieval" for something to which it has never belonged: a discipline detached from—and even resistant to—the white supremacist ideology of European exceptionalism.[5]

5. This scholarly appropriation of the "medieval," the move to transform the concept into a neutral historiographical category, is not new. Joachim Kurtz's (2018) description of

Although Charlottesville now serves as the watershed moment that thrust the field into crisis and galvanized its scholars toward change, that moment arrived with the force of a movement because of the groundwork of medievalists who have long agitated this politically dormant field. In the late 1990s and early 2000s, a series of books and edited collections developed the subfield of postcolonial medieval studies, in which there were two distinct yet overlapping branches: one that tackled the field's complicity with colonial systems (including that of the university) and one that transgressed the traditional borders of what counted for "medieval" topics. Much of this work was comparative, interdisciplinary, and transgressive. Although the more institutionally appealing global medieval studies has since replaced it, this subfield nonetheless helped create the conditions of possibility for our current moment of internal reckoning and potentially productive instability. The intention here is not to excavate origins but to suggest that the current crisis has been brewing for decades, producing insight along the way. Scholars such as Kathleen Davis and Nadia Altschul as well as Kathleen Biddick, Jeffrey Jerome Cohen, Jacqueline de Weever, John Ganim, Geraldine Heng, Patricia Clare Ingham, Ananya Jahanara Kabir, Sharon Kinoshita, Barbara Lalla, Kathy Lavezzo, María Rosa Menocal, Michelle R. Warren, and Deanne Williams, among others, laid the foundation for current discourses that place white supremacist medievalism in relation to the field itself, for their work has shown the politics of the field and the important role that medievalists hold in not only making the medieval but also undoing it.

The Global Middle Ages and the English Department

In a recent essay in *boundary 2*, Joe Cleary (2021: 145) traces the colonial history of the English department and writes:

> If the expansion of the English language across the globe and the morphology of English literature departments have now grown so familiar as to appear wholly unremarkable, it is important to remember that neither the dominance of "global English" nor the current

---

the Middle Ages as a "colligatory concept" illustrates how "medieval" can come to mean a middle period, such as in the case of Chinese historiography, that does not inherently return to a Eurocentric gaze. However, such usage means the "middle" periods across the globe do not always match up synchronically to achieve the aims of interconnectivity sought by the "Global Middle Ages."

structures of English departments were ever inevitable; there are histories to both. The more self-critically aware we are of the contingent nature of the present fundamentals of the English department, the more we may be open to changing things in the future, if change indeed is what literary scholars want.

Cleary argues that the crisis of the English department in an era of "global English" stems as much from external circumstances such as student enrollment and the contraction of the humanities as it does from the inadequacy of its internal structures. Cleary's injunction invites an examination of the place of medieval literature in the English department.[6]

Kathleen Biddick's 1998 monograph *The Shock of Medievalism* revealed that the Early English Text Society (EETS) was founded in 1864 with the explicit aim of using the apparatus of historical research to authorize the imperial dominance of English. The EETS founders made the unequivocal statement, "We are banded together to trace out the springs, and note the course, of the language that shall one day be the ruling tongue of the world, which is now the speech of most of its free men" (quoted in Biddick 1998: 93). Biddick's research exposed how the field of medieval studies developed within the nationalist and imperialist agendas of the modern university. She shows how language and literature departments incorporate medieval literature as a foundation for their colonial structures. *Beowulf,* for example, became the beginning of the English canon, and EETS disseminated their modern editions of Middle English literature in India's colonial education system before they made their way into England's curriculum (Lampert-Weissig 2010: 27). In French, *La chanson de Roland (The Song of Roland)* became "a precocious assertion of French national sentiment [that] performed important cultural work as the Third Republic strove to overcome the humiliation of the Franco-Prussian War and formalize its colonization of Algeria" (Kinoshita 2006: 15). This structure of literary study asks medievalists to sublimate the multilingualism of our research materials and present them to students as a buttress for nationalist, imperialist, and monolingual understandings of culture and belonging (Hsy 2013). Doing so entrenches the idea that it was not until Europe set sail for conquest that the world was in motion—or existed at all.

As a maneuver away from these epistemologies, English depart-

---

6. These debates are already happening; notably, the University of Leicester cut its English language and medieval studies program in January 2021 (Jagot 2021).

ments have rapidly embraced the global turn in medieval studies. From an institutional vantage point, global medievalist positions serve DEI aims insofar as they enable a diversified syllabus and may even cultivate a more diverse faculty. But global medievalists in English departments are still in English departments; that is, they still teach within the parameters of a nationalist linguistic structure that is tethered to a white and male-dominated English literary canon. However diverse the reading list, these courses ultimately circle back to English, even if only in the linguistic form in which their global medieval texts are delivered to students or, because of the nature of major and minor requirements, in the points of reference students make to other texts in their curricular background. Thus, a global medieval English framework cannot simply deliver global literatures of the premodern world; doing so ignores what we already know about the imperializing moves of global literature: "For all its claims to inclusiveness, it cannot quite conceal the asymmetrical arrangement of power that structures it as an apparatus and a field" (Mufti 2016: 5). Instead, the global Middle Ages in an English department demands an inward-facing critique of the legacies of race and imperialism that medieval English was formed to reproduce and buttress within the Western academy.[7] This meeting point presents a productive instability for the future of both fields and of other disciplines that coalesce around myths of linguistic nationalism.

Global narratives about the Middle Ages speak back against the very construction of history that the "medieval" helped form: the idea, that is, that *modern* Europe, and its epistemologies of whiteness, is the birthplace of cultural and scientific invention, of artistic and intellectual genius. The "global turn" explores new methods of teaching and research that focus not only on Europe, or even the diversity of medieval Europe, but also on the global significance of a flourishing world outside Europe whose economic, intellectual, and cultural advancements far outpaced Europeans. It has drawn into the field some of history's most influential empires, such as the Mali, Mongol, and Khmer. As medievalists demonstrate how the Middle Ages was a time not of European isolation but of global trade and cross-cultural exchange—evidenced through art, architecture, literature, religion, and material goods—they contravene the notion of the "Middle Ages."

This epistemological project repositions not only space but also time within our construction of history. Geraldine Heng (2014) has argued that

---

7. See also Momma 2012, which details how modern philology shaped the study of English literature within a context of English imperialism.

a global Middle Ages activates a framework of overlapping temporalities through which multiple modernities materialize and thereby counter the myth of modern European exceptionalism. At the same time, Sylvie Kandé (2009) has made the case that although the notion of an "African Middle Ages" asserts the inclusion of Africa's precolonial history within a European timescale that systematically and maliciously erased that history, it nonetheless necessitates Africa's inclusion in world history on Europe's terms—and those terms have consequential limitations. To the extent that a "global medieval" framework requires Europe's presence and its timescale, it forecloses the possibility of necessary frameworks that eschew Europe entirely.

Global has become a shorthand term for diversity and inclusivity, where it stands opposed to isolationism; and when thinking especially about the Middle Ages, that isolationism readily translates into white supremacist rhetoric and myths of white heritage. So the "global Middle Ages" signals an inclusive Middle Ages where the whole world—not just Europe—is represented. But as Mufti (2016: 13) has argued about world literature, "hidden inside [it] is the dominance of globalized English." The global has a perspective. In *Reading the Global*, Sanjay Krishnan (2007: 1) intervenes in the trend toward taking the "global" as an empirical concept that describes "a transparent comprehension of the world"; he argues that

> the global describes a mode of thematization or a way of bringing the world into view. It does not point to the world as such but at the conditions and effects attendant upon institutionally validated modes of making legible within a single frame the diverse terrains and peoples of the world. A "global perspective" ought not simply be taken to mean that the world is grasped in its entirety but should alert the reader to the way in which the world is constituted—rendered visible and legible—through a particular style of perspectivizing that is as useful as it is dangerous. (4)

Krishnan's analysis, crucially, calls for a critical reading practice when taking a global frame. A central question driving any such project must be, From whose perspective is the "global" world being seen?

Thus, what is the perspective instituted by the fusion of *global* and *medieval*? A global Middle Ages can unmask the colonial gaze that the politics of periodization obscures. As a practice, not a system or "one-world talk," to use Mufti's formulation of the ongoing imperialism of global frameworks, the global Middle Ages can make the perspective of medieval studies the *object*, not subject, of critique. It can expose the colonial, racial logic that has underscored and sustained knowledge about the past and its use within modernity's hegemonic structures. The global Middle Ages could be a Eurocentric gaze on the world that reformulates itself within the language and apparatus of the modern liberal university (Melamed 2011, Ferguson 2012), or it could be an entry into that gaze to destroy it from the inside out, an option that yet hovers with Audre Lorde's prudent warnings about the "master's tools."

The opening of Biddick's essay "Bede's Blush: Postcards from Bali, Bombay, Palo Alto," included in *The Shock of Medievalism*, builds from Umberto Eco's insight that medievalists are dreaming the Middle Ages, dreams that are "midway between Nazi nostalgia and occultism" (quoted in Biddick 1998: 83). These dreams, Biddick argues, began in the Renaissance and have since become a nightmare:

> In their sleepwalking, humanists invented a Middle Ages as a place and time of non-origin and formed an identity essentially informed by a claim of what it was not. Nation-states of the nineteenth century, in contrast, produced a place and time, a Middle Ages, to stage the cultural origins of the "Western animal" (Eco's term). At the end of the twentieth century, such overdetermined constructs of the Middle Ages haunt medieval studies as a double bind of origin and non-origin. (83)

Medievalists are still caught in this double bind. Some are what Biddick calls "pastists"—those who treat the past as a bounded period radically different from modernity—and some are what she calls "presentists"—those who hold up a mirror to the Middle Ages and ask it to reflect histories of our modern or postmodern identities. These two camps, she suggests, "debate over the epoch in which to locate radical 'past' alterity instead of questioning desires for such a boundary as an effect of specific historiographic metanarratives" (83). In other words, what would happen if we stopped treating the Middle Ages as a *pre*-modern space of either absolute difference or contiguous reflection, and started thinking of it as a construct in which the national and imperial formations of the nineteenth century are ever-present?

If the Middle Ages are a dream, a fantasy—a nightmare—that engenders white European, cis-heteropatriarchal, Christian superiority, then it is time to wake up. Speaking specifically about the field of early American literature, but germane to medieval studies as well, Joanna Brooks (2006: 319) has posed the question, "Do the stories we tell about the past have the power to call us into a new relationship with the present?" To narrate the past is to create the present and open up the future. However, it is not only stories of a premodern past that medievalists must tell but modern stories too. The historical figure of Belle da Costa Greene has emerged in recent years as a celebration of the field's diversity and a symbol for its commitment to future inclusion and equity. But Greene's story also shows how white heritage production and Orientalism were part of the development of medieval studies and integral mechanisms in its process of becoming.

Belle da Costa Greene:
Racial Passing and a Global Medieval Archive

The Pierpont Morgan Library in Manhattan helped establish medieval studies in the United States, and it still offers one of the most extensive archives of medieval manuscripts. I was fortunate to visit the Morgan during the summer of 2019, when I called up M. 723, a fourteenth-century French manuscript from Picardy that contains Hayton of Armenia's *La fleur des histoires d'Orient* and Marco Polo's *Le livre des merveilles d'Asie*. M. 723 is a European manuscript, but one that captures the interconnected world of medieval Eurasia as well as extensive Mongol-European relations. It falls within a "global medieval" framework, and it has been at the Morgan since 1927. As I carefully turned each page of this beautifully illuminated codex, careful not to rub the ink or crease the vellum, I was astounded to turn to 68r and find its entire right-side column covered in the writing of a modern hand. On the left-side column of 68r is the medieval scribe's copy of Hayton of Armenia's Colophon, neatly written across twenty-three of the column's twenty-six lines. On the right-side column is a full translation in modern English, likewise spanning the same number of lines so that the original text and its translation appear neatly together, in parallel fashion. "Translation" is written at the top, a header to what follows. The next three folios are blank (68v–69v), but then 70r once again presented me with modern handwriting, prominently displayed: in the center of the folio, underlined, reads "Marco Polo / Le Livre des Merveilles d'Asie" followed by a loose translation: "(The Book of Messer Marco Polo)"—a title page for the medieval text! To view modern handwriting in a medieval manuscript, particularly one so carefully preserved at so prestigious an institution, is a shocking experience. However, I soon learned to whom this modern hand belonged, and it no longer seemed surprising. The hand belonged to the woman who purchased the manuscript and, almost one hundred years ago, prepared it for researchers precisely like myself: Belle da Costa Greene, the librarian and director who helped found the Morgan Library and built its original archive.

Belle da Costa Greene was a luminary in the rare book world of the first half of the twentieth century. In 1905, J. P. Morgan hired Greene, who was at the time working at the Princeton University library, to catalog and purchase rare books, manuscripts, and art for his personal collection. Her curatorial expertise turned this collection into a world-renowned public library for research, and she became one of the most important librarians in modern American history. A note in the *Times Literary Supplement* (1949: 436) about the library's twenty-five-year anniversary celebration since opening to the public credits and praises Greene for the collection: "It is in [Greene's] honour that this rich and various selection has been put on show; and this is no formal compliment, for these acquisitions bear testimony to her judgement, knowledge, practical abilities and above all her sense of quality." In fact, this entire notice about the anniversary celebration is about Belle Greene even though it is titled "A Great Institution," a testament to just how synonymous they were. She came to define the Morgan Library by the time she retired in 1948, and her presence is still important to visitors today. The library's audio tour tells visitors that Greene was "known as the soul of the Morgan Library," and her name serves as the example entry on the sign-in sheet in the reading room: she has a prompt 4:00 p.m. sign-out time, when the reading room closes each weekday. In July 2019, a bronze bust of Greene created by the artist Jo Davidson was installed next to the fireplace in the East Room. Greene thus continues to reside within the library with an honor that respects the centrality she held during her lifetime.

Greene also holds a place of significance within medieval studies. In 1939, the Medieval Academy of America (MAA) inducted her as a fellow, an elected membership granted "to honor major long-term scholarly achievement within the field of Medieval Studies."[8] While Greene had a wide range of intellectual interests, her archive reflects a particular commitment to the Middle Ages. In her festschrift, a massive volume of five hundred pages and nearly four hundred images edited by Dorothy Miner (1954), about half of the articles focus on medieval subjects. In fact, Greene's unprecedented work at the Morgan coincided with the formation of medieval studies in the United States: the MAA was founded in 1925, only one year after the library became public in 1924. She not only curated extensive medieval manu-

8. See "Fellows and Corresponding Fellows," Medieval Academy of America (website), https://medievalacademy.org/page/fellows (accessed April 1, 2023).

scripts but made them accessible to scholars in ways that aided the expansion of medievalist research. Notably, Hope Emily Allen, a famous medievalist known for her work on Margery Kempe, wrote to Greene asking for her help on an edition of Wynkyn de Worde's *Treatise of Love*.[9] Greene also collaborated with Max Farrand, her counterpart at the Huntington Library, to devise systems that would make their materials accessible to students who "cannot afford to 'go East' or 'go West,'" a collaboration she thought would "prove that both libraries have passed beyond the merely 'collectors' state, and are now interested, mainly in making their important original material available to serious students wherever located."[10] Her interests were not in antiquarianism (as they had been for Morgan) but in scholarly research.

Greene's incredible contribution to the field—and historical research more broadly—has warranted her a place of honor within the MAA, and in recent years, her racial identity has also prompted discussions about the field's past diversity and its commitment to inclusion and equity in the present. Greene lived her public life as a white woman, but her Black heritage was confirmed by historian Jean Strouse in her 1999 biography of J. P. Morgan, published about fifty years after Greene's death in 1950. She was born into a prominent family in the Black community of Washington, DC, in 1879. Her mother was Genevieve Ida Fleet Greener, a pianist and music teacher. Her father was Richard T. Greener, the first Black man to graduate from Harvard College and a well-known activist for civil rights during Reconstruction. According to historian Heidi Ardizzone (2007), Greene began to pass for white as early as eight years old, soon after the family moved to New York in 1887. Richard was often away for work and his relationship with Genevieve became increasingly strained, leading to divorce in 1897. Ardizzone has surmised that as she became more estranged from her husband and the color line became increasingly rigid in the 1880s, Genevieve gradually turned away from her Black social circles and started to live as white. By 1900, Genevieve and her children had dropped the final *R* of *Greener* in all official documents, giving them a new name that would have separated them from Richard and his continued prominence in the Black community. Ardizzone suggests that they started using this name as early as 1894, when Greene was fifteen. Greene and one of her brothers also added

9. Hope Emily Allen to Belle da Costa Greene, March 27, 1940, Director's Files, 1903–1948, Box 1374, Morgan Library and Museum, New York.
10. Belle da Costa Greene to Max Farrand, November 17, 1930, Director's Files, 1903–1948, Box 1367, Morgan Library and Museum, New York.

"da Costa," a Sephardic surname that helped them fashion a Portuguese ancestry that could account for their darker complexion.[11] Born Belle Marian Greener, she lived most of her life Belle da Costa Greene.

Medievalists now celebrate her as the first Black fellow of the MAA. In 2018, Nahir Otaño Gracia spearheaded efforts to institute a scholarship fund specifically for medievalists of color, and the MAA named it in Greene's honor. The following year, Tarrell Campbell organized the Belle da Costa Greene conference at his home institution of Saint Louis University, which featured three prominent medievalists as keynote speakers, themselves all women of color: Monica Green, Seeta Chaganti, and Dorothy Kim. Shavauna Munster (2019) reflected on her experience at the conference, writing, "discussions regarding scholars who have overcome adversity and have succeeded in making their voices heard are indispensable to medievalists of color, like myself, who have occasionally felt their work was not pertinent to the field due to that lack of representation." In a predominantly white field like medieval studies, Munster's words resonate with my own experience as a mixed-race Asian American scholar. Medievalists of color can often feel like outsiders who must prove we belong not only in terms of expertise but because of our identities, too. But when I visited the Morgan in 2019 and stood in Greene's original office, the magnificent North Room with two levels of rare books, ornate ceiling paintings, and a bust of Boccaccio on the mantel, I was struck with a sense of connection that translated into belonging.[12] Knowing that a pivotal influence on our field was, in fact, a Black woman has had significant impact on medievalists of color. Particularly for Black scholars in the field, she is a hidden figure whose celebration within the MAA makes a powerful statement about resistance and achievement in the face of US anti-Black racism.

At the same time, Belle Greene's prominence as a symbol for diversity also exposes "the walls" of exclusion, to return to Ahmed's metaphor, that continue to enclose medieval studies, particularly in relation to the global turn. Within Greene's archive at the Morgan, we can glimpse how her curatorial choices sought to apprehend a diverse, global world, while also aiding a white Euro-American heritage project. In William Courtenay's

11. Greene's choice of the name Da Costa seems significant, as it connects her to the Jewish diaspora and particularly the history of the Conversos (Bodian 2008).
12. I am grateful to Christine Nelson, who was the Drue Heinz Curator of Literary and Historical Manuscripts at the time, for offering me a personal tour of the library and Greene's office.

(1982: 20) article on the growth of medieval studies in America between 1870 and 1930, he describes the European scholars who came to the United States before and during World War II; he explains that what they found "in the universities, colleges, and institutes of America [was] a world in which the Middle Ages were studied and appreciated not only as a period in its own right but as part of the cultural past of America." As Courtenay articulates here, the formation of medieval studies in the United States imported European culture as a heritage with elite status.[13] One need only stand in the original entrance of the library to see this dynamic. The foyer, known as the Rotunda, transports visitors to Renaissance Italy, which was Morgan's goal: there are grand marble columns and a marble floor, for example, and blue and white stucco reliefs based on the Villa Madama in Rome, designed by Raphael. Belle da Costa Greene's project at the library was to help build a cultural institution in the likeness of European cultural institutions, imbuing a comparable intellectual and aesthetic value that Europe held (and still holds) in the American imaginary.

Medieval England was of particular significance to Morgan. Circling the ceiling of the East Room, the original main library, are roundels depicting allegorical figures that represent the arts and sciences as well as portraits of historical men who represent various contributions to Western culture. In the roundel dedicated to the printing press is a portrait of William Caxton, not Gutenberg. In fact, it was Greene's purchase of sixteen of Caxton's early print books that secured her position as Morgan's private librarian and launched her reputation as a powerful player on the rare books and manuscripts circuit. In 1908, only two years into her job, she went on her first trip to Europe for a book auction of Lord Amherst's personal collection, which included the coveted Caxton editions. Through a savvy and skillful negotiation before the auction even began, she convinced Amherst to sell these gems to her privately, successfully swooping in on established book dealers with years more experience.

Although the medieval collection Greene curated was mostly European, it was not exclusively so. In other words, you would not have found (then or now) a collection of medieval manuscripts reflecting a fantasy of racial homogeneity or European isolation. Many of the manuscripts, including M. 723, would merit inclusion in bibliographies for archival research on the global Middle Ages. For example, in 1912, Greene acquired M. 500,

13. See Miyashiro 2019 for a discussion about how this use of the Middle Ages was part of the US settler-colonial project.

a thirteenth-century bestiary that Ilkhan Ghazan, the ruler of the Mongol Ilkhanate of Persia, commissioned around 1295. In Greene's festschrift, Richard Ettinghausen (1954: 460) credits Greene with the acquisition, writing, "Miss Greene's unerring eye has provided us not only with a magnificent series of paintings, but also with the earliest Persian binding so far found to which an exact date can be attributed." In 1911, Greene purchased an important collection of ninth-century Coptic manuscripts that reflect the history of Christianity in Egypt.[14] And the last item she acquired before her retirement in 1948 was an illuminated Gospel Book from Ethiopia (M. 828).

If this archive contributed to the development of an American medieval studies as a heritage discipline, then what does it mean that a *global* Middle Ages held a role in that process of (white) heritage production? Although this archive does not reflect a fantasy of racial homogeneity or European isolation, it does capture a fantasy of Western dominance. The myth of European superiority, which emerged through the apparatus of modernity, rests on the desire for—and ownership over—the non-European world. Part of the importation of European culture to an elite American institution like the Morgan Library is the importation of an *apprehended* non-European world, whose histories and cultures are working in service of the development of an American culture imbued with an imperial—not geographically isolated—European heritage. In other words, the global medieval archive here, included within the heritage of an American medieval studies, is steeped in Western colonialism.

The correspondence between Greene and Charles Read, who was the curator at the British Museum and who guided her through the acquisition of the Coptic manuscripts, exposes these larger geopolitics that contextualize that acquisition. Read writes to Greene, "They [the dealers] first made sure that the mss would not be seized by the British government, as stolen out of Egypt, as of course they were."[15] His remark here is a crucial reminder that the colonial gaze of Orientalism inflected the development of the American medieval archive. It is not Asia and Africa that matter in the acquisition of these materials but rather their *use* within the archive, which could turn, to use Edward Said's (1978: 115) own words, "vast geographical domains into treatable, manageable, entities." Within the Orientalist

---

14. See Achi 2018 for more about this significant acquisition at the Morgan.

15. Charles Read to Belle da Costa Greene, December 3, 1911, ARC 1310: Morgan Collections Correspondence, Charles Hercules Read file, Morgan Library and Museum, New York.

gaze, "directly dealing with Oriental source material . . . helped a European to know himself better" (117). Rather than the erasure or dismissal of the non-European world, a desire for and apprehension of that world under-scores Greene's collection of medieval manuscripts and its significance in the heritage project of a nascent American medieval studies—and this process has implications for the production of whiteness.

Greene's inscriptions in M. 723 reflect her deep commitment to the study of the Middle Ages—indeed, to a *global* Middle Ages: as the librarian, she is guiding the researcher through the manuscript, insuring that we can follow its contents. She also wrote small pagination marks in the corners of many of the library's manuscripts, a point Dorothy Kim analyzed in her key-note at the Belle da Costa Greene conference. As recounted by Munster (2019), Kim argued that these corner markings "can be viewed simply as categorization notes or as a literal attempt by Greene to mark her place in a history that is largely Eurocentric." The inscriptions I stumbled upon in M. 723 further evidence Kim's supposition, but they are not on the peripheral edges of the folio; they are in the column where the medieval scribe would have written. To write directly and so extensively in the manuscript reflects her confident ownership over it. In his memorial to Greene, Curt F. Bühler (1957: 643) refers to the Morgan Library as "HER library," and indeed so too were the manuscripts. Her handwriting delivers her expert scholarship alongside the hand of a fourteenth-century scribe whose writing passes along the words of a fourteenth-century author. Through her direct inscrip-tions in the manuscript, Greene is inscribing herself into an elite, white American culture, one that would have excluded her had she not passed for white. She is claiming ownership over what she believed was that elite white culture's heritage. M. 723 thus confronts the reader with the layers of mean-ing that accrete through time as these materials come into our purview.

The valuable manuscripts that she curated, in the library she built, reflect a medieval past that held significance in Greene's present. Her hand-writing in M. 723 is a material illustration of the way we stamp the past with ourselves, how we cannot ever remove ourselves from the meaning we make, the knowledge we produce, in our archive. But this entanglement goes both ways: just as we make the past, the past makes us. Examining Greene's inscription compelled me to think about how she—and her par-ticular racial identity—matter to this encounter. The phenomenon of racial passing in the twentieth-century United States directly exposes the insta-bility of race, while also inherently pointing to the sociopolitical investment in its fixity (an insistent attachment to biology, the body, visibility). Passing captures both the elusive nature of race and the desire for racial order at once. As Anne Anlin Cheng (2019: 14) has put it, "Race is a dream of embodiment that speaks, paradoxically, through abstract forms." Greene exposes how racial formations are contingent, unstable, and reliant on external relations—and that even medieval manuscripts could play a role in one's self-constitution.

Greene's relationship to her archive is one of racial becoming—through the materiality of her manuscripts, she adopts and affirms an inclusion into whiteness. Likewise, so too can the medievalist replicate this racial becoming. I would like to suggest that as Greene's own identity emerges within the present encounter with her archive, the instability of racial formations presents itself as a crucial point of analysis for parsing the implications of a global medieval turn today. The fact of unstable racial formations means that whiteness is potentially always up for grabs: one can become white—not just in appearance but also *in service*. Even a global Middle Ages, a concept whose aim is certainly to counter white Eurocentrism, can work in service of the white Euro-American hegemony. Mufti (2016: 90) offers medievalists a productive guidepost for approaching the global in our field: "Far from being mutually exclusive ideological formations, Anglicist and Orientalist ideas and practices coexisted productively in the cultural and educational institutions inaugurated by colonial power."

The "Medieval" Undone

The global Middle Ages can undo the coherence of the "medieval" and thereby the coherence of medieval studies; from there, other formations that have held it together or been held *by* it—such as the English department—become undone as well. This turn exposes the obsolescence of the structures and methods that have defined the discipline, and we cannot merely patch up their inadequacies with a wider geographic scope. But how do we do this work of undoing when we are doing it within the very framework we are trying to undo? This is the question many medievalists are grappling with. Demonstrating the necessity of branching out beyond strictly academic spaces, Dorothy Kim and Mary Rambaran-Olm have led important discussions across social media and other public forums about white supremacist medievalism and its continuing hold on medieval studies (Kim 2016, 2017, 2019a; Rambaran-Olm 2018, 2019; Rambaran-Olm and Wade 2021). Rambaran-Olm's (2021: 388) scholarship has also demonstrated how periodization "operates within the framework of white supremacy, prompting scholars to view time both episodically and linearly rather than as a complex web."[16] In a special issue of *New Literary History*, Rambaran-Olm models the historical analysis she calls for, in which she weaves together an analysis of "how BIPOC scholars have often been erased from Early English studies" (393) and her research on two early medieval figures—Hadrian and Archbishop Theodore of Canterbury—who both migrated to England (from Africa and Tarsus, respectively) and had significant influence on its cultural development, but whose non-European origins scholars have sublimated to produce narratives of English exceptionalism.

An emergence of special journal issues (among others, see Whitaker 2015; Kim 2019a; Bychowski and Kim 2019; Andrews and Beechy 2020; Rambaran-Olm, Leake, and Goodrich 2020) has contributed peer-reviewed scholarship that pushes the bounds of the field to include critical theories previously dismissed as anachronistic to the period (see also Wade 2022). For example, Tarren Andrews's special issue of *English Language Notes* explores the compatibility—or incompatibility—between medieval studies and critical Indigenous studies (see also Duperron and Edwards 2021). Andrews (2022: 2) emphasizes that any collaboration between these fields must begin with medievalists slowing down and "extending invitations" to Indigenous scholars, being careful not to appropriate and to consider "the ethics of kinship and reciprocity that we owe Indigenous peoples, places, and communities who have labored to craft Indigenous studies as an academic field." Andrews pinpoints the way scholars will jump to show inclusion without the care such collaboration requires.

Within a cluster of essays in the *Cambridge Journal of Postcolonial Literary Inquiry* that centers the work of Geraldine Heng, Seeta Chaganti (2022: 126) calls for medievalists to "act in solidarity with fields that have formed themselves in the crucibles of radical missions," and she focuses specifically on the multiple fields that constitute critical ethnic studies. She makes the crucial point that "solidarity means looking beyond the invention of a better medieval studies" because, she argues, what this work of transforming the field ultimately requires is the work of "transforming the world" (130). Matthew Vernon (2018), Cord Whitaker (2019), and Jonathan Hsy (2021) have examined how appropriation of the Middle Ages has oper-

16. The special issue in which Rambaran-Olm's essay appears is a publication emerging from the RaceB4Race colloquium, hosted at the Arizona Center for Medieval and Renaissance Studies under the leadership of Ayanna Thompson, which advances research on race in medieval and early modern studies, conducted particularly by scholars of color.

ated not only as a force for white supremacism but as a resistance practice within communities of color. Their work shows how medievalism serves as a site of racial conflict wherein white supremacist oppression regenerates yet also meets resistance. This push and pull within medieval studies has mobilized the crisis within the field, generating a productive conversation about where we go from here.

The essays in this present special issue join these medievalists to examine how the current crisis can move us forward. They take up the question of what the "medieval" itself does—and impedes—as a category around which to formulate knowledge production. The collection begins with a question: "*Cui Bono*: Who Is the 'Medieval' For?" The first three essays explore how, as a historiographical category, the usefulness of the "medieval" has clear limits. Raha Rafii (2023: 44) opens the section with the crucial reminder that the concept of a Middle Ages serves "a progressive history that culminate[s] in a phase called the European Enlightenment and 'modernity,'" one in which non-Western societies exist frozen in time, in a barbaric and backward past "where they deviate from notions of 'appropriate' social and political development, often in relation to an adequately 'secular' public sphere." Rafii offers a critical analysis of "Islamic history" as it exists as an epistemological construct of Western academic study. She shows how both "Islamic" and "medieval" function as binaries to modernity, co-constituting the notion of "Western civilization" within a model of progressive history. Rafii thus argues that the starting point for parsing the extension of the global Middle Ages to Islamic studies—the concept of an Islamic "medieval" period—should focus on how "academic institutions, colonialist and neo-imperialist geopolitics, and neoliberal market forces have long instrumentalized the nature of knowledge produced about Muslims" (34). Orientalism remains the structural lens of the Western academy in which studies of Islam and Muslims have fueled persistent and ongoing Islamophobic violence, from the US invasion of Iraq to Narendra Modi's Hindu nationalist policies in India. Rafii makes clear that the "medieval" benefits narratives of civilizational progress and Western subjectivities, the solution to which lies beyond the Western academy and its models of knowledge production.

Julie Orlemanski's essay steps inside the institutional investments of a scholarly journal, *postmedieval: a journal of medieval cultural studies*, to consider what advantages "medieval" may bring to an undoing of Western knowledge production. From her embedded vantage point as an editor of the journal, Orlemanski traces its history as it emerged from a working group, BABEL, which was formed specifically to push back against the field's traditional epistemologies. In tracing this genealogy, she shows how a transgressive movement at the edges of the field inched its way to the center but, in so doing, came to work in service of academia's capitalist structures. Orlemanski (2023: 72) thus explores what is still possible from within that space, acknowledging the challenge that "to be *postmedieval* is simultaneously to undo the medieval and to propagate it. It is to draw others into the time frame of the West even as we try to warp and crack the grid." She poses the possibility that, when confronted through critical exploration, "terms like *global, the Middle Ages,* and *theory* can be catalysts to confront the Eurocentrism, transnational flows of capital, dominance of English, and politics of time that make those words significant for us" (79). To remain within the institutions of the Western academy is to never "escape from what we critique, [because] we are also constituted by it" (79), but the unsettledness that such critique, generates, Orlemanski argues, is the next step forward within a discipline tethered to the corporate university and its historical foundations of colonialism.

Michelle R. Warren's (2023: 85) essay looks far into the future—ten thousand years—to consider what the "medieval" means when *our now* has long receded into a new middle period between "the beginning and the possible end of human civilization." Warren shows how, from the perspective of geologic time and the inevitable effects of our climate crisis, the concept of a "long now" readily links us in the second millennium to those in the first and the fourth. Undoing periodization undoes time, but, as Warren considers, does it undo its politics and colonial complicities? Warren analyzes the Long Now Foundation, a tech project founded in the 1990s that created the 10,000-Year Clock and the 10,000-Year Library, to argue that tech medievalism "creates a retrofuturist framework for 'the long now' in which the medieval is both precedent and prediction" (85). Warren's analysis reveals the ways in which the medieval features at various points to both project the colonialism of time on the distant future and install connections across vast temporal distances that can eliminate the imperializing notion of anachronism.

In the second part, "Disciplinary Dilemmas," three essays explore deeply ingrained disciplinary formations and epistemologies that have shaped the study of medieval literary and cultural histories, and likewise pose barriers to forging new methods of study. To parse the emergence of the global Middle Ages as a salve to medieval studies' Eurocentrism, Adam Miyashiro turns to debates already staged in the field of comparative literature about the Eurocentrism of "world literature." He enjoins medieval-ists to excavate lessons already learned outside of medieval studies and to take seriously the impossibility of situating medieval literature and objects of study within disciplinary frameworks founded on nationalism, monolingual-ism, and geographic isolation. As he demonstrates that the trade networks of the medieval Mediterranean reached as far as northern Europe, and how material evidence reveals contact between the economies of the Abbasid Empire and the kingdom of Mercia, Miyashiro also reveals the necessity for medievalists to expand their citational practices beyond medieval studies. He ends his essay with a proposal not merely to redefine the borders of periodization but to critique their political motivations. He argues that mak-ing the Middle Ages a global concept "reinscribes traditional narratives of modernity that European colonial encounters in subsequent centuries have defined" (Miyashiro 2023: 118). He thus asks the question at the core of our current disciplinary dilemma: "How can medievalists break out of the Euro-centrism endemic to the contemporary study of the Middle Ages?" (118). He suggests that one methodology is to eschew periodization entirely and follow the networks that have shaped the materials of our study, however far—in time and space—they take the scholar.

However, as Shokoofeh Rajabzadeh details in her essay about her experience as a doctoral student with precisely these aims of breaking free of disciplinary limitations for the sake of epistemological integrity, pushing for these changes comes at a deep personal cost with no promise of return. Her advocacy work at the University of California, Berkeley, taught her unexpected lessons about how medieval studies sustains its exclusionary structures. Her efforts to expand the medieval studies program to include courses on Arabic language and literature, and training in areas such as postcolonial theory and critical race studies, were met with resistance not only from the professors who governed the curriculum but also her peers. Her analysis leads her to the conclusion that "it is in that *middle* space, where students are not yet professionals but also no longer strictly students, where the disciplining of the 'middle' is determined" (Rajabzadeh 2023: 143). Her essay also reveals how it is, ironically, the crisis in the humanities that causes medievalists to cling to the field as it has been rather than view it as an occasion for transformation so that the study of this interconnected past continues and is not lost to the commodification of higher education.

Christopher Livanos and Mohammad Salama's (2023) essay, which follows Rajabzadeh's, shows precisely why the disciplinary changes that Rajabzadeh was calling for in her graduate program have implications for scholarship both within and beyond medieval studies. They examine the harmful persistence of a Biblicist approach to scholarly analyses of the Qur'an, a method borne out of Islamophobic medieval Christian exegesis, which they attribute to the connection between the European Middle Ages and the modern university. Their analysis reveals how the work of Peter the Venerable, a twelfth-century Benedictine Abbot of Cluny, and other anti-Muslim polemicists created the earliest translations of the Qur'an, which continue to influence the anti-Muslim sentiment that permeates contemporary studies of the Bible in the Western academy. They thus demonstrate how central medieval texts are to contemporary studies. As a Christian-focused and Eurocentric field, medieval studies has not intervened in the continued influence of Peter the Venerable, and crusade ideologies more broadly, on scholarly engagement with the Qur'an. If medievalists intend to globalize and transform the field's Christian-Eurocentrism, then they must contend with how anti-Muslim medieval commentaries and translations of the Qur'an have filtered into our current academic systems. If Euro-medievalists viewed Arabic and Islamic studies as equally important linguistic and historical contexts for their studies, a core point Rajabzadeh made to her colleagues, they could disrupt the Islamophobic methodologies that persist not only in medieval studies but other fields as well—in this case, Qur'anic studies.

The final section, "Critical Possibilities," answers the call of Miyashiro's essay to eschew periodization. Medieval studies has traditionally excluded or marginalized critical theories that have emerged and developed to elucidate modernity's systems of power because of their anachronist application to premodernity, a period before Europe's global imperial dominance, racial capitalism, and the formation of the nation-state. However, the medieval-modern divide is itself the result of Eurocentric epistemologies, and these three essays demonstrate how medieval materials deepen and nuance concepts such as Orientalism and race once our scholarly methods no longer tether them to modernity—or parameters defined by periodization. Periodization can stagnate our capacity to theorize while also reifying the white Eurocentric hold on scholarly inquiry. Opening modern critical theories to premodern contexts begins to crack the epistemological foundation that has so thoroughly bound white Eurocentrism and modernity.

Mariah Min's essay elucidates how the long history of Christian Europeans racializing Jewish people in the Middle Ages informs the anti-Semitism of Nazi ideology. She argues that this history is relevant beyond the academy, which she demonstrates in her opening discussion of Whoopi

Goldberg's comments on *The View*, whose understanding of race led her to mistakenly claim that the Holocaust was not about race. Turning to the Chaucer classroom, where medievalists are eager to include voices of color to diversify a white syllabus but not necessarily to interrogate white epistemologies, Min (2023: 184) argues that critical attention to race is the only way "to appreciate the sharpness of [this work's] critical teeth." She makes a case against the concept of "medieval race studies" because its boundedness gives "license to regard the nonmedieval . . . as peripheral," when it is the present that offers ways of seeing the past (184).

Anne Le (2023: 190) takes up a similar problem with the concept of "medieval Orientalism," which "entrenches the medieval-modern divide, an epistemological barrier" that cuts off historical texts from contributing to the development of modern theory. Although medievalists have successfully revealed the way that medieval literature presents the Christian West and Muslim East in a relationship not of binary opposition but of ambivalent interchange, they have not contextualized this ambivalence as a tool of Orientalism; instead, it has served to show how these texts were *not* Orientalist. Le turns to a medieval French text to make the case that the characteristic ambivalence between the Christian protagonist and his relationships with his Muslim adopted mother (later wife) and peers shows how, in fact, ambivalence underscores the way medieval French literature advanced a discourse of Latin Christian supremacy. She argues that post-Saidian theories of Orientalism have likewise shown the machinations of ambivalence in Orientalist discourse; thus, she makes the point that scholarly dialogue across the medieval-modern divide would aid the development of theories of Orientalism for both medievalists and nonmedievalists alike.

Shoshana Adler's essay explores the critical insight that queer theorists can bring not only to local interpretations of medieval poetry but also to how we understand emotional attachments across disparate temporalities. Adler (2023: 213) uses the medieval figure of the leper, a symbol that "marks historical distance" while also generating "emotional recognition," to expound the affective conditions that drive the recursive histories of white supremacist medievalism. She argues that "circuits of desire" (213) animate white supremacists' attachment to the Middle Ages as white heritage, and thus queer theory offers a promising framework for tackling the problem. If emotional attachment underscores the connection between the medieval past and white supremacists, then it stands to reason that merely correcting the historical record is not a sufficient response from scholars. Adler demonstrates how the concept of "spoiled history" in queer studies, in which cherished objects become de-idealized without displacement, offers a paradigm for medievalist scholars who, she argues "are uniquely positioned to produce attachment genealogies of a period whose special status *needs* spoiling" (218).

Elizabeth J. West concludes "The 'Medieval' Undone: Imagining a New Global Past" with an afterword that both reflects on its collected essays and explores its implications for her research in Africana studies. West shows how her investigations into the lives of enslaved Africans and African-descended peoples in the Americas led her to the pre-1500 history of the Temne people in West Africa, who experienced forced removal and migration trauma during the expansion of Islam in the Middle Ages. West's foray into "global medieval" histories, she argues, enriches our present understanding of the impact of cultural DNA on how enslaved Africans experienced the Middle Passage and the development of generational trauma. For West (2023: 243), global medieval studies has opened new epistemological pathways for exploring how "Africans arrived *tabula inscripta* to the shores of the Americas from their forced voyages across the Atlantic" in ways that continue to hold significance. West also suggests, as she reflects on the conversations generated through these essays, that even if it is impossible to "dismantle the embedded racist epistemology that is the master tool of Western intellectualism, part of the struggle is to not leave it uncontested" (245). Contesting and challenging from within, West reminds us, constricts the spaces for its institutional regeneration.

These eleven essays, including the introduction and afterword, raise questions about disciplinary formation and the productive possibilities that emerge through crisis. The authors work across different disciplines and fields, but each intersects with medieval studies, and together they show the necessity for building critical frameworks and methodologies that reimagine medieval studies as not, to return to Biddick's (1998: 16) words, "a discipline based on expulsion and abjection and bound in rigid alterity, but one permeable to the risk of futurity." The present crisis requires interdisciplinary collaboration and risk-taking: to imagine a new global past is to imagine a new, unbounded present, one open to the possibility of an obsolete "Middle Ages," a concept undone by our own epistemological progress.

References

Achi, Andrea. 2018. "Illuminating the Scriptorium: The St. Michael Collection and Monastic Book Production in the Fayyum Oasis, Egypt during the Ninth and Tenth Centuries." PhD diss., New York University.

Adler, Shoshana. 2023. "Spoiled History: Leprosy and the Lessons of Queer Medieval Historiography." In Lomuto 2023: 211–32.

Albin, Andrew, Mary C. Erler, Thomas O'Donnell, Nicholas L. Paul, and Nina Rowe, eds. 2019. *Whose Middle Ages? Teachable Moments for an Ill-Used Past.* New York: Fordham University Press.

Andrews, Tarren. 2020. "Indigenous Futures and Medieval Pasts: An Introduction." In Andrews and Beechy 2020: 1–17.

Andrews, Tarren, and Tiffany Beechy, eds. 2020. "Indigenous Futures and Medieval Pasts." Special issue, *English Language Notes* 58, no. 2.

Ardizzone, Heidi. 2007. *An Illuminated Life: Belle da Costa Greene's Journey from Prejudice to Privilege.* New York: Norton.

Biddick, Kathleen. 1998. *The Shock of Medievalism.* Durham, NC: Duke University Press.

Bodian, Miriam. 2008. "Hebrews of the Portuguese Nation: The Ambiguous Boundaries of Self-Definition." *Jewish Social Studies* 15, no. 1: 66–80.

Brooks, Joanna. 2006. "Working Definitions: Race, Ethnic Studies, and Early American Literature." *Early American Literature* 41, no. 2: 313–20.

Bühler, Curt F. 1957. "Belle da Costa Greene." *Speculum* 32, no. 3: 642–44.

Bychowski, M. W., and Dorothy Kim, eds. 2019. "Visions of Medieval Trans Feminism." Special issue, *Medieval Feminist Forum* 55, no. 1.

Chaganti, Seeta. 2022. "Solidarity and the Medieval Invention of Race." *Cambridge Journal of Postcolonial Literary Inquiry* 9, no. 1: 122–31.

Cheng, Anne Anlin. 2019. *Ornamentalism.* Oxford: Oxford University Press.

Cleary, Joe. 2021. "The English Department as Imperial Commonwealth; or, The Global Past and Global Future of English Studies." *boundary 2* 48, no. 1: 139–76.

Courtenay, William J. 1982. "The Virgin and the Dynamo: The Growth of Medieval Studies in North America, 1870–1930." In *Medieval Studies in North America: Past, Present, and Future*, edited by Francis G. Gentry and Christopher Kleinhenz, 5–22. Kalamazoo, MI: Medieval Institute.

Davis, Kathleen. 2008. *Periodization and Sovereignty.* Philadelphia: University of Pennsylvania Press.

Davis, Kathleen, and Nadia Altschul, eds. 2009. *Medievalisms in the Postcolonial World: The Idea of "the Middle Ages" outside Europe.* Baltimore, MD: Johns Hopkins University Press.

Davis, Lisa Fagin. 2021. "MAA News." *Medieval Academy Blog*, June 3. https://www.themedievalacademyblog.org/maa-news-from-the-executive-director-5/.

Duperron, Brenna, and Elizabeth Edwards. 2021. "Thinking Indigeneity: A Challenge to Medieval Studies." *Exemplaria* 33, no. 1: 94–107.

Elliott, Andrew B. R. 2017. *Medievalism, Politics, and Mass Media: Appropriating the Middle Ages in the Twenty-First Century.* Suffolk, UK: D. S. Brewer.

Ettinghausen, Richard. 1954. "The Covers of the Morgan Manafi Manuscript and Other Early Persian Bookbindings." In *Studies in Art and Literature for Belle da Costa Greene,* edited by Dorothy Miner, 459–73. Princeton, NJ: Princeton University Press.

Ferguson, Roderick A. 2012. *The Reorder of Things: The University and Its Pedagogies of Minority Difference.* Minneapolis: University of Minnesota Press.

Heng, Geraldine. 2014. "Early Globalities, and Its Questions, Objectives, and Methods: An Inquiry into the State of Theory and Critique." *Exemplaria* 26, nos. 2–3: 234–53.

Heng, Geraldine. 2022. "The Literature of the Global Middle Ages." In *Teaching the Global Middle Ages,* edited by Geraldine Heng, 27–47. New York: Modern Language Association of America.

Hsy, Jonathan. 2013. *Trading Tongues: Merchants, Multilingualism, and Medieval Literature.* Columbus: Ohio State University Press.

Hsy, Jonathan. 2021. *Antiracist Medievalisms: From Yellow Peril to Black Lives Matter.* Leeds: Arc Humanities.

Ingham, Patricia Clare, and Michelle R. Warren, eds. 2003. *Postcolonial Moves: Medieval through Modern.* New York: Palgrave Macmillan.

Jagot, Shazia. 2021. "Students from All Backgrounds Need Access to the Literature of Every Age." *Times Higher Education,* January 31. https://www.timeshigher education.com/blog/students-all-backgrounds-need-access-literature -every-age.

Kandé, Sylvie. 2009. "African Medievalisms: Caste as a Subtext in Ahmadou Kourouma's Suns of Independence and Monnew." In Davis and Altschul 2009: 301–24.

Kim, Dorothy. 2016. "The Unbearable Whiteness of Medieval Studies." *In the Middle,* November 10. https://www.inthemedievalmiddle.com/2016/11/the-unbearable -whiteness-of-medieval.html.

Kim, Dorothy. 2017. "Teaching Medieval Studies in a Time of White Supremacy." *In the Middle,* August 28. www.inthemedievalmiddle.com/2017/08/teaching -medieval-studies-in-time-of.html.

Kim, Dorothy, ed. 2019a. "Critical Race and the Middle Ages." Special issue, *Literature Compass* 16, nos. 9–10.

Kim, Dorothy. 2019b. "White Supremacists Have Weaponized an Imaginary Viking Past." *Time,* April 12. https://time.com/5569399/viking-history-white -nationalists/.

Kinoshita, Sharon. 2006. *Medieval Boundaries: Rethinking Difference in Old French Literature.* Philadelphia: University of Pennsylvania Press.

Krishnan, Sanjay. 2007. *Reading the Global: Troubling Perspectives on Britain's Empire in Asia*. New York: Columbia University Press.

Lampert-Weissig, Lisa. 2010. *Medieval Literature and Postcolonial Studies*. Edinburgh: Edinburgh University Press.

Le, Anne. 2023. "Different and Familiar: *Les enfances Renier* and the Question of Medieval Orientalism." In Lomuto 2023: 189–209.

Livanos, Christopher, and Mohammad Salama. 2023. "A Bridge Too Far? Ludovico Marracci's Translation of the Qur'an and the Persistence of Medieval Biblicism." In Lomuto 2023: 145–69.

Livingstone, Jo. 2017. "Racism, Medievalism, and the White Supremacists of Charlottesville." *New Republic*, August 15. https://newrepublic.com/article/144320/racism-medievalism-white-supremacists-charlottesville.

Lomuto, Sierra. 2016. "White Nationalism and the Ethics of Medieval Studies." *In the Middle*, December 5. https://www.inthemedievalmiddle.com/2016/12/white-nationalism-and-ethics-of.html.

Lomuto, Sierra. 2019. "Public Medievalism and the Rigor of Anti-racist Critique." *In the Middle*, April 4. https://www.inthemedievalmiddle.com/2019/04/public-medievalism-and-rigor-of-anti.html.

Lomuto, Sierra. 2020. "Becoming Postmedieval: The Stakes of the Global Middle Ages." In Rambaran-Olm, Leake, and Goodrich 2020: 503–12.

Lomuto, Sierra, ed. 2023. "The 'Medieval' Undone: Imagining a New Global Past." Special issue, *boundary 2* 50, no. 3.

Melamed, Jodi. 2011. *Represent and Destroy: Rationalizing Violence in the New Racial Capitalism*. Minneapolis: University of Minnesota Press.

Min, Mariah. 2023. "Undoing Medieval Race Studies." In Lomuto 2023: 173–88.

Miner, Dorothy, ed. 1954. *Studies in Art and Literature for Belle da Costa Greene*. Princeton, NJ: Princeton University Press.

Miyashiro, Adam. 2019. "Our Deeper Past: Race, Settler Colonialism, and Medieval Heritage Politics." In Kim 2019a: 1–11.

Miyashiro, Adam. 2023. "Race, Medieval Studies, and Disciplinary Boundaries." In Lomuto 2023: 107–21.

Momma, Haruko. 2012. *From Philology to English Studies: Language and Culture in the Nineteenth Century*. Cambridge: Cambridge University Press.

Mufti, Aamir R. 2016. *Forget English! Orientalism and World Literatures*. Cambridge, MA: Harvard University Press.

Munster, Shavauna. 2019. "Conference Spotlight: Celebrating Belle da Costa Greene at Saint Louis University." *Medieval Academy of America Graduate Student Committee Newsletter* 11, no. 1.

Orlemanski, Julie. 2023. "What Is 'Postmedieval'? Embedded Reflections." In Lomuto 2023: 57–81.

Rafii, Raha. 2023. "Making Islam (Coherent): Academic Discourse and the Politics of Language." In Lomuto 2023: 33–55.

Rajabzadeh, Shokoofeh. 2023. "Fighting for the Middle: Medieval Studies Programs and Degrees within Higher Education." In Lomuto 2023: 123–44.

Rambaran-Olm, Mary. 2018, "Anglo-Saxon Studies [Early English Studies], Academia, and White Supremacy." *Medium*, June 27. https://mrambaranolm.medium .com/anglo-saxon-studies-academia-and-white-supremacy-17c87b360bf3.

Rambaran-Olm, Mary. 2019. "Misnaming the Medieval: Rejecting 'Anglo-Saxon' Studies." *History Workshop*, November 4. https://www.historyworkshop.org .uk/misnaming-the-medieval-rejecting-anglo-saxon-studies/.

Rambaran-Olm, Mary. 2021. "A Wrinkle in Medieval Time: Ironing Out Issues Regarding Race, Temporality, and the Early English." *New Literary History* 52, nos. 3–4: 385–406.

Rambaran-Olm, Mary. 2022. "Sounds About White: Review of Matthew Gabriele and David M. Perry's *The Bright Ages* (Harper Collins, 2021)." *Medium*, April 27. https://mrambaranolm.medium.com/sounds-about-white-333d0c0fd201.

Rambaran-Olm, Mary, M. Breann Leake, and Micah J. Goodrich, eds. 2020. "Race, Revulsion, and Revolution." Special issue, *postmedieval* 11, no. 4.

Rambaran-Olm, Mary, and Erik Wade. 2021. "The Many Myths of the Term 'Anglo-Saxon.'" *Smithsonian Magazine*, July 14. https://www.smithsonianmag.com /history/many-myths-term-anglo-saxon-180978169/.

Said, Edward W. 1978. *Orientalism*. New York: Pantheon.

Schuessler, Jennifer. 2022. "Medieval Scholars Spar on a Modern Battlefield: Twitter." *New York Times*, May 6. https://www.nytimes.com/2022/05/06/arts/medieval -race-twitter.html.

"A Great Institution." *Times Literary Supplement*. July 1, 1949, p. 436.

Vernon, Matthew X. 2018. *The Black Middle Ages: Race and the Construction of the Middle Ages*. New York: Palgrave Macmillan.

Wade, Erik. 2022. "Skeletons in the Closet: Scholarly Erasure of Queer and Trans Themes in Early Medieval English Texts." *ELH* 89, no. 2: 281–316.

Warren, Michelle R. 2023. "The Medieval of the Long Now." In Lomuto 2023: 83–103.

West, Elizabeth J. 2023. "Afterword: In and beyond the Boundaries of Medievalism." In Lomuto 2023: 233–46.

Whitaker, Cord, ed. 2015. "Making Race Matter in the Middle Ages." Special issue, *postmedieval* 6, no. 1.

Whitaker, Cord. 2019. "The Middle Ages in the Harlem Renaissance." In Albin et al. 2019: 80–88.

Wollenberg, Daniel. 2018. *Medieval Imagery in Today's Politics*. Leeds: Arc Humanities.

Young, Helen. 2016. *Race and Popular Fantasy Literature: Habits of Whiteness*. New York: Routledge.

Young, Helen, and Kavita Mudan Finn. 2022. *Global Medievalism: An Introduction*. Elements in the Global Middle Ages. Cambridge: Cambridge University Press.

Part 1. *Cui Bono*: Who Is the "Medieval" For?

Making Islam (Coherent): Academic Discourse and the Politics of Language

---

Raha Rafii

Medieval studies is at a moment of reckoning. The current battle over its role in white supremacist ideology,[1] playing out on a massive public scale as whitewashed fantasy "medieval" epics and revived medieval European imagery, has created an urgent insistence by some Euro-medievalist scholars to reexamine its Eurocentrism in light of a "Global Middle Ages" (Young 2019; see also, for example, Heng 2021; Holmes and Standen 2018: 1–2; Frankopan 2019: 5–10). At first glance, an expanded "Middle Ages" that diversifies the concept of the "medieval" would appear to be an obvious solution by simply including a wider swath of cultures, geographies, and societies. However, the parameters of a "global" Middle Ages remain undefined; in more limited terms, it can range from an analysis of the interaction of non-European cultures with "medieval Europe," to an inclusion of disparate non-European cultures that fall within the "medieval period" in order

---

1. Such roles include the creation and justification of the racialized category of "Anglo-Saxon" that is "often reconstructed to include fictitious narratives to promote political messages of patriotism, imperialism, or racial superiority" (Rambaran-Olm 2019).

boundary 2 50:3 (2023)   DOI 10.1215/01903659-10472331   ©2023 by Duke University Press

to get a "wider" sense of the world.[2] Alternatively, it can refer to installing a "Middle Ages" within a society's own history that does not necessarily correspond temporally to the European Middle Ages (Heng 2021: 23). Regardless, the notion of expanding the "Middle Ages" on a global scale does not actually address the problem of the existence of a European "Middle Ages" in the first place, which requires an interrogation of its role in establishing the supremacy of Europe as the model of social progress and modernity. Such an analysis is crucial in light of extending the "Global Middle Ages" to teaching Islamic history, or to even speak of an Islamic "medieval" period.

Unraveling the role of the "medieval" in European history, along with the development of a European Christian identity in contrast to that of an amorphous Islamic "Orient," is crucial to understanding why the concept of any "Middle Ages" is never a neutral one. Furthermore, the conceptualization of an academic Islamic "medieval" period, particularly in the English-speaking world, has not unfolded in a linear trajectory. Rather, it exists within a matrix in which academic institutions, colonialist and neo-imperialist geopolitics, and neoliberal market forces have long instrumentalized the nature of knowledge produced about Muslims. The authority wielded by academic institutions, and the university in particular, enabled such institutions to function as sites for the production and vindication of Orientalist scholarship as well as its weaponization. As such, the periodization of "Islamic history"—including but not limited to a "medieval" Islamic period—created an identifiable, essentialized, Sunni-normative and Arabocentric "Islam" that was the opposite of "modernity." Islam, Muslims, and Islamic history were thus permanently enclosed in a "medieval" age characterized by violence and backwardness; subsequently, US foreign policies and post–September 11 defense funding would both exploit and influence the academic study of Muslims and this linkage to "medieval" violence.

Despite previous attempts at highlighting the methodological prob-

2. For example, in 2019 the Medieval Academy of America held its annual meeting with the theme of "The 'Global Turn' in Medieval Studies" (MAA 2019). However, its scheduling of "Global Ages" and non-European presenters and panels in parallel time slots significantly reduced the audience for these panels. Although its journal *Speculum* revised its submission guidelines in 2021 to more evenly include "European, Arabic, Byzantine, Hebrew, and Slavic studies," the use of "Arabic" still indicates an "inclusion" relevant only to certain areas of Western Europe. See "Guidelines for Submissions," Medieval Academy of America (website), https://www.medievalacademy.org/page/submission_guideline (accessed July 1, 2022).

lems of the periodization and geographic delimitations of Islamic history, university teaching and hiring practices continued to reinforce Orientalist approaches to Islamic history, thus assuring their persistence. The university, although far from the only institution engaged in problematic dynamics, is thus implicated at multiple points in this matrix; in fact, its role in validating and perpetuating the Orientalist scholarship that was produced in justification of, and in tandem with, European colonialist administration is inextricable. Orientalist scholarship exists within a colonialist dynamic of subjugating Muslim societies to comparison, classification, and evaluation with regard to Eurocentric norms. In this respect, Orientalism retains a structural power imbalance in which the Muslim "Other" has become an object of academic study; such knowledge is then weaponized to govern the colonial subject, engage in detailed polemics to undermine Islamic modes of authority, and engender a mode of "objective" authority to narrate civilizational decline or backwardness. More subtly, the creation of an authoritative "expertise" on Islam and Muslims through Orientalist scholarship has resulted in the utilization of the academic history of Islam as a mode of violence, both epistemological and physical.

Through this institutional system, Orientalists[3] and their heirs accrue social capital as "experts" in defining the parameters of Islam and Islamic history in order to weaponize them in service against racialized Muslim groups and societies. To this effect, the renowned Orientalist and Columbia University professor Joseph Schacht took the stand in 1964 as an expert witness to argue against Malcolm X that the Nation of Islam was not a normative Muslim, and therefore religious, organization (Felber 2017). On an even broader scale, Princeton University Orientalist Bernard Lewis (1990), despite his academic specialization in premodern textual studies, exploited his credentials to write sweeping and Islamophobic articles about a range of contemporary Muslim-majority societies, push for the US invasion of Iraq, and entrench the neoconservative exploitation of Islamic and Middle East

3. Zachary Lockman (2010: 68, 79–80) traces the founding of "modern" Orientalism to the Arabist Silvestre de Sacy (1758–1838) and notes the influence of Ernest Renan (1823–1892) on the "Semitic" characterization of Islam. The Anglophone tradition of Orientalist scholarship on "Islamic civilization," and the Arabic juristic tradition in particular, is based heavily on the work of nineteenth-century Orientalists compiling sources and writing in English, German, French, and Dutch, such as Christiaan Snouck Hugronje, Ignaz Goldziher, Theodor Nöldeke, D. S. Margoliouth, Reinhart Dozy, and M. J. De Goeje. One can find more names in the first edition of Brill's *Encyclopaedia of Islam*, with a similar Arabic and philological focus (Hodgson 1974: 40).

studies.[4] While unimaginable death and destruction would rain upon Iraqis in their own homeland for decades, Lewis continued to violently shape US foreign policy until the ripe old age of one hundred and one (van Bladel 2020: 168; Gardner 2018). Whether individual scholars produce scholarship with these goals explicitly in mind or not makes little difference; the colonialist— and, later, neo-imperialist—institutions that give authority to Orientalist scholarship entrench it in uneven power dynamics in which the West is granted an "objective" authoritative status regarding Muslims and their societies. The apologist emphasis on mere scholarly interest and engagement only serves to distract from academic Orientalism's role as the justifying ideology of violent European colonialism. Understanding the persistent nature of these dynamics means that scholars producing knowledge about Muslims must reckon with the Euro-Christian polemical roots of academic Orientalism. Such a reckoning includes the transition of Orientalist scholarship to the academic discipline of "Islamic history," which Western scholars created as a foil for "Western civilization."

The Conceptualization of "Islamic History"

The centering of institutionalized learning is fundamental to understanding the academic history of Islam as a history of unsettled layers. The fact that I am saying "academic" and writing in English implies the context of the "West," which, in turn, contains the idea of "European civilization."[5] How-

4. Lewis was the Founding Chairman of the Association for the Study of the Middle East and Africa (ASMEA), which holds its own conference and publishes its own journal. The officers and staff have strong links to the military and conservative or hawkish US policy think tanks; see "ASMEA Officers," ASMEA (website), https://www.asmeascholars.org /asmea-officers (accessed July 1, 2022); "Academic Council," ASMEA (website), https:// www.asmeascholars.org/academic-council (accessed July 1, 2022).
5. Kevin van Bladel (2020: 152–54) discusses the rise of the term *civilization* in nineteenth-century Europe (referring to European civilization) as a way to account for "all the major patterns of human history" and its later application to "Islamic civilization." Furthermore, "Europe" itself is a construct, built on Hellenic notions of cultural otherness and not physically distinct from Asia as a continent in any geographic sense. The designation "Europe," as opposed to Northwest Asia, is very much a sociopolitical construct meant to create a contradistinction to non-European, non-Christian, and/or nonwhite societies. However, as Anthony F. Aveni (1989: 8–9) noted, the concept of "the West" can expand this sociopolitical context to the "industrialized Americas, and the background cultures out of which have sprung present ideas, attitudes, customs, and patterns of behavior—those traits that lead us to think of all these aforementioned people as

ever, this idea does not extend to all of "Europe," a concept with fuzzy borders; rather, it draws from its northwestern regions, and by extension, a specific cultural and Christian heritage that would eventually beget scientific racism and colonialist subjugation, post-Enlightenment "modernity," and the concept of the modern university itself. This particular development creates the illusion of objectivity, of cold, hard logics, of impartial truths—of "History." The implied universality of the concept of history is further evident in the naming of the discipline of "philosophy of history," in which unmarked history or History with a big *H* refers to the European context as foundational, if not primary. Whereas anything Western is multivarious, detailed, and nuanced, "Islam"—itself a concept with shifting boundaries—is a black box. It has to be, because "Islam" has been the very concept against which logic, modernity, and "the West" is defined. To impose the academic concept of history on "Islam" to match Orientalist norms of "civilization," "progress," and "decline" only adds a scientific veneer to mere constructs. It is to render ideas and events relating to Islam either reductive or strange, but always as merely poor copies of other "Near Eastern" prototypes.[6] Islam thus becomes an object of inquiry that only the Western scholar is able to survey, categorize, and determine from an analytically objective standpoint.[7] Yet despite the constructed and problematic nature of these concepts—"Europe," "Western," "Near East," "Islamic," "history"—the entrenchment of these terms in both academic and popular discourse, along with the poverty of conceptual alternatives that are widely coherent, necessitate utilizing the terms even in critique of them. As Geraldine Heng (2021: 22) observed, "all attempts at naming the past thus pointed to the inescapability of the conceptually and politically freighted nature of the

---

essentially 'the same'"; at the same time, it can also be restricted to "Anglo-Franco-Hispanic" European cultural contexts.

6. Although the revisionist approach to Islamic history has roots in the work of earlier Orientalists, it is most closely associated with John Wansborough in modern academic Islamic studies. For relatively recent examples, see Donner 2012; Powers 2009, 2014; see also what is perhaps the most well-known example in the last few decades, Crone and Cook 1980.

7. Western epistemologies are not limited to the geographic regions of the so-called West but include anywhere Western academic epistemologies are practiced, rewarded, and invested in. This phenomenon is also evident in its appropriation by non-Western intellectuals, such as the discussion of different "golden ages" in Islamic history and the "evolution of civilizations" by the nineteenth-century Ottoman Levantine intellectual Jurjī Zaydān (Ogle 2015: 143).

language we had to use in order to participate in academic discourse"; this inescapability also points to the limits of what such discourse can attain within an academic framework.

The issue of the "medieval" or "Middle Ages" in Islamic history thus cannot be understood outside of the framework of both *Islamic* and *history* as slippery terms themselves. The acknowledgment of the problematic nature of the term *Islamic*, which tends to define Muslim activity and thought primarily through a limited canon of religious texts, has led to several scholarly attempts at circumventing the term. Some of these attempts can result in ethnonationalist histories that essentialize Islamic history to Arabs and Arabic cultural production instead, including influential texts such as Philip K. Hitti's *A History of the Arabs* and Albert Hourani's *A History of the Arab Peoples*. Acknowledging the problematic nature of "Arab" and "Arabic" as a solution in place of "Islamic," the University of Chicago's Marshall Hodgson was one of the few historians to critically evaluate the discipline of "Islamic history" in depth over fifty years ago. Hodgson (1974: 40–41, 31) focused his analysis on the problematic prevalence of Arabic-centric, text-based approaches to Islamic studies and inadequate frameworks of analysis for "cultural forms for studying the pre-Modern cities societies." His coinage of the term *Islamicate* created a distinction, albeit unexplained, between "religion" and "culture," casting a wider net to include architectural forms as well as non-Muslim activities in Muslim-majority societies, although Hodgson's framework focused on Southwest Asia. In using the term, Hodgson also aimed to move academic discourse on Islamic history away from Arabs and Arabic as "essentially" Islamic and from Persian/Turkish literatures and cultural groups as mere "influences" (31). However, Hodgson's notion of "civilization" as an interdependent grouping of literary traditions of "high culture" still hewed closely to the idea of grand overarching narratives (33). Furthermore, Hodgson's understanding of history as a "date-bound" discipline resulted in his use of the terms *Classical* and *Middle* periods as framing concepts, culminating in "Gunpowder Empires and Modern Times" (23). Such a tripartite division was also driven by the mundane necessity of the University of Chicago's three-semester academic year (van Bladel 2020: 165).

Fred Donner, also professor at the University of Chicago and former president of the Middle East Studies Association, would later bring up the question of the designation of "Islamic history" as a separate category in the first place. Yet Donner's discussion asserts the necessity of periodization to capture the diversity of Islamic cultures, and thus appropriate forms of periodization, rather than on the problem of periodization itself. What is most telling, however, is his critique of Western scholars "inheriting" periodization from the Muslim scholars they studied; Donner (2014: 29) states that the concomitant "subdivision of world history into pre-Islamic and Islamic eras" was flawed because it was a "faith-based" worldview not appropriate for the "secular" discipline of history, reinforcing the idea of the Western academic framing of history as fundamentally objective. His criticism of Western academic scholars "inheriting" Muslim periodization also belied the fact that Western scholars, in addition to privileging scholarly male output, ultimately chose certain forms of historical writing, such as dynastic chronicles, over other narrative forms to exemplify "Islamic history." Such chronicles fit into their own values of empire-building and "rise and fall" narratives, alongside the designations of "golden" and "classical" eras. For all their supposed objectivity, Western scholars ultimately reinforced a Sunni narrative as unmarked "Islamic history" through this emphasis of a linear, dynastic chronology, thus rendering other, non-Sunni histories deviant by default.

Shahab Ahmed (2015: 32) built on Hodgson's framework of an expanded, "Islamicate" civilization to integrate what he called the Balkans-to-Bengal complex, a geographic region he centered due to its stated importance as "home to the absolute demographic majority of Muslims on the planet." In his emphasis on moving away from essentializing Islamic history to the period of the earliest Muslims in Southwest Asia, Ahmed focuses on the years 1350–1850 CE, what he calls a half-millennium "post-formative" period before the "violent irruption of modernity" (81–82). Ahmed chose to fix and segment a time range in order to geographically expand his lens of analysis and demonstrate the depth of an "Islamic" diversity which would not need neologisms like *Islamicate*, despite analytically cutting out other, arguably equally important geographies such as Southeast Asia and much of Africa. Despite his insistence on a cultural trickle-down trajectory that included a wider array of social groups, he nonetheless utilizes Hodgson's civilizational paradigm of high culture. Ahmed reconstitutes this paradigm as "the elite and cultivated Sunnī and Shīʿī elites of the Balkan-to-Bengal complex," although he did not differentiate between "religion" and "culture" as mutually exclusive categories as Hodgson did (80, 116). Ahmed neither labels his periodization nor explains the significance of the end dates he has chosen, which roughly coincide with Muslim military and political expansion into both the Balkan and Bengal regions as its beginning and the eventual fall of Mughal rule to the British empire as its end. However, merely designating a time range by years in order to critique Orientalist notions of "Islamic" does not prevent Ahmed from falling into Orientalist paradigms in other ways. Although Ahmed does not use the term *Middle Ages* or even *Islamic* for his periodization, in his zeal to move away from a historical trajectory that centers Muslim communities in Southwest Asia he instead maps on to a slightly modified British Orientalist conceptualization of South Asian history. His lens of analysis thus reinforces the idea of an Islamic interlude that exists between an "ancient" Hindu period and the advent of modernity with the British (Flatt 2022: 177).

While discussions of the "Islamic" and the "Islamicate" have attempted to widen these concepts beyond normative, text-based parameters, they do not consider the problematic nature of the predominant divisions of "history," particularly in relation to notions of "Western civilization."[8] Instead we have the problem of relativity, of the pretensions of precision to fundamentally fuzzy and imprecise categories. One of the main issues regarding the concept of the "medieval" or "Middle Ages" is that it is by definition relative. It is the "middle" in relation to other fuzzy yet designated periods, and thus must be distinguished from them in some way. It is ironic that these designations of the "middle," as in the Islamic Middle Ages or even the "Middle East," are not effectively dealt with as mutable, problematic boundaries. Instead, they function as vacuums into which Western epistemologies inject their own ideas about specific peoples, cultures, and religious traditions. Thus, the "Middle East" (along with its parallel the "Near East"), despite its highly shifting and arbitrary designation(s), is now mainly analyzed as a fixed geographic region alongside North Africa (Yilmaz 2012: 24–28; Bonine 2012: 63–74). Furthermore, because the concept of a fixed geography serves several functions—including US military and domestic policy interests—it is transformed into an actual, effective category with real economic and political consequences. These ideological terms thus create their own reality, a reality embedded in violence and control.

The use of the terms *medieval* and *Middle Ages* for European history is equally imprecise. In this context, the medieval/Middle Ages continued to conceptually exist alongside the "Dark Ages"—designating a period of intellectual "darkness" and internecine warfare—rather than displac-

---

8. More anthropologically oriented approaches, such as that of A. Kevin Reinhart (2020), tend to not address periodization explicitly; for example, Reinhart divides time for Muslims into "pre-modernity" and "modernity," although he idealizes Muslim premodernity as a time of wider diversity than after the modern rise of literacy, mobility, and expanded media.

ing it entirely as a more "neutral" term. Although many academic Euro-medievalists now work against the limited notions of gender, race, sexuality, violence, and power hierarchies attributed to these earlier periods, the concept of the medieval in popular culture maintains its hold as racially white, chivalrous fairy tale as well as dirty, superstitious, and violent social spectacle. The equation of violence in particular with the "medieval" is a persistent, important one, particularly when non-Western societies are depicted as never having fully left it behind.

Orientalist Legacies

Unsurprisingly, the weaponization of knowledge about Muslims comes out of the earliest formal studies of "Islam" by European Christians who saw it as a theological as well as imperial threat. Islam was not only reduced to the figure of Muhammad, the "false prophet," but Muhammad was made a false parallel to the figure of Christ, as was the Qur'an to the Bible. The Qur'an, in turn, became the focus by which Christian, particularly Protestant, theologians chose to direct their polemics when not inveighing against the "seductive" internal enemy of Catholicism. Unlike Catholics, however, the imagined Mohammedan was an outsider threat precisely because he was filtered through the threat of the Ottoman Empire. When Thomas Jefferson acquired his Qur'an translation, it was not to acknowledge the enslaved African Muslims and their descendants who worked in the former British colony, possibly even on his own plantation, but to manage nascent American diplomacy with the Ottomans in dealing with naval matters in the Mediterranean.

In these earlier polemics, Islam was Muhammad, Qur'an, and Arabic; Persian and Turkish were either relegated to "secular" pursuits like historical prose or poetry or used to administer colonial bureaucracies.[9] It was for this reason—along with missionizing—that well-established European universities like Cambridge, Harvard, and Leiden endowed their Arabic-

---

9. As Paul Babinski (2020: 27–28, 46) notes—with a special focus on German Orientalists—"the European study of Persian has its origin in Istanbul," where Ottoman Turkish was the language of various guides to understanding texts in Arabic and Persian, the latter particularly due to global trade and "the establishment of the Dutch and British East India Companies." Turkish later became a subject of its own as a means for diplomatic relations with the Ottomans, another arm of colonial expansion (Babinski 2020: 183; Hodgson 1974: 39).

language chairs, whose longevity they proudly yet selectively still relate to prospective Arabic majors.[10] European biblical studies, with their study of Hebrew alongside Greek, expanded to the study of other related Semitic languages, linking and subsuming Arabic under the label. The explosion of archaeology in the nineteenth century onward, particularly in Egypt and Mesopotamia, helped mix the various Semitic- and non-Semitic-language cultures of Southwest Asia and North Africa into an amorphous Orient. In turn, "Oriental studies" evolved as the handmaiden of colonialism. Oriental studies would also set the standards for the academic study of "Islam" and Muslims, as prioritized by non-Muslims in a world dominated by European colonialism.

However, Islamic history, as defined by Orientalists, did not fit into a Western model of progressive history. The development of the idea of a "Middle Ages" or "medieval" period for Europe had a specific rationale: its history had to be depicted as one of ultimately leading to progress. For nineteenth-century European historians, the Middle Ages gave way to the Renaissance, which in turn gave way to the Enlightenment period of "rational and secular thought" (Le Goff 2017: 106).[11] Since European historians depicted "the West" as the sole inheritor of the "Greek and Roman" cultural and imperial traditions, then it, too, had sole ownership of the concept of civilizational progress. Its colonial dominance and later, supposed economic and democratic achievements were proof enough.

European Orientalists thus made sense of societies in which Muslims predominated through a parallelism that became more acute with the designation of "Islamic civilization" in the nineteenth century CE (van Bladel 2020: 152). Once segmented alongside European history—itself divided into the progressive narrative of "Dark Ages," "Renaissance," and "Enlightenment"— Islamic history was not only made coherent but made to fit into and contribute to Western history itself. However, Islamic civilization could only be understood as a brief interlude in this trajectory, in which, as Hodgson

10. "History of Islamic Studies at Harvard," Prince Alwaleed Bin Talal Islamic Studies Program at Harvard University, https://timeline.islamicstudies.harvard.edu/home (accessed July 1, 2022).
11. Jacques Le Goff (2017: 105–6), a French historian who argues that the Renaissance should be seen as part of the Middle Ages and not a distinct period, places the transition to the modern period in the mid-eighteenth century, which he considers a distinct break because of agricultural reforms; the invention of the steam engine and modern industry, science, and technology; and anti-monarchical movements—namely, the French Revolution.

(1993: 6) drily noted, it was "permitted to hold the torch of science, which properly belonged to the West, until the West was ready to take it over and carry it forward."

The "Medieval" as Historical Period

Within Western academic institutions, very little has changed since the nineteenth century. Instead, the periodization of Islamic history has shifted to renaming rather than reconsidering the nature of periodization itself. Although value-laden terms like *Golden Age* have mostly fallen out of favor (at least in academic publications), they are essentially subsumed into "classical Islam." The "classical" itself is seen as the interregnum between two other increasingly used designations, "Late Antiquity" and "medieval." Whereas Late Antiquity is meant as a corrective to include the "rise of Islam" within the wider context of Byzantine, Sasanian, and Greco-Roman history, the medieval period does not seem to function more than as a catch-all term between the classical period—so called because supposed foundational literary and legal genres developed in this period, with everything else following considered derivative—and the "Age of Empires" of the sixteenth century onward. Whereas the relevant empires implied in this designation are the Safavid, Mughal, and Ottoman empires, the rising dominance of European colonialism underwrites this designation. Other attempts at avoiding period designations by instead referring to ranges in time—the "eleventh to sixteenth centuries" instead of "medieval"—do not address the issues of what the purpose of these time ranges are, and why they (or any time range) should be set off from any other period.[12] Furthermore, these designations in the Common Era—what used to be AD (anno Domini)—are quite effective in demonstrating how nakedly derivative these periodizations are and how they function as an imposition of Western time. By "Western time"

---

12. For example, MEM's peer-reviewed academic journal, *al-'Usur al-Wusta* (the Arabic calque for the "Middle Ages") avoids any labeled periodizations within its stated time range of 500 to 1500 CE, even though they coincide with the period starting with Late Antiquity (generally associated with the "rise of Islam" in the sixth century CE) until the advent of European colonialism and the "Age of Empires" in the sixteenth century CE. See "About the Journal," *al-'Usur al-Wusta: The Journal of Middle East Medievalists*, https://journals.library.columbia.edu/index.php/alusur/about (accessed July 1, 2022). The period of 500-1500 CE is also the standard periodization of the "medieval" period for European history, where the beginning is the fall of the Roman Empire and the end is the "Renaissance" (Heng 2021: 23).

I do not refer to the Christocentric accounting of time through AD or CE, although it would be tempting to mark it in those terms as another layer of othering. Rather, this kind of calendrical accounting is not merely a religious convention or theological worldview but a kind of normativity widely established and entrenched—made "common"—through colonization and subsequent neo-imperialist international financial and economic systems (Ogle 2015: 199–200); its Christocentric features are thus secondary. Indicating or converting a time range of the medieval period into *hijrī* years obfuscates the fact that the designations of "Late Antiquity" and "early," "classical," and "medieval" Islamic periods are still in service to Western notions of European history and progress, and thus remain a colonizing gesture.

Furthermore, despite the problematic nature of periodization and its unclear temporal parameters, there remains the irony that, within academic and other contexts, these periodizations nonetheless function within fixed boundaries of geography and social class—whether explicitly stated so or not. These geographical and socioeconomic assumptions—centering male scholars, the Arabic language, and Southwest Asia as the default for Islamic history—assume certain areas as "latecomers" in the timeline of Islamic history. This framing creates both an artificial peripheralization in academic studies under the rubric of "medieval Islamic history" while putting forth a history that makes certain Muslim populations vulnerable to nationalist revisionist rhetorics of foreignness and invasion in non-Muslim-majority countries (Flatt 2022: 185).

The "Medieval" as Metaphorical Violence

Ultimately, what academics call history, Islamic history, or medieval history is what is valued from a Eurocentric perspective. These designations thus tell us more about the people doing the research than the people they research. The very existence of academic production of knowledge then brings up the question: what is the point of "history"? We have already established that the concept of the "classical," "Dark Ages," and "medieval" were in service to a progressive history that culminated in a phase called the European Enlightenment and "modernity." The medieval in particular was meant to be a violent contrast to the humanism of the post-Enlightenment West up through our own age, despite the fact that the nineteenth through twenty-first centuries have been a continuous, ever-expanding circus of violence: colonialism and violent occupation; brutally unequal and impoverishing international financial systems; hoarding and monopolizing of food, housing, vaccines, and natural resources; destructive and genocidal wars; and environmental degradation on massive scales not previously possible. The irony of this conceptualization is that these violent notions of the "medieval" are mapped onto non-Western societies at the points where they deviate from notions of "appropriate" social and political development, often in relation to an adequately Westernized and "secular" public sphere.

We can see these examples in Anglophone news coverage of the rise of the Islamic State of Iraq and Syria/the Levant (ISIS/ISIL) in 2014. Even analyses that pushed back against the designation of ISIS/ISIL as Islamically "medieval" conflated it with the early seventh century—that is, the beginnings of Islam—betraying their prejudice of a historical "sameness" of Muslim communities that are not considered adequately Westernized (e.g., Kotkin 2021). US President Barack Obama, in an attempt to rhetorically avoid feeding into Islamophobia when referring to ISIS/ISIL, referenced the Christian Crusades as a historical Western counterpoint. However, rather than deemphasizing an inherent violence in Muslim communities, he merely implied that Muslims were not the only group capable of "religious" violence (Simon 2015). Furthermore, his commentary did not question the idea of ISIS/ISIL as a "medieval" throwback, neatly sidestepping questions of US foreign policy and invasion in the creation of such a group, with its deft use of both military and media technology. Policy analysts regularly referred to Taliban rule in Afghanistan as "medieval," despite being the result of Soviet and US training and proxy war fighting as well as subsequent power vacuums; some analysts even insisted that a historical medieval lens was necessary to illuminate modern geopolitical issues precisely because they involve Muslims trapped in a "medieval" context (Barfield 2010). Again, this strategy—whitewashing current systems of violence by appending violent spectacles as "medieval" and attributing them as inherent to non-Westerners—is a sleight of hand to show that the history of the West was solely of progress, thus justifying colonization and the "civilizing mission." The centering of women and women's rights, and later LGBTQ rights, as another measure of progress and backwardness/"medievalness" in Muslim communities created yet another element by which Western nation-states could paper over their own spotty records and present themselves as beacons of freedom while justifying both colonization and neo-imperialist invasion.

Both the colonialist and neo-imperialist attributions of backwardness to Muslims and Islam have become so rhetorically effective that they are utilized as political strategy and rhetoric by postcolonial nation-states anxious to present themselves as "modern." A prominent example is the legal instrumentalization of British Orientalist scholarship by Hindu nationalists to define Islamic religious boundaries. Such courts refer to colonial-era "Anglo-Muhammadan" legal treatises as sources of authority, enabling a nominally secular court to directly engage in interpreting Islamic jurisprudence and Muslim religious practice to the exclusion of Indian Muslim communities themselves (Rafii 2022). Narendra Modi, the Prime Minister of India and head of the Hindu-nationalist BJP party, responded to the court case banning triple talaq—a form of husband-initiated instant divorce—by announcing it as an advancement of women's rights that finally did away with an "archaic and medieval practice" (*BBC News* 2019). Such discourse builds on Orientalist conceptualizations of an Islamic "medieval" period stretching from Ghurid rule in the twelfth century until consolidation of British power in the eighteenth century, which in turn created a contrasting "classical" period of a timeless, monolithic Hindu and Sanskrit culture; the "Islamic" interlude is thus utilized in modern political rhetoric as one of foreign and backward Muslim elements (Flatt 2022: 177). The equation of induction into the British empire and, by extension, the liberalism of modernity—in stark contrast to ruling Muslim forces—is integral to Modi's emphasis on ignoring complicated legal and social phenomena surrounding Muslim communities in service to "women's rights." The fact that triple talaq had existed in its current form in the Indian legal system as a result of British colonialism is stripped in favor of its depiction of a timeless yet medieval "Islamicness."

Yet despite the colonialist baggage of Orientalist scholarship and its legacies, it is still lauded for its methodological "rigor" in various academic disciplines in Islamic studies due to its philological focus on written languages and texts. Although most Western academic Islamic studies scholars now would not accept a focus on texts as a stand-in for entire societies, cultures, and religious traditions, the idea that Islamic studies can be reduced and quantified to a set of legal and theological texts and historical chronicles, particularly in Arabic, is a persistent one. Even with the many discursive analyses of Edward Said's influential *Orientalism* and other writings in the last few decades, there has been a recent resurgence of support for the Orientalist philological tradition among Islamic studies academics in the West, both explicit (Daneshgar 2020)[13] and implied (Stew-

13. Majid Daneshgar (2020: 179) claims that the Orientalist tradition, by demanding access to sources irrespective of "believer" status, is "inclusive and pluralistic" and encourages scholarly engagement and productive critique. However, his assertion that

art 2018),[14] divorcing Oriental scholarship from its colonialist context. The Arabic-centric, textual approach to Islamic studies, along with its Oriental-ist periodization, has been further reinforced through its integration into university teaching and job advertisements, particularly by nonspecialists (Morganstein Fuerst 2020: 916). The ability to hire only one specialist for most departments further aids in the essentializing of "Islam" as an object of inquiry; as Ilyse Morganstein Fuerst observed in her survey of faculty job advertisements, "for Islam, one scholar is enough; and that one ought to reflect Arabic, the Middle East, or a command of texts" (919). Morganstein Fuerst traces this issue to a lack of integration of religious studies discourse into nonspecialists' rudimentary framing of Islamic studies in job searches, although she also noted the pressures of student enrollment and curricu-lum building.

The overlap of Islamic studies with area studies—specifically, "Near East" or "Middle Eastern" studies—presents additional challenges. While many Near East/Middle Eastern studies departments serve to diversify "the Middle East"—usually inclusive of Southwest Asia and North Africa—beyond Islamic or even religious studies, the fact that Islamic studies tends to be primarily homed in Near East/Middle East departments[15] as opposed to other area studies reinforces this problematic conflation to which Mor-ganstein Fuerst refers. Furthermore, post–September 11, programs in Islam and the Middle East became filtered heavily through defense studies (Lock-man 2010: 239); Arabic (and to a lesser degree, Persian and a few other Central/South Asian languages) enjoyed a period of government funding mainly to filter South, Southwest, and Central Asia through extractive mili-

---

Orientalism was "passion-based, not power-based" whitewashes Oriental studies as a form of scholarship embedded in the justifying ideology of empire irrespective of an indi-vidual scholar's own declared commitments (180).

14. Devin Stewart (2018: 157–58) defends Orientalist philology (without naming it thus) in direct response to Aaron Hughes's criticism that Islamic studies would improve with "more rigorous engagement with recent theories in religious studies." Stewart's coun-terproposal for the "improvement" of academic Islamic studies is the emphatic return to Orientalist philological training that prioritizes Arabic, European languages for second-ary sources, "fundamentally religious texts," and "the main religious sciences of Islam" (188–91).

15. Although Charles Kurzman and Carl W. Ernst (2016: 332–33) note that religious stud-ies departments, which grew out of an original concentration on biblical studies and Prot-estant theology, function as "a second academic home" to Islamic Studies, "even among these departments the commitment to Islamic studies varies considerably."

tary and political lenses, which were expediently established as a means to access lucrative federal positions and contracts.

Recent cuts to government humanities funding—and even entire humanities departments—have also laid bare this expedient positioning of knowledge in general and Islamic studies in particular. Advocacy for funding has depended on three general responses: that studying the humanities is just as market-viable as business or STEM concentrations; that the knowledge gained through humanities training will aid in addressing current issues of racism/Islamophobia/stereotyping that have policy impacts, as in journalistic coverage; and that "knowledge for its own sake" is enough merit. However, it should be clear by now that this adage is a trope of faux innocence, especially when it comes to Western academic Islamic studies and the weaponization of both the "Islamic" and the "medieval" as binaries to "modernity." The production of knowledge as a means of categorizing, comparing, and even surveilling does not exist in a vacuum.

The "Global" Middle Ages

The idea of a "Global Middle Ages" ultimately does very little to address these issues. Although Geraldine Heng (2021: 19) acknowledges the expedient nature of the term, she nonetheless utilizes it to posit a new framework in order to move beyond centering European time. As an example, to counteract the depiction of the Industrial Revolution as a unique and foundational Western achievement, she proposes tracing multiple "industrial revolutions" throughout the histories of other societies. Such an approach would make premodern societies "intelligible" as well as erode the artificial constructs of premodernity, modernity, and postmodernity (10). Yet this framework cannot address the problem that it is still Western conceptions of European achievements that set the standards of what is of historical importance in the first place, of what is worthy of tracing through time. Under Heng's rubric, there would be no historical achievement in the world that Europe had not already attained, a far cry from eroding notions of Western exceptionalism. Unfortunately, this process shows that decentering European history does not automatically decenter Western subjectivities.

However, Heng's exposition of premodernities/modernities/postmodernities existing simultaneously is a crucial one. As previously noted, periodization often traces the activities of an elite, rarefied segment of society, especially because written history has been recorded by an elite, rarefied segment of society. The very notion of "modernity" is relative to Western parameters of European history and progress. Scholars implicitly utilize "modernity" to indicate the degree to which non-European societies compare with the technological, scientific, and social "advances" of Europe at the time the comparison is made; yet this concept is so regularly taken for granted that it is rarely defined. This forces us to revisit the question: What is the purpose, or more accurately, the narrative behind periodization, and what constitutes historical "achievement"? Whereas there can be value in locating major historical changes from long-established modes of living or thinking, the primary focus on novelty on a grand scale is problematic. How Euro-medievalists determine an event as a "major historical change," as in the Black Plague in Europe, is also teleologically defined. Instead of highlighting the "Industrial Revolution" and locating it in other periods and cultures, scholars need to reconsider what it is they are implicitly celebrating: Human agency on a grand scale over other humans and natural environments? Mass accumulation of power by a male-dominated capitalist class? Even the definition of "industrial revolution" is not stable; what historical development counts as "industrial revolution"? Its scale? Its labor and environmental impact? Enduring technologies? Individual leadership?

Is history confined to being a series of disruptions? The emphasis on innovation and newness is a teleological one, again based on the notion of history as one of progressive improvement culminating in the "Enlightenment." What would the study of history look like when scholars move away from this model? Instead of prioritizing industrial revolutions, to value instead stewardship of the environment, including its noninvasive forms? History, as well as anthropology, has yet to fully discard the primitive/civilized model—a challenge, since academic history has been a narrative of civilizations explaining the rise of a very specific kind of capitalist urban society. While there is excellent research on microhistories, gendered labor, diverse human experiences of gender and sexuality, and subaltern history, these appear in parallel to the standard chronological and political segmentations of history as the Classical Age, Golden Age, and so on, reproduced in teaching and textbooks ranging from K–12 education to required college courses. Without restructuring the teaching of "history" at these levels, these other interventions in historical framing remain the haven of the privileged few, thus greatly minimizing their impact.

Academia and Its Critics

Having determined that all these terms and conceptualizations are problematic, where do we go from here? The notion of expanding the concept of the medieval through the Global Middle Ages is ultimately one of inclusivity—that is, bringing more regions into the fold—rather than one of alternative epistemologies. As much as there is debate about nodes, centers, and peripheries, as well as multiple forms of modernities existing at the same time, these do not include questioning the idea of cutting up time and subjecting it to order in the first place. Inclusivity does not ultimately change the framework or parameters in which scholarship functions; it merely subjects more sources to it. So, despite the integration of regional histories, microhistories, and histories of the subaltern, scholars continue to operate in the same West-determined notions of periodization and historical value. Heng skillfully critiqued alternate ideas of extended cores and peripheries, as well as Lila Abu-Lughod's extension of the world-systems analysis to the pre-1600s (Heng 2020: 46), observing that "for the world's inhabitants, every place is the center of the world" (12). Yet even her exhortation to move away from grand narratives of history and her framework for not "privileging zones, regions, oceans, or societies; types of economic or other forms of organization; or types of ḥabitus or environments" cannot avoid an implicit comparison with European and Eurocentric periodization if overarching West-centric frameworks remain in place (55).

A persistent problem, as both Morganstein Fuerst (2020) and Heng (2021: 52) note, is the outsized role of the job market in reproducing outdated and West-centric frameworks, which determine research and teaching agendas. Academic realities do not allow much space for liminalities and discomfort—not for teaching undergraduate students nor for academic publishing, which in the last few years has pushed for grand claims, "relevance," and wide appeal. The ability to expose students to different ways of historical thinking will always be limited when it is aimed at undoing Eurocentric periodizations inculcated since primary and secondary school. The academic publishing and marketing model, driven by disciplinary norms, is now mostly moving away from grand sweeping histories, such as those of Patricia Crone (2003) and Richard Bulliet (1990), yet now pushes scholars to render mostly narrow scholarly contributions relevant on a grand scale. Beside the discussion of what frameworks and methodologies to use, the nature of academic disciplinary reproduction and publishing, particularly in relation to the academic job market and university rankings, will continually replicate these ideas.

There have also been recent calls to decolonize various academic disciplines, including history, particularly through course syllabi. However, as Eve Tuck and K. Wayne Yang (2012: 19) have noted, when calls for decolonization focus on education advocacy and scholarship rather than dismantling settler-colonial systems, decolonization becomes a mere metaphor, ironically reifying structural settler dominance. Furthermore, academic institutions are not innocent institutions. They are built to construct distance between an elite group and the populace through access to power, socioeconomic status, and other resources. In North America, as well as other regions with colonial histories, academic institutions are built on stolen and appropriated land, and they produce knowledge that erases this history or justifies it. On a wider scale, universities create systems that hoard and manipulate information about the communities they research without their consent. Furthermore, the academic commitment to the supremacy of Western "civilization" is evident not only in the way modern universities package the "medieval" as an object of study but also in the way they utilize the medieval and early modern periods "to understand their own colonial formations" (Miyashiro 2023: 113). Recognizing universities as exporters of colonialist modes of knowledge production, if not as colonialist and settler institutions themselves, is crucial to understanding what decolonization processes actually entail and, thus, the limits of the university itself.

However, as much as we can critique the West-centric framing of academic Islamic history and the concept of the "medieval," structural linguistic and academic contexts trap us in utilizing these terms. Knowing that terms are problematic does not mean they will be easily discarded, especially when wider coherence is necessary and older, Eurocentric terms are still reiterated through popular culture. The act of mere renaming—for example, "Oriental studies," with the implied sense of the premodern past, to Islamic/Near Eastern studies—is much like substituting "sub-Saharan Africa" for "the racially tinged phrases 'Tropical Africa' and 'Black Africa'": it simply repackages the same colonialist paradigms into more precise-sounding terms (de Haldevang 2016). Creating different designations, whether geographic or temporal, will not free academics from their problematic paradigms, nor will it mitigate the violent results of the knowledge they produce. As students enter the academic world working to hone new historical methods and outlooks, academic disciplines will nonetheless reproduce hegemonic approaches because even as scholars shift Eurocentric paradigms, they do not break them.

It is thus crucial to look beyond academics, with its market forces of publishing and student enrollment, to understand what other ways history has been construed in relation to storytelling, identity, and being. The expansion of modern primary and secondary school education, an extension of colonialist knowledge production, has created authoritative institutions in which texts and grand narratives are standardized while undermining oral traditions and community storytellers. The field of Orientalism, with its emphasis on texts and, by extension, the small, elite percentage of a population that could write, has in the same way severely undermined the concept of cultural local histories, poetic narratives, and storytelling as authoritative histories in their own right. This is not to say that notions of orality do not exist in Orientalism or that other disciplines, such as anthropology, do not focus on storytelling and communal narratives as a primary research area. However, it is one thing to research these areas and quite another to integrate different modes of epistemologies into institutional ways of seeing the world, to move beyond categories that have been embedded in massive structural violence culminating in one of the most violent and extractive periods in human existence. To do so would be to acknowledge the limitations of academic knowledge, in that it can never truly be comprehensive; even the search for different nodes and peripheries will always leave gaps, either in detail or general content. Historical academic research entails a fundamental aspiration to maximalism; it envisions a world in which information is always out there simply waiting to be found as soon as a researcher decides to undertake the research or has the funds to do so. It does not question its rights to do so.

As a progenitor of several academic disciplines, Orientalist scholarship rarely considers the conditions for its own existence; despite multiple critiques post–Edward Said, it has not had the forced, albeit minimal, confrontation of its colonial legacy on a disciplinary scale the way that anthropology or the social sciences have. Academic history thus rarely considers the context of the information it has gathered, or hoarded, from other cultures and even socioeconomic groups, which it weaponized and used in service of suppression of alternative forms of knowledge in its grand stakes to hegemony. This is particularly true of Oriental studies and its legacies, which proponents depict as a history of intellectual curiosity both divorced from its role in colonialism and as an innocent foundation on which to further build "Islamic" and area studies.

Ultimately, the issues concerning the nature of the "medieval" and Islamic history itself are questions about the nature of the university's production of knowledge, with its problematic historical foundations as well as its exponentially increasing rankings- and profit-driven model. It is thus invested in constant expansion and the continuation of its disciplinary models, if only because addressing the issue of its role in problematic productions of knowledge would undermine its institutional authority. The fact that the categorization of Islamic history around the "medieval" has effects beyond epistemological violence means that substantively addressing it cannot be left solely to the university and must ultimately go beyond the university itself.

References

Ahmed, Shahab. 2015. *What Is Islam? The Importance of Being Islamic*. Princeton, NJ: Princeton University Press.

Aveni, Anthony F. 1989. *Empires of Time*. New York: Basic Books.

Babinski, Paul. 2020. "World Literature in Practice: The Orientalist's Manuscript between the Ottoman Empire and Germany." PhD diss., Princeton University.

Barfield, Thomas. 2010. "Is Afghanistan 'Medieval'?" *Foreign Policy*, June 2. https://foreignpolicy.com/2010/06/02/is-afghanistan-medieval-2/.

BBC News. 2019. "Triple Talaq: India Criminalises Muslim 'Instant Divorce.'" July 30. https://www.bbc.com/news/world-asia-india-49160818.

Bonine, Michael E. 2012. "Of Maps and Regions: Where Is the Geographer's Middle East?" In *Is There a Middle East? The Evolution of a Geopolitical Concept*, edited by Michael E. Bonine, Abbas Amanat, and Michael E. Gasper, 56–99. Stanford, CA: Stanford University Press.

Bulliet, Richard. 1990. *The Camel and the Wheel*. New York: Columbia University Press.

Crone, Patricia. 2003. *Pre-industrial Societies: Anatomy of the Pre-modern World*. Oxford: Oneworld.

Crone, Patricia, and Michael Cook. 1980. *Hagarism: The Making of the Islamic World*. Cambridge: Cambridge University Press.

Daneshgar, Majid. 2020. "I Want to Become an Orientalist, Not a Colonizer or 'Decolonizer." *Method and Theory in the Study of Religion* 33, no. 2: 173–85.

de Haldevang, Max. 2016. "Why Do We Still Use the Term 'Sub-Saharan Africa'?" *Quartz Africa*, September 1. https://qz.com/africa/770350/why-do-we-still-say-subsaharan-africa/.

Donner, Fred. 2012. *Muhammad and the Believers: At the Origins of Islam*. Cambridge, MA: Harvard University Press.

Donner, Fred. 2014. "Periodization as a Tool of the Historian with Special Reference to Islamic History." *Der Islam* 91, no. 1: 20–36.

Felber, Garrett. 2017. "Malcolm X in the Courtroom." *Black Perspectives*, February 25. https://www.aaihs.org/malcolm-x-in-the-courtroom/.

Flatt, Emma J. 2022. "The Worlds of South Asia." In *Teaching the Global Middle Ages*, edited by Geraldine Heng, 177–93. New York: Modern Language Association Press.

Frankopan, Peter. 2019. "Why We Need to Think about the Global Middle Ages." *Journal of Medieval Worlds* 1, no. 1: 5–10.

Gardner, David. 2018. "Bernard Lewis, Historian of the Middle East, 1916–2018." *Financial Times*, May 25.

Heng, Geraldine. 2021. *The Global Middle Ages: An Introduction*. Cambridge: Cambridge University Press.

Hodgson, Marshall. 1974. *The Classical Age of Islam*. Vol. 1 of *The Venture of Islam: Conscience and History in World Civilization*. Chicago: University of Chicago Press.

Hodgson, Marshall. 1993. *Rethinking World History*. Cambridge: Cambridge University Press.

Holmes, Catherine, and Naomi Standen. 2018. "Introduction: Toward a Global Middle Ages." In "The Global Middle Ages," edited by Catherine Holmes and Naomi Standen. *Past and Present* 238, supplement 13: 1–44.

Kotkin, Joel. 2021. "It's Not Just the Taliban: We in the West Are Embracing Medievalism, Too." *Newsweek*, August 25. https://www.newsweek.com/its-not -just-taliban-we-west-are-embracing-medievalism-too-opinion-1623102.

Kurzman, Charles, and Carl W. Ernst. 2016. "Islamic Studies in US Universities." In *Middle East Studies for the New Millennium: Infrastructures of Knowledge*, edited by Seteney Shami and Cynthia Miller-Idriss, 320–48. New York: New York University Press.

Le Goff, Jacques. 2017. *Must We Divide History into Periods?* Translated by Malcolm DeBevoise. New York: Columbia University Press.

Lewis, Bernard. 1990. "The Roots of Muslim Rage." *Atlantic*, September 1. https:// www.theatlantic.com/magazine/archive/1990/09/the-roots-of-muslim-rage /304643/.

Lockman, Zachary. 2010. *Contending Visions of the Middle East: The History and Politics of Orientalism*. Cambridge: Cambridge University Press.

MAA (Medieval Academy of America). 2019. *Ninety-Fourth Annual Meeting, Medieval Academy of America: The Global Turn in Medieval Studies*. Program schedule. https://www.medievalacademy.org/resource/resmgr/pdfs/2019 philadelphiaprogram.pdf.

Miyashiro, Adam. 2023. "Race, Medieval Studies, and Disciplinary Boundaries." In "The 'Medieval' Undone: Imagining a New Global Past," edited by Sierra Lomuto. Special issue, *boundary 2* 50, no. 3: 107–21.

Morganstein Fuerst, Ilyse. 2020. "Job Ads Don't Add Up: Arabic + Middle East + Texts ≠ Islam." *Journal of the American Academy of Religion* 8, no. 4: 915–46.

Ogle, Vanessa. 2015. *The Global Transformation of Time, 1870–1950*. Cambridge, MA: Harvard University Press.

Powers, David S. 2009. *Muhammad is Not the Father of Any of Your Men*. Princeton, NJ: Princeton University Press.

Powers, David S. 2014. *Zayd*. Princeton, NJ: Princeton University Press.

Rafii, Raha. 2022. "Karnataka High Court's Interpretation of Islamic Sources: Ḥijāb Is Not 'Part of Essential Religious Practice in Islam.'" *Islamic Law Blog*, May 27. https://islamiclaw.blog/2022/05/27/karnataka-high-courts-interpretation -of-islamic-sources-ḥijab-is-not-part-of-essential-religious-practice-in-islam/.

Rambaran-Olm, Mary. 2019. "Misnaming the Medieval: Rejecting 'Anglo-Saxon' Studies." *History Workshop*, November 4. https://www.historyworkshop.org.uk /misnaming-the-medieval-rejecting-anglo-saxon-studies.

Reinhart, A. Kevin. 2020. *Lived Islam: Colloquial Religion in a Cosmopolitan Tradition*. Cambridge: Cambridge University Press.

Simon, Evan. 2015. "Historians Weigh In on Obama's Comparison of ISIS Militants to Medieval Christian Crusaders." *ABC News*, February 6. https://abc news.go.com/Politics/historians-weigh-obamas-comparison-isis-militants -medieval-christian/story?id=28787194.

Stewart, Devin. 2018. "A Modest Proposal for Islamic Studies." In *Identity, Politics, and Islam*, edited by Matt Sheedy, 157–200. Sheffield, UK: Equinox. https:// www.equinoxpub.com/home/identity-politics-and-the-study-of-islam/.

Tuck, Eve, and K. Wayne Yang. 2012. "Decolonization Is Not a Metaphor." *Decolonization: Indigeneity, Education, and Society* 1, no. 1: 1–40.

van Bladel, Kevin. 2020. "A Brief History of Islamic Civilization from Its Genesis in the Late Nineteenth Century to Its Institutional Entrenchment." *al-'Usur al-Wusta* 28, no. 1; 155–73. https://journals.library.columbia.edu/index.php /alusur/article/view/8412/4308.

Yilmaz, Huseyin. 2012. "The Eastern Question and the Ottoman Empire: The Genesis of the Near and Middle East in the Nineteenth Century." In *Is There a Middle East? The Evolution of a Geopolitical Concept*, edited by Michael E. Bonine, Abbas Amanat, and Michael E. Gasper, 11–35. Redwood City, CA: Stanford University Press.

Young, Helen. 2019. "Whitewashing the 'Real' Middle Ages in Popular Media." In *Whose Middle Ages? Teachable Moments for an Ill-Used Past*, edited by Mary C. Erler, Thomas O'Donnell, Nicholas L. Paul, and Nina Rowe, 233–42. New York: Fordham University Press.

What Is "Postmedieval"? Embedded Reflections

Julie Orlemanski

Apostrophic Overture

What does it mean to declare yourself *postmedieval*? It means you're standing on the far side of the Middle Ages, at some point *post-* or after. According to the familiar chronology, it's a position that would seem to make you modern. But you haven't said you're modern, have you? You've used this peculiar term, cobbled together, which keeps the medieval before our eyes.

What does it mean to say you're *postmedieval*? Maybe you were medieval once, but now you're over it. You were part of medieval studies, say, and were "medieval" by the transferred property of your subject matter. But you've moved past that; you're in recovery now: postdivorce, postcleanse, *postmedieval*.

Or maybe that's wrong. Maybe you've never been medieval—just like people say, we have never been modern (Latour 1993). But such words, *medieval* and *modern, postmedieval* and *postmodern*, will not stay paral-

boundary 2 50:3 (2023)   DOI 10.1215/01903659-10472345   ©2023 by Duke University Press

lel. Declaring yourself modern is a very modern thing to do, even if you've been mistaken all along. *Medieval*, on the other hand, was coined afterward, outside the Middle Ages. Saying you're medieval is like saying you're dead: your speech-act contradicts you. To talk about medieval things is to be saying all along, I'm postmedieval.

So, what are you if you're *postmedieval*? You're "a journal of medieval cultural studies," as your subtitle reads. The two halves of your name embody a hesitation—a repetition and an antithesis, *not-A* and *A*. They form a situation, sprawling across the historical boundary.

What are you doing when you announce you're *postmedieval*? You're speaking English; I noticed that. You intone an English word composed from Latin roots: *post, medium, aevum*. As we talk about it, we make reference to a particular scheme of history, one that we rely on and play within. To say you're *postmedieval* is to feel the imperial, cosmopolitan language of Latin, idiom of the Roman Empire and Western Christendom, stretch itself out into the terms of a globalizing English.

Whose name is *postmedieval*? It is the property and asset of Springer Nature, a German-British academic publishing conglomerate formed in 2015, from the merger of Springer Science+Business Media, Holtzbrinck Publishing Group's Nature Publishing Group, Palgrave Macmillan, and Macmillan Education. Before then, from *postmedieval*'s founding in 2010, Palgrave Macmillan owned the name and contents—itself the outcome of the 2000 merger of St. Martin's Press and Macmillan Publishers. On May 6, 2015, the new Springer Nature CEO Derk Haank announced, "Taking a unified one-company approach will enable us to have a global view" (Springer 2015). *Postmedieval* falls within this one-company approach, this global view.

If you say you're *postmedieval* but decline to say you're *modern*, it could be because you're postmodern. Is that it? Postmodern is postmedieval without being modern. As Kwame Anthony Appiah (1991: 342–43) clarified now more than thirty years ago, the "structure of the modern/postmodern dichotomy" across the spheres where it operates is that "in each of these domains there is an antecedent practice that laid claim to a certain exclusivity of insight, and in each of them 'postmodernism' is a name for the rejection of that claim to exclusivity, a rejection that is almost always more playful, though not necessarily less serious, than the practice it aims to replace." Those who came before you may have claimed a universal standard—but you've come after that and come against it. Of course, it is difficult to say (following Appiah) whether the *post-* in *postmodernism* is the *post-* in *postmedieval*. They might have a common object of repudiation, modernity's "claim to a certain exclusivity of insight." Yet they call up history differently.

How has the meaning of *postmedieval* changed? If Google Ngrams and anecdotal evidence are indicative, the "postmodern" moment is now some time ago, decaying steadily since maybe 2002. Has something happened to the *post-* in *postmedieval* as "postmodernism" recedes? Meanwhile, other rumored aftermaths drift over us—postcolonial, posthumanist, posthistoricist, postracial, postlapsarian—and continue to alter what we hear in "postmedieval."

When we're declaring you're *postmedieval*, where are we standing, you and I? Do you want to go somewhere else? Are there places where no one knows your name, or the time inside your name?

The present essay explores the special issue's topic, "The 'Medieval' Undone: Imagining a New Global Past," by asking what it has meant, and what it could yet mean, to be postmedieval. It does so by telling a specific institutional history, that of *postmedieval: a journal of medieval cultural studies*, which was launched in 2010 and continues to the present. I take it that part of the remit of this issue of *boundary 2* is to entertain the potential obsolescence of "the medieval," particularly in intellectual frameworks responsive to decolonial and antiracist work on the politics of time. Is medieval studies post-"medieval," many of the assembled essays can be understood to ask—or should it be? What follows, then, is an oblique approach to those questions. It is both a brief history of the recent past, particularly at the intersection of medieval studies and theory, and an effort to think toward the futures that the term *postmedieval* at once catalyzes and obstructs. Even a perfunctory scan of the journal's title illustrates the difficulty of leaving the medieval behind. The bold *post-* is belied by the call to a "medieval cultural studies." Our shared title here, "The 'Medieval' Undone," stages a similar vacillation, by foregrounding the term that may, or may not, be up for overcoming. In the case of *postmedieval*, such ambivalence has been the occasion for scholarly thought, collaboration, and labor over the thirteen or so years of the journal's existence.

I take up the writing of this essay from a decidedly embedded, interested perspective since I am currently coeditor of *postmedieval* and have previously been an author and book reviews editor there. I focus on two episodes of the journal's history, its launch in 2010 and its transition to new editorial leadership in 2021. Unsurprisingly, the journal's preoccupations shifted somewhat between those points. When it began, *postmedieval* was on a mission to scramble linear history, challenge the norms of medieval studies, and explore the matrix of themes and practices that might be called postmodernism. More than a decade later, some of that remains, though the mood is less impish, periodization feels less tractable, and the topics of concern have altered, with the scale of the globe now a pressing matter conceptually and in the day-to-day workings of the journal.

Some of what I do in the pages that follow is simply describe the journal and note its circumstances and development. Across these changes, I pay attention to a disposition for which the name *postmedieval* serves as a useful emblem. As the start of this essay is meant to dramatize, *postmedieval* at once avows and disavows a connection to the Middle Ages and medieval studies. It links itself to a regime of periodization while also staking a position beyond it, over it, *post-*. The rather contradictory moniker seems to me helpful for capturing not only the journal's ambivalence toward the "medieval" but also the secondariness, the belatedness and incompletion, of its gesture of turning away. "Postmedieval" is a species of what Jacques Derrida calls paleonymics, or the practice of "retain[ing], provisionally and strategically, *the old name*." For Derrida's (1988: 21) deconstruction, paleonymics is a tactic for "effective *intervention* in the constituted historical field" and a means to "graft" what has been "subordinated, excluded, or held in abeyance" onto the old term. In retaining *medieval*, *postmedieval* has done something similar, not just terminologically but in institutional practice—attempting to intervene in a field, to alter it, through ceaseless contact with the old name's power.

Or, to say it another way: articles published in *postmedieval* attain their legibility within a discursive field shaped by such large-scale formations as medieval studies, the humanities, the globalizing research university, and academic publishing (to name a few). The discursive field thus constituted has a history, a history that materially shapes the distribution of the journal's resources and labor, access and authority. It conditions *postmedieval* at every point, and we can trace to it such banal facts as that we are published in English, the Gregorian calendar keeps our time, our content is owned by Springer Nature, and certain of our submissions wind up published while others do not. The term *medieval* is, among other things, a metonymy for this field, a crucial word drawn from the system and made to stand for it. From the journal's beginning, this discursive field and the conditions of possibility it imposes have been a major part of what *postmedieval* has wished to speak about. It has sought to challenge aspects of its own framework of comprehensibility and its material support—even as

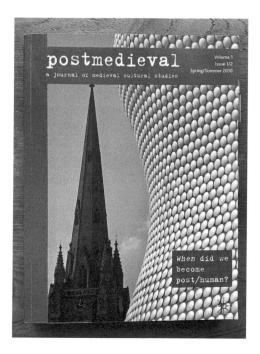

Figure 1 Cover of *postmedieval* 1, no. 1–2 (2022). Digital JPEG image, 960 × 1280 pixels. Courtesy of Julie Orlemanski.

its utterances have remained part of that system, humming on its circuits. Obviously such a situation is in no way unique to *postmedieval*; it pertains to any reflexive critique that gains recognition in the vast apparatus of academia. But the journal has inhabited the double bind with particular intensity. The tensions between *post-* and *medieval*, between what we say and the conditions of our saying it—those are not, finally, avoidable contradictions. They derive from the larger institutional and sociohistorical processes within which our thinking has been labored over, materialized, circulated, and valued.

postmedieval Then: 2010

The journal *postmedieval* launched in the summer of 2010 with a double issue entitled "*When* Did We Become Post/Human?" Across the issue's cover (fig. 1), a church spire spikes, framed in the foreground by the sinuous curve of a space-age surface. The building in the background is St. Martin in the Bull Ring, an 1871 reconstruction of a thirteenth-century parish church, by J. A. Chatwin, a British architect known for his neo-Gothic designs. In the foreground the Selfridges department store undulates, its curved facade a skin of thousands of aluminum disks, designed and built by the firm Future Systems in 2003. The two buildings embody two fantasies of time, nostalgic and futuristic. Together they comprise a close-cropped fragment of the cityscape of Birmingham, UK, a city known for its crucial role in the disciplinary history of cultural studies as it developed at the Centre for Contemporary Cultural Studies, which opened at the University of Birmingham in 1964.

The cover photograph, by Richard Ridge, is printed in crisp black and white, though the stone of St. Martin has a reddish tint, as if hand-colored. A band cuts across the top, framing the journal's title: *postmedieval: a journal of medieval cultural studies*. The words are printed in a stylized typewriter font, their edges ragged as though struck on an inked ribbon. With its hand-colored photograph, exaggerated typography, and found pastiche of architectural styles, the inaugural cover of *postmedieval* mixes temporal codes. It declines to picture the Middle Ages any way but phantasmally—both as Victorian reconstruction and as the projection of twenty-first-century viewers, who think they know how to map the grammar of "medieval" and *post-* on to the visual field. The cover thus aptly embodies *postmedieval*'s stated mission "to bring the medieval and modern into productive critical relation" and its hope "that a concerted focus on the *question* of the relations between the medieval and modern in different times and places will help us take better stock of the different roles that history and various processes of historicizing have played in the shaping of various presents and futures" (Joy and Seaman 2009). These phrases, which I quote from the journal's prospectus, emphasize a multiplicity of temporal relations. The cover's playful juxtaposition of styles unmoors us from historical sequence and promises a kind of temporal freedom. "Medieval" as it appears here has little to do with the tripartite succession of antiquity, the Middle Ages, and modernity. What matters instead is the boundary of past and future, apparently perforated and breached at innumerable points.

Folding back the cover and leafing through the front matter, one finds the usual details about whose work and authority have coalesced in the issue. Eileen A. Joy and Craig Dionne were the issue's editors, under the overall editorial leadership of Joy and Myra Seaman, with Holly Crocker acting as book reviews editor. At the time of publication, all were faculty members in US English departments, an index of the journal's intellectual and institutional center of gravity. Of the issue's thirty-three articles, twenty-three were by scholars in English departments, and all the authors appear to have had university affiliations.[1] The list of fifty-four editorial board members on the inside cover casts a wider disciplinary net, though one firmly grounded in the institution of the university.

Alongside the masthead and table of contents, however, a more unusual claim for the journal's leadership appears. Up until 2021, the first page of every printed issue announced that *"postmedieval: a journal of medieval cultural studies* is published in association with the BABEL Working Group" and then recounted the group's story. Founded in 2004, BABEL was "a collective and desiring assemblage" made up "primarily of medievalists but also including persons working in other areas" (Joy and Dionne 2010b).[2] In text printed under a black-and-white reproduction of Pieter Bruegel's "The Great Tower of Babel" (ca. 1563), members of BABEL are described as "working to develop new cross-disciplinary alliances between the humanities, sciences, social sciences, and the fine arts in order to formulate and practice new 'critical humanisms,' as well as to develop a more present-minded medieval studies and a more historically-minded cultural studies" (Joy and Dionne 2010b). Readers who were familiar with BABEL will recall that it was an organization looser and more protean than a learned society. In a retrospective essay about editing *postmedieval*, Lara Farina and Myra Seaman (2022: 91) recall that BABEL "preferred voluntary and often spontaneous collaboration" rather than elected officers or a fixed roster of membership. Despite its lack of formalized structures, for the decade running from 2005 to 2015, BABEL was a dynamic force in medieval studies— orchestrating, for instance, a series of important biennial conferences. The BABEL ethos was to be irreverent, playful, experimental, antihierarchical, and eager to invite you—yes, *you!*—under the circus tent of its operations. As a graduate student, I found it extravagantly hospitable. There were no fixed procedures that governed the connection of BABEL to *postmedieval*, except that anyone who declared themselves a BABEL member could claim a subscription discount. Nonetheless, the "desiring assemblage" shared with *postmedieval* an attitude of institutional restlessness, trying to twist away from the conventional grounds of scholarly exchange.

The prospectus for *postmedieval* that Joy and Seaman drafted in 2008–9 to pitch the journal to Palgrave Macmillan outlines some of its intel-

---

1. Also represented are the disciplines of French, German, philosophy, history, archaeology, theater, comparative literature, and cognitive neuroscience.
2. This quotation is cited from Joy and Dionne 2010b, but it also appears in subsequent issues.

lectual genealogy. *Postmedieval* was a slightly belated emergence from the intellectual foment that swirled around the medievalist uptake of theoretical discourses like feminism, queer theory, psychoanalysis, poststructuralism, and postcolonialism. In the prospectus, Joy and Seaman (2009) observe that *postmedieval* would find its place alongside other medieval studies journals engaged with "contemporary theoretical approaches" and "theoretically-inflected historicisms," like *Exemplaria* (founded in 1989), *New Medieval Literatures* (1997), and the *Journal of Medieval and Early Modern Studies* (1997). The prospectus, together with BABEL's early sponsored publications and the first issues of the journal, offer a clear sense of the scholarship that most influenced *postmedieval*'s start.[3] Titles cited most frequently include Kathleen Biddick's *The Shock of Medievalism* (1998), Carolyn Dinshaw's *Getting Medieval: Sexualities and Communities, Pre- and Postmodern* (1999), Paul Strohm's *Theory and the Premodern Text* (2000), Glenn Burger and Steven Kruger's edited collection *Queering the Middle Ages* (2001), and Jeffrey Jerome Cohen's *Medieval Identity Machines* (2003). All of these are highly reflexive works of scholarship that meditate on theory's generative role in the interpretation of the medieval past. Most were produced under the aegis of English departments.[4]

The phrase "medieval cultural studies," in the journal's subtitle, is now less familiar than it once was. It seems to have come into circulation starting with a much-discussed 1995 conference, "Cultural Frictions: Medieval Cultural Studies in Post-modern Contexts."[5] Many of the papers from "Cultural Frictions" were subsequently published in a special issue of *New Literary History* in 1997, which, as Michael Uebel noted in his introduction, represented not so much "a 'new' approach to the Middle Ages" as "new approaches"—"a new eclecticism" (Uebel and Smith 1997: 158–59). Meanwhile in 1998, the journal *Studies in Medievalism* published a special issue entitled "Medievalism and the Academy," part 2, "Cultural Studies," edited by David Metzger, with subsections called "The Question of Difference," "The Question of Theory," "The Question of Woman," and "The Question of God," and a note lamenting that it had not been possible "to include the 'Question of Sexuality' in this list" as well (Metzger 1998: 10n1). Medieval

---

3. For other BABEL-sponsored publications, see Joy et. al 2007; Joy and Neufeld 2007.
4. *The Shock of Medievalism*, by Biddick, a historian, is the exception.
5. For the conference program, see "Cultural Frictions: Medieval Cultural Studies in Post-modern Contexts," https://web.archive.org/web/19980124064935/http://www.georgetown.edu/labyrinth/conf/cs95/ (accessed March 13, 2022). I am grateful to Mary Kate Hurley for discovering the location of this material online.

cultural studies in these early, rangy instantiations was thus a gathering place for a range of questions and approaches. If these articulations shared something, it was the refusal of neutral or objective historicism. Writing in 2006 in *Medieval Cultural Studies: Essays in Honour of Stephen Knight*, Ruth Evans, Helen Fulton, and David Matthews emphasized the overlaid, compacted nature of the materials proper to medieval cultural studies, drawn from the coimbricated archives of the Middle Ages and medievalism (or the later reception of the period). The methodology reminds us that we necessarily "deliver a version of the medieval past that is not identical with that past's sense of itself" and that the specificity of our own versions of the past testifies to the ongoingly situated and interested uses to which history is put (Evans, Fulton, and Matthews 2006: 2).

In their prospectus for *postmedieval*, Joy and Seaman (2009) match these prior articulations by adopting a self-consciously pluralistic paradigm:

> It will be admitted that attempts to define "cultural studies," in any period, have been vexed over the years, although it has very distinct histories in the U.K. (where it was originally connected to the founding of the Birmingham Centre for Contemporary Cultural Studies in 1964, which had definitive Marxist, Frankfurt School, and Gramscian orientations) and America (where it has been most often associated with the analysis of subjective relations to the ephemera of mass popular culture). For the purposes of this journal, we take as a given that cultural studies do not comprise a unified field of approaches and objects, but rather constitutes an open field of inter- and multidisciplinary debate regarding the material, discursive, and other relations between cultural objects, practices, and institutions and the realms with which they come into contact: history, society, politics, commerce, religion, globalism, the body, subjectivity, and the like. To develop and practice a *medieval* cultural studies will be to ask, not only what longer historical perspectives can provide to contemporary cultural theories, but also how the Middle Ages—its mentalities, social forms, culture, theology, political and legal structures, ethical values, and the like—inflect contemporary life and thought.

The marked eclecticism of this approach—which declines to decide among methods or topics and instead embraces them all on a flattened plane of possibility—is recognizably postmodernist. The coimplication of present and past in "medieval cultural studies" tends to create a temporal kaleidoscope, in which different historical conjunctures abruptly form and dissolve.

The first issue of *postmedieval* sets up a series of mirrorings and displacements among notions of the medieval, the postmedieval, and the postmodern—starting, as I have mentioned, with the cover image. Since the issue has as its title and theme, *"When* Did We Become Post/Human?," contributions foreground topics like technology, new media, robots, cyborgs, and other sci-fi topoi linked to the self-transcendence of the human. Over the course of the issue, those elements are remixed with the literature and culture of the Middle Ages and early modern period. Contributors reject truisms about historical sequence by highlighting intimacies between the futuristic and archaic. For instance, Ruth Evans in her essay criticizes the presentism of much posthumanist thought, evident in its fascination with the latest developments in bioengineering. As a corrective, Evans offers a "temporal recalibration" and a different "way of slashing the post/ human." She focuses not on the emergence of specific technologies but on the enduring practice of incorporating nonbiological props into embodied selves—as in, in her example, the medieval arts of memory. The props may change, but the posthuman condition does not. Thus, in Evans's (2010: 65) formulation, "the 'post' is simultaneously present, future, and past, and the past is correspondingly folded into the 'post'—and the 'human' is decisively relocated as an entity distinct from the Enlightenment ideal of 'Man.'" Enlightenment "man" and his close relation, the liberal humanist subject, pop up across the issue, avatars for that "certain exclusivity of insight" propounded by modernity, with its pretensions to rationalization and universality (Appiah 1991: 342).

Julian Yates (2010: 224), an early modernist, warns in his article of the tenacity of chronological sequence, despite the challenges brought to it:

> No matter how many brilliant, vital, anti-teleological protestations there are to the contrary—that "we have never been modern"; that "we have never been human" but have always been "embodied"; that we have always been "natural-born cyborgs"; or that "humanism" not the "human" is what finally resides in the "post-human"—the pull to mere chronology in the preposition "post" threatens to posit the "post-human" merely as what comes next, nominalizing the term, and so sloughing it off as a category, a type of being, an ontology, even an anthropology, and so a valid reference.

Against this tendency, Yates, Evans, and other contributors argue for the antichronological possibilities of the *post*-. The issue's title, *"When* Did We Become Post/Human?," emerges as something of a joke. What are offered are rejections of punctual historical emergence and, in its place, alternative proposals.[6] In their editorial introduction, Joy and Dionne (2010a: 6) make this explicit: "We propose that the post/human present and future are predicated upon a plurality of different, discontinuous and heterogeneous temporalities: there are many different Nows existing alongside each other and within each of them, multiple pasts—pasts in which the human never was entirely itself." Here again is the flattened temporal plane, where "different Nows" yield "multiple pasts," spread out for interpretation.

The pluralism of this approach is reflected in the format of the issue. Though it is quite long, almost three hundred pages, its thirty-three contributions are short; most are eight or nine pages. The brief articles reflect *postmedieval*'s preference for evocative encounter over ironclad demonstration. As the prospectus explains, a large number of short pieces allow "for the fullest possible disciplinary and other perspectives on a particular subject" (Joy and Seaman 2009). In a similar spirit, BABEL's conferences and sponsored sessions were pioneers of the five-minute presentation, often self-consciously theatrical, which helped shift understandings of what scholarly discourse could be. Meanwhile, *postmedieval*'s use of sidenotes limited the scale of the paratextual apparatus that could accompany any given article. The layout made room for the proper crediting of ideas, but in scale and design, it departed from the conventions of traditionally authoritative medievalist scholarship, in which massive footnotes testified to scholarly rigor. Finally, though *postmedieval* always maintained the practice of peer review, it also experimented with how to make that process less hierarchical and more inclusive and transparent.[7] If journals like *Speculum* had claimed for themselves a "certain exclusivity of insight" (in Appiah's terms), then *postmedieval* rejected that claim by trying something else.[8]

To track the intellectual currents that led up to the journal's founding is to encounter the now partly obsolescent medium of the blog. I found it a little dizzying, in preparing this article, to go back through web pages from the late aughts and be reminded of the scale and quality of such writing. In

6. For an expression of fierce dissent from this overall tendency, see Bartolovich 2010.

7. For instance, the journal experimented with a practice called "crowd review"; see "Crowd Review," *postmedieval*, Palgrave Macmillan (website) https://www.palgrave.com /gp/journal/41280/about/crowd-review (accessed September 3, 2022).

8. *Speculum: A Journal of Medieval Studies*, published by the Medieval Academy of America, is the most widely distributed journal of medieval studies and one of the most prestigious. I invoke it as an authoritative standard-bearer.

2023, social media tends to favor brevity, image and video over text, and semiprivate modes of address and archiving. By contrast, in 2010 writing on the internet was substantial public prose—often slablike paragraphs of argument, citation, and reflection. The articles that *postmedieval* began publishing shared features with these blog posts (and not infrequently began their existence in connection with them). For instance, *postmedieval* welcomed first-person and informal modes of address, exploratory approaches to research (rather than comprehensive mastery), a length shorter than traditional academic articles, and topical arguments that intervened directly in present-day controversies. Moreover, the editors sought to democratize authorship much as blogs had done, by seeking out and supporting contributors who did not (or not yet) have traditional academic credentials.

One especially important online forum for medieval English literary studies at the time was the blog *In the Middle* (*ITM*), created in 2006 by Jeffrey Jerome Cohen, then a faculty member in English at George Washington University in Washington, DC.[9] Blogging responsibilities were soon shared among Cohen, Eileen Joy, Karl Steel, and Mary Kate Hurley. The fact that Steel and Hurley were both graduate students when they started writing there traduced some of the field's gatekeeping norms. The verve of Steel's and Hurley's posts and their place in much-read intellectual exchanges were refutations of any sense that medievalists only gradually, cautiously, worked their way into positions where they could address the field. The accessibility of authorship was an affordance of internet publishing in general, where one could write briefly, experimentally, comically, and audaciously, and no one could stop you. Under Cohen's leadership, *ITM* developed a reliable community of readers, who often became guest bloggers in turn. *Postmedieval*, like *ITM* and the BABEL Working Group, sought to push back against academic paradigms of wary intellectual apprenticeship. People who were not tenured faculty consistently proposed and edited special issues, organized *postmedieval*-sponsored conference sessions, published articles, and otherwise set the terms for intellectual conversation in the journal.

There were limits, though, to what this inclusion could accomplish. In the case of *postmedieval*, though a relatively wide array of voices were welcomed in its pages, they were gathered into a unit of intellectual property "owned absolutely by the Publisher"—as editorial contracts stipulated.

9. For a thoughtful reflection on blogging, *ITM*, and "Internet-assisted collaboration" in medieval studies, see Cohen 2010.

Seaman recalls, "At the time, we were not as attuned to the differences that might exist between academic and commercial journal publishers, nor had opportunities for open access publication made their way into academic journal publishing" (Farina and Seaman 2022: 93). Editors were required to agree (as they continue to have to) that "all Intellectual Property Rights in the Journal including the title of the Journal, the subscribers list, the content in print and electronic format and all associated good will are, and shall remain, the sole and exclusive property of the Publisher."[10] These were not exceptional stipulations, though they were serious ones, of consequence for the journal's future. Meanwhile, aspirations for inclusion ran into other constraints—on the time, labor, and resources of potential authors. *Postmedieval* began publishing in the aftermath of the 2008 recession, a point when the number of tenure-line academic positions in the humanities fell sharply and did not rebound. Though the journal's editors were eager to feature the often brilliant work of precariously employed academics, questions necessarily arose about how this unpaid work would be supported and whether it should be undertaken at all. Such uncertainties became only more urgent as time went on.

A *postmedieval* article in 2010, then, was a corporate asset, "sole and exclusive property of the publisher." It was also an artifact of intellectual expression, wherein thinking about the past, under the pressure of theoretical reflexivity, took shape. These ontologies jostled against one another in the life of the journal. In answering "*When* did we become post/human?" contributors to *postmedieval*'s inaugural issue documented their reactions to phenomena with similarly mixed natures. The humanities appear in the issue's pages as both the reflex of a hegemonic liberal order and the imperiled grounds for studying the past. The Middle Ages is a fragile collection of traces and the malignant construction of still active chauvinisms. Humanism is exclusionary and homogenizing, yet BABEL seeks "to formulate and practice new 'critical humanisms'" (Joy and Dionne 2010b). Such entities— the humanities, humanism, the Middle Ages, medieval studies, and *postmedieval* itself—solicit both critique and defense, rejection and repair. Such rivenness, I would suggest, cannot be eliminated from our relation to the past and our means of studying it—though different scholarly formations certainly adopt different tactics for managing those divisions. In 2010, *postmedieval*'s approach was additive and paratactic, broadly compatible with

10. Agreement for editorial services for *postmedieval: a journal of medieval cultural studies*, signed September 13, 2011.

the pluralism of postmodernism. Over the next decade, as the cultural energies of postmodernism ebbed and transformed, it was the global scale of contemporary affairs that would become a major conceptual and methodological issue for the journal, at the same time that the transnational movements of capital continued to shape publication.

Interlude

Between 2010 and 2021, *postmedieval* published four issues per year, almost all of them guest edited and built around specific topics. To look back at these issues is to see important subfields taking shape and finding new articulations—for instance, "The Animal Turn" (guest edited by Karl Steel and Peggy McCracken in 2011), "Disability and the Social Body" (guest edited by Julie Singer in 2012), "Ecomaterialism" (guest edited by Jeffrey Jerome Cohen and Lowell Duckert in 2013), "Making Race Matter in the Middle Ages" (guest edited by Cord J. Whitaker in 2015), "Facing Up to the History of Emotions" (guest edited by Stephanie Downes and Stephanie Trigg in 2017), and "Medieval Intersex: Language and Hermaphroditism" (guest edited by Ruth Evans).[11] Meanwhile, individual articles experimented with new modalities of scholarship.[12] The constant rotation of editorial authority allowed different versions of medieval studies to take shape in the journal's pages.

In 2015, Lara Farina joined Myra Seaman as coeditor, and Eileen Joy shifted into a more advisory role while continuing to manage the journal's social media accounts. Holly Crocker stepped down as book reviews editor in 2016, and I took over those responsibilities. All of us who had assumed such editorial roles up to 2021 were white women who had found tenure-track appointments in US English departments. There was, then, a kind of provincialism in the journal's record of leadership, though it also testified to the role of feminist scholars in building and leading platforms for new conceptual work in medieval studies.

Also in 2015, a corporate merger created Springer Nature and swallowed Palgrave Macmillan up into its ever more sprawling global processes. As Farina and Seaman (2022: 93–94) summarize: "The buyout is reflec-

---

11. For the list of issues, see "Volumes and Issues," *postmedieval*, SpringerLink, https://link.springer.com/journal/41280/volumes-and-issues (accessed March 17, 2022).
12. Lara Farina has recently enumerated some examples of "serious play with the form and style of scholarship" in the journal; see *postmedieval* Editorial Board 2021: 25–26.

tive of the past decade's trends in scholarly publishing, which has seen the predominance of increasingly fewer and larger presses, as smaller companies and university presses have folded, been absorbed, or lost institutional support in an era of tightening budgets." In the fallout of the merger, I watched as Farina and Seaman performed herculean labors to keep the journal's busy production schedule going. In their retrospective essay, they recall the "obstacles to innovation and adaptation" that the merger made clear: "restricted accessibility; rigid standardization of processes and format; refusal to decentralize proprietary processes; and corporate structures that defer decision-making" (Farina and Seaman 2022: 94). Springer Nature showed no interest in maintaining individual subscribers or print circulation, so the journal gradually became available only through institutional subscriptions to its electronic version.

Meanwhile, as time passed, the wider ecosystems of medieval studies and scholarly discourse continued to change. Blogging faded.[13] The casualization and precarity of academic labor continued to accelerate. The "desiring assemblage" of the BABEL Working Group hosted its final large-scale conference at the University of Toronto in fall of 2015 and afterward entered a process of dispersal. Some of the ambitions it had pursued for a more accessible and equitable medieval studies were taken up by other organizations, both new (e.g., Medievalists of Color) and established (e.g., the Medieval Academy of America), not to mention less formalized groups, like the activist-scholars leading medieval trans studies (including, among others, M. W. Bychowski, Micah James Goodrich, Blake Gutt, Dorothy Kim, and Alicia Spencer-Hall). Indeed, it is perhaps fitting that one of BABEL's final actions under its own name was to organize an open letter in 2018 in solidarity with a newer organization, Medievalists of Color. With more than six hundred signatories, the letter protested the International Congress on Medieval Studies' (ICMS) decision to reject multiple sessions cosponsored by Medievalists of Color, most notably two sessions organized by Shokoofeh Rajabzadeh and cosponsored by the Graduate Medievalists at Berkeley student group. The letter objected to the lack of transparency attendant on the ICMS selection process and argued that sessions addressing medieval race, globality, public-facing scholarship, and a self-

13. For instance, *In the Middle* had 105 posts in 2016, 87 in 2017, 40 in 2018, and 12 in 2019. Numbers drawn from the blog archive at *In the Middle*, https://www.inthemedieval middle.com/ (accessed March 17, 2022).

critical medieval studies warranted multiple appearances in the program.[14] ICMS subsequently did institute a more transparent process to decide the program, with a rotating roster of contributing reviewers. The letter was the final time the BABEL Working Group would conjure a large medievalist collective under its name.

In 2020, *postmedieval* celebrated its ten-year anniversary with two coedited special issues: "Critical Confessions Now," edited by Abdulhamit Arvas, Afrodesia McCannon, and Kris Trujillo; and "Race, Revulsion, and Revolution," edited by Mary Rambaran-Olm, M. Breann Leake, and Micah James Goodrich. As these issues showed, the journal remained a vibrant publication in the field, where authors and editors were taking risks and trying out new modes of addressing medieval studies. But once these issues appeared, nothing remained in the publication pipeline, and the journal approached a crossroads.

postmedieval Now: 2021 and After

It remains the case today that to be *postmedieval* is simultaneously to undo the medieval and to propagate it. It is to draw others into the time frame of the West even as we try to warp and crack the grid. It is to invite a welter of language traditions to appear, but in English. It is to perform, and to solicit, a great deal of collaborative labor within the horizon of a for-profit company. Some of these conditions can be and have been challenged and renegotiated; doing so has been the labor of institutional change, eked out in legal, material, financial, social, intellectual, and aesthetic terms. But while specific circumstances can often be altered, the larger pattern is not one we are likely to put behind us: we will not become unproblematically *post-*, unburdened of historical baggage, at least not without change at a scale far beyond that of an academic field. In what is left of this essay, I reflect on *postmedieval* since 2021 and the journal's ongoing, necessarily unsettled, responses to its own conditions of possibility.

Starting in 2020, Seaman and Farina were thinking about stepping down from their editorial roles. Seaman had been leading *postmedieval* for more than a decade; Farina, for five years. Yet they felt uneasy recruiting future editors for what had often felt to them like undersupported work. As book reviews editor, I was part of the conversations about *postmedi-*

14. For the text of the letter and its signatories, see Steering Committee of the BABEL Working Group 2018.

eval's future. We faced several constraints. Springer Nature owned the journal's name and contents. If the current editors simply resigned and refused to oversee the transition to new leadership, the publisher could pick new editors themselves, and *postmedieval* would continue in "zombie" form— tethered to its name and its back issues but unmoored from the intellectual community that had established it. But even if the editors decided to abandon the journal's name and contents to Springer and take their editorial vision elsewhere, it was no easy matter to find a publisher ready to support the resource-intensive processes of journal production, like typesetting, distribution, and archiving. The task would amount to starting a new journal.

As it turned out, Springer agreed to make a further financial investment in *postmedieval* by funding a part-time managing editor, someone who would be compensated for taking on some of the administrative labor and copyediting that Seaman and Farina had been doing entirely on their own. That concession made staying at Springer seem feasible. It was under these renegotiated conditions of labor, but without a change to the journal's ownership, that three new editors took over at the start of 2021: Sara Ritchey, Shazia Jagot, and me. At the time, Ritchey was an associate professor of history at the University of Tennessee, Knoxville; Jagot, a lecturer in the Department of English and Related Literature at the University of York; I was an associate professor of English at the University of Chicago.

One of the first tasks the three of us faced was putting together an editorial board. The members of the previous *postmedieval* board had served for eleven years, so it was time for new leadership. As we set about drafting invitations, Ritchey, Jagot, and I found ourselves in a distinctly different position from the one that Seaman and Joy had occupied in 2009, when they were pitching their prospectus to Palgrave Macmillan. Then, the incipient publication had needed the authorizing endorsements of a large and prestigious board to make its case to the publisher. Now *postmedieval* was well established, but we faced other challenges. We had no equivalent to the BABEL Working Group—no energetic, utopian "assemblage" who claimed us, much less one whose aspirational openness could push against the strictures of academic publishing. We needed to build a coalition, an alliance of scholars representing different disciplines and subfields, who could help us recognize new possibilities.

At the forefront of our considerations was one of the most widespread trends in contemporary medieval studies, the imperative to think about not just the temporal mediation of the Middle Ages but its geopolitics as well—an imperative often synecdochally figured by the phrase "the global Middle Ages.'"[15] The energy behind this trend is indicated by the number of journals recently founded on the topic, including the *Medieval Globe* (founded 2014), *Medieval Worlds* (founded 2015), and the *Journal of Medieval Worlds* (founded 2019). During the editorial transition, in the various conversations that Farina, Seaman, and I had with potential editors and with longtime readers of *postmedieval*, we heard repeatedly about the desirability of shifting the journal's center of gravity outside of medieval England and outside of literary studies. Ritchey, Jagot, and I assumed our editorial roles with these goals in mind. Since *postmedieval* had an established identity already, it would require scholars from different backgrounds staking a claim in the journal to refashion what it could be.

Of course, the ironies and complications coiled in the "global Middle Ages" are many. The Middle Ages is often narrated as the era just prior to planetary circumnavigation and for that reason crucially *not* global. Medievalists thinking at the scale of the globe have thus seemed to trespass into the domain of modernity. Some have criticized the subfield for imposing Eurocentric schemes of periodization where they do not fit. Yet others have seen it as a means to dismantle European exceptionalism from within. Geraldine Heng (2014: 236) analyzes this ambiguity and considers the fact that scholars of non-European cultures "have *themselves* begun to conjure with terms like the 'medieval' and 'the Middle Ages.'" She continues: "References to 'the Islamic Middle Ages,' 'medieval Japan,' or 'medieval India' can perhaps be seen both as the hegemonic ineluctability of European studies' influence in the academy, and also as efforts of goodwill in positing the utility of structuring overarching heuristic paradigms across geographic zones through attention to features and characteristics that suggest resemblance or analogy" (236–37).[16]

Critical reflection on the Janus-faced character of the "global Middle Ages," seemingly poised between the promulgation and unraveling of Eurocentrism, has been encouraged by the increasing interest in medieval studies in the politics of time. Some scholars have focused on the violent and disciplinary character of the early modern period's construction of historical difference. Kathleen Davis takes a different tack in her 2008 *Periodization and Sovereignty*, where she argues that the periodization of "medieval" and "modern" took shape via nationalist claims to territorial sovereignty in the eighteenth and nineteenth centuries. The medieval, on Davis's account,

---

15. The phrase was evidently coined by Geraldine Heng in 2003; see Heng 2021: 4.
16. For a more recent discussion, with similar implications, see Heng 2021: 21–22.

was a colonial invention. While the medievalisms so important to *postmedieval*'s founding often sought to multiply temporal relations—"many different Nows existing alongside each other and within each of them, multiple pasts" (Joy and Dionne 2010a: 6)—the field has come increasingly to focus on the intransigence and coercion of time's structures.

For the new editors, the risks and promises of a more geographically encompassing "medieval" were on our minds as we worked to assemble the new editorial board, which we hoped would include disciplines, language traditions, geographic locales, and perspectives heretofore little featured in the journal. At the time of writing, we have twenty board members, who bring expertise in fields and languages including musicology, Byzantine studies, art history, medievalism, religious history, Jewish studies, Ethiopian studies, the environmental humanities, film studies, Chinese, Arabic, Persian, Hebrew, Japanese, French, the Mediterranean, the Indian Ocean, premodern critical race studies, manuscript studies, and the digital humanities.[17] The board is also varied in terms of where members live and work. In addition to ten US-based members and three in the United Kingdom, members are based in Australia, Ireland, Germany, Morocco, the United Arab Emirates, Turkey, and Bosnia and Herzegovina.[18] As with so many aspects of academic labor, the position is unremunerated except for an electronic subscription and a small quantum of prestige. In inviting scholars to join the board, we invite them to join the journal's "we," an entity that seeks both to extend itself and transform itself in their inclusion.

Questions remain as to why those in other fields should be expected to give their time and expertise to collaborate under the sign of the "medieval"—not to mention its peculiar cousin, the "postmedieval." After all, thinkers working on geographic areas other than Western Europe have often reflected critically on their fields' encounters with the "Middle Ages." For instance, in his 2018 monograph Thomas Bauer argues at length against the *islamisches Mittelalter* (the "Islamic Middle Ages"), contending that it distorts both historical explanation and ideological perception (see also Varisco 2007; Rafii 2023). Michael Puett, a scholar of Chinese history, notes, "When the ancient-medieval-modern narrative began to be applied

---

17. For board bios, see "Editorial Board," *postmedieval* (website), Google Sites, https://sites.google.com/view/postmedieval/about/editorial-board (accessed March 19, 2022).
18. For information about where board members work, see "Editorial Board," *postmedieval*, Palgrave Macmillan (website), http://www.palgrave.com/gp/journal/41280/about/editorial-board (accessed March 19, 2022).

to China by Western scholars in the nineteenth and twentieth centuries, the concern was precisely to ask why China had failed to emerge into the 'the modern era' as the West had" (Davis and Puett 2015: 4). Daud Ali provides a useful capsule history of how the period has been applied to South Asia. As Ali (2012: 7) recounts, both Orientalist and nationalist scholars in the early twentieth century made use of the tripartite scheme of "ancient," "medieval," and "modern" to gloss the progression of "Hindu," "Muslim," and "British" epochs.[19] The rise of Marxist-inflected social history in the late 1950s and 1960s intensified interest in "Indian feudalism" as a means of analyzing and comparing modes of production (8–9). Ali tracks the gradual obsolescence of "the medieval" in south Asian historiography, but the specter of the benighted medieval past makes a surprising return, in what Ali identifies as historians' new interest in early modernity, especially the proposal of "indigenous" rather than exogenous (European) sources of change between the sixteenth and eighteenth centuries. This scholarship often focuses on geographically far-flung trading markets and the activities of merchant capitalists. Ali writes: "The arguments for 'early modernism' or 'early modernity' in South Asia however, have often relied, rather ironically, on the very tropes of the 'medieval' once used to consign the Mughal Empire itself to a backward 'medieval period.' At this level, early modern historiography has not so much rectified images of medieval stagnation as simply pushed back their boundaries to pre-Mughal times" (12). On Ali's account, the glamour of discovering globalizers and modernizers in one's archive leads to the repetition of earlier schemes of periodization, albeit now with new protagonists.

Connectivity, circulation, and material and economic exchange are the focus of much scholarship on global early modernity.[20] In a conversation with Kathleen Davis about "Periodization and 'The Medieval Globe,'" Michael Puett cautions against the trend of challenging the medieval/early modern divide by importing the topics of trade, contact, and exchange into the study of the Middle Ages:

> Even if finally removed from a claim of "early modernity"—finally removed, in other words, from a claim that these global networks of trade were breaking down earlier, more insular societies and moving us toward a modern, globalized world—we need to be careful that we are not implicitly celebrating these networks for precisely this very

19. For another and more recent consideration of the "compromise" of employing "medieval" in South Asian historiography, see Flatt 2022.
20. For a helpful overview of scholarship on "global early modernity," see Strathern 2018.

reason. In other words, we risk falling into the danger of the "early modernity" paradigm even if we have dropped the term. (Davis and Puett 2015: 12)

As part of the same conversation, Davis points out the ideological sympathy between a global historiography and neoliberal economics. The critical historiography of medieval studies has rendered it common knowledge that the discipline's foundations and ongoing conventions took shape as part of nationalist, imperial, and colonial projects of nation-states. Yet, Davis suggests, the new hegemony of globalization demands new sites of critique, particularly in light of the possibility that "globalization *needs* the de-nationalizing of that temporal frame we call the Middle Ages" (Davis and Puett 2015: 2, emphasis original). Davis continues:

> Unpicking the attachments of a foundational Middle Ages to the national histories of northwestern Europe, and reconfiguring them as global, stretched across trade routes, enmeshed economies, and intercultural experience, is precisely what is necessary for globalization—particularly its economic forms—to have a legitimizing past. . . . We medievalists, situated within the corporate university and responsive to its call for global studies, seem poised to deliver such a past, and we would do well, I think, to keep the inherent dangers of this larger context in mind. (2–3)

Davis invites us to scrutinize the urgency of the "global Middle Ages" in our present moment. Does our work create a "legitimizing past" for the transnational mobility of capital? What Davis calls the corporate university has its parallel in corporate publishing, and I have already quoted Springer Nature CEO Derk Haank announcing, "Taking a unified one-company approach will enable us to have a global view." Inviting a multinational roster of board members and authors to invest their labor in *postmedieval* cannot be cleanly separated from Haank's "global view." Nonetheless, how to react to Davis's warning, or what to do as we "keep the inherent dangers of this larger context in mind," is far from obvious. The lesson cannot be to go backward to a reactionary embrace of national frameworks or willful ignorance of global connections, and indeed, no scholars are suggesting this. Responding to the knot of globality and periodization will have to be worked out in practice, with all our tools of critique and self-scrutiny to hand.

The ambiguities that accompany the extension of the "medieval" outside of Europe recur and repeat in the extension of other concepts as well. Take "theory." *Postmedieval* defines its mission as "publish[ing] theoretically driven scholarship on premodernity and its ongoing reverberations."[21] From its founding, it has assumed the role of theoretical upstart, challenging pretensions to historicist objectivity dominant in the field. But theory only looks like an underdog from certain angles and particular points of view. At a *postmedieval* board meeting in April 2021, one of our new board members, Mahnaz Yousefzadeh, pointed out the geopolitical hierarchy that often shapes the status of "theory" in premodern fields, determining who gets to theorize and on what basis. "Theory" is most readily accepted in Anglo-American English departments, where poststructuralist approaches eventually reached wide acceptance. "Theory" often claims the powers of conceptual synthesis and timely intervention, against the details of philological argument and positivist historiography. Yet the theoretically driven scholar's lack of interest in establishing basic chronologies or textual editions often depends on the ready availability of such resources—the fruits of well-established scholarly fields, accessible in well-stocked research libraries and buttressed with modern language translations and other aids to access. Theory's confidence in speaking on behalf of wider archives can seem to mirror existing hierarchies and the West's acquisitive, globalizing knowledge practices.

An observation related to Yousefzadeh's has recently been made by Justin Stearns, a scholar of premodern Islamic intellectual history. He remarks in a published conversation, "[On occasion, when] I look at our Europeanist colleagues, I am struck with something you could call 'theory envy,' as I see there a much deeper explicit engagement with a wide variety of contemporary theoretical approaches" (Şahin et al., 2021: 204). Stearns continues: "This is in part a reflection of our fields not yet having fully digested the ocean of unedited manuscript sources with which we are faced, but we are also struggling to find the right master narratives with which to contextualize these materials and to articulate them to others outside our fields" (204). As the comments of Stearns and Yousefzadeh register, scholarly fields come to "theory" variously, and the concept is marked by its circulation through globalized hierarchies of knowledge production. If one wants to avoid an anti-intellectualist rejection of "theory" but at the same time to challenge theory's provincialism, it is important to acknowledge the asymmetries of its circulation, to make these the occasion for critique and change.

21. For a full mission statement, see "Overview," *postmedieval*, Palgrave Macmillan (website), http://www.palgrave.com/gp/journal/41280 (accessed March 11, 2022).

Writing in 2004, Rey Chow criticized the discipline of comparative literature for its extension of the European category of "literature" across the globe. She writes, "The grid of intelligibility here is that of literature as understood in Europe, and historical variations are often conceived of in terms of other cultures' welcome entries into or becoming synthesized with the European tradition" (Chow 2004: 294). She points out that this configuration "stabilizes Europe as the grid of intelligibility to which may be added more and more others" (304). The role that Chow identifies "literature" as playing—providing a conceptual grid for inclusion and comparability—is also played by "theory" and the "medieval." Adding "comparative," "global," or *post-* as qualifying modifiers constitutes a profoundly ambiguous gesture, the effects of which cannot be preemptively exonerated from giving new life to old categories and old hierarchies. This is the "risk" that Derrida (1981: 5). identifies in "put[ting] the old names to work": "To put the old names to work, or even just to leave them in circulation, will always of course, involve some risk: the risk of settling down or regressing into the system that has been, or is in the process of being, deconstructed." And yet this is the practice that Derrida recommends, of paleonymics, or retaining the "old name so as to destroy the opposition to which it no longer quite belongs, or to which in *any* event it has never *quite* yielded" (4).

Regarded critically, terms like *global, the Middle Ages,* and *theory* can be catalysts to confront the Eurocentrism, transnational flows of capital, dominance of English, and politics of time that make those words significant for us. The conclusion of the "Apostrophic Overture," above, has asked, "Where are we standing, you and I? Do you want to go somewhere else? Are there places where no one knows your name, or the time inside your name?" To go somewhere else entirely, where no one knows the medieval, would mean abandoning *postmedieval*'s project. That might be a good thing, the right thing to do with our limited time on earth. Yet it is not what *postmedieval* has done, nor could it do so without becoming entirely other than itself. Instead, sutured to medieval studies, academic publishing, and the corporate university, the journal also churns with the impulse to go elsewhere and be otherwise. This is part of the engine of its thinking, which propels it forward, in the directions it does move and the ways it does change. We cannot simply escape from what we critique, when we are also constituted by it. The trick is to figure out what to say and do next.

References

Ali, Daud. 2012. "The Historiography of the Medieval in South Asia." *Journal of the Royal Asiatic Society*, 3rd ser., 22, no. 1: 7–12.

Appiah, Kwame Anthony. 1991. "Is the Post- in Postmodernism the Post- in Post-colonial?" *Critical Inquiry* 17, no. 2: 336–57.

Bartolovich, Crystal. 2010. "Is the Post in Posthuman the Post in Postmedieval?" In Joy and Dionne 2010b, 18–31.

Bauer, Thomas. 2018. *Warum es kein islamisches Mittelalter gab: Das Erbe der Antike und der Orient*. Munich: C. H. Beck.

Chow, Rey. 2004. "The Old/New Question of Comparison in Literary Studies: A Post-European Perspective." *ELH* 71, no. 2: 289–311.

Cohen, Jeffrey Jerome. 2010. "Blogging the Middle Ages." In *Geoffrey Chaucer Hath a Blog: Medieval Studies and New Media*, edited by Brantley Bryant, 29–42. New York : Palgrave Macmillan.

Davis, Kathleen, and Michael Puett. 2015. "Periodization and 'The Medieval Globe': A Conversation." *Medieval Globe* 2, no. 1: 1–14.

Derrida, Jacques. 1981. *Dissemination*. Translated by Barbara Johnson. Chicago: University of Chicago Press.

Derrida, Jacques. 1988. "Signature Event Context." Translated by Samuel Weber. In *Limited Inc*, 1–23. Evanston, IL: Northwestern University Press.

Evans, Ruth. 2010. "Our Cyborg Past: Medieval Artificial Memory as Mindware Upgrade." In Joy and Dionne 2010b, 64–71.

Evans, Ruth, Helen Fulton, and David Matthews. 2006. "Introduction: Stephen Knight and Medieval Cultural Studies." In *Medieval Cultural Studies: Essays in Honour of Stephen Knight*, edited by Ruth Evans, Helen Fulton, and David Matthews, 1–6. Cardiff: University of Wales Press.

Farina, Lara, and Myra Seaman. 2022. "Editing *postmedieval: a journal of medieval cultural studies*." *New Chaucer Studies: Pedagogy and Profession* 3, no. 1: 90–99.

Flatt, Emma J. 2022. "The Worlds of South Asia." In *Teaching the Global Middle Ages*, edited by Geraldine Heng, 177–93. New York: Modern Language Association of America.

Heng, Geraldine. 2014. "Early Globalities, and Its Questions, Objectives, and Methods: An Inquiry into the State of Theory and Critique." *Exemplaria* 26, no. 2–3: 234–53.

Heng, Geraldine. 2021. *The Global Middle Ages: An Introduction*. Cambridge: Cambridge University Press.

Joy, Eileen, and Craig Dionne. 2010a. "Before the Trains of Thought Have Been Laid Down So Firmly: The Premodern Post/Human." In Joy and Dionne 2010b, 1–9.

Joy, Eileen, and Craig Dionne, eds. 2010b. "When Did We Become Post/Human?" Special issue, *postmedieval* 1, no. 1–2.

Joy, Eileen A., and Christine M. Neufeld, eds. 2007. "Premodern to Modern Human-isms: The BABEL Project." Special issue, *Journal of Narrative Theory* 37, no. 2.

Joy, Eileen A., and Myra J. Seaman. 2009. Journal prospectus for *postmedieval: a journal of medieval cultural studies* (April). https://www.siue.edu/%7Eejoy/postmedievalProspectus.htm (accessed March 5, 2022).

Joy, Eileen A., Myra J. Seaman, Kimberly K. Bell, and Mary K. Ramsey, eds. 2007. *Cultural Studies of the Modern Middle Ages.* New York: Palgrave Macmillan.

Latour, Bruno. 1993. *We Have Never Been Modern.* Translated by Catherine Porter. Cambridge, MA: Harvard University Press.

Metzger, David. 1998. Introduction to "Cultural Studies." Part 2 of "Medievalism in the Academy." Special issue, *Studies in Medievalism*, no. 10: 3–12.

postmedieval Editorial Board. 2021. "'What Might a Journal Be?': Reflections from the *postmedieval* Editorial Board." *postmedieval* 12, no. 1–4: 15–27.

Rafii, Raha. 2023. "Making Islam (Coherent): Academic Discourse and the Politics of Language." In "The 'Medieval' Undone: Imagining a New Global Past," edited by Sierra Lomuto. Special issue, *boundary 2* 50, no. 3: 33–55.

Şahin, Kaya, Julia Schleck, and Justin Stearns. 2021. "*Orientalism* Revisited: A Con-versation across Disciplines." *Exemplaria* 33, no. 2: 196–207.

Springer. 2015. "Springer Nature Created Following Merger Completion." Press release, May 6. https://www.springer.com/gp/about-springer/media/press-releases/corporate/springer-nature-created-following-merger-completion/256626.

Steering Committee of the BABEL Working Group. 2018. "Letter of concern, ICMS / Kalamazoo 2019," July 18. https://docs.google.com/forms/d/e/1FAIpQLSd ReGZAQJiSSDWTRV0kT2tO2b9LEaAPLTjDJGCeH6auDczBhA/viewform (accessed March 17, 2022).

Strathern, Alan. 2018. "Global Early Modernity and the Problem of What Came Before." In "The Global Middle Ages," edited by Catherine Holmes and Naomi Standen, 317–44. *Past and Present* 238, supplement 13.

Uebel, Michael, with D. Vance Smith. 1997. Introduction to *New Literary History* 28, no. 2: 157–59.

Varisco, Daniel Martin. 2007. "Making 'Medieval' Islam Meaningful." *Medieval Encoun-ters* 13, no. 3: 385–412.

Yates, Julian. 2010. "It's (for) You; or, The Tele-t/r/opical Post-human." In Joy and Dionne 2010b, 223–34.

The Medieval of the Long Now

Michelle R. Warren

Nothing undoes the medieval quite like the passage of time. Decades turn to centuries to millennia—and the medieval becomes less and less the middle of anything. This slippage is hard to perceive because periodization organizes so many institutions and so much of society and culture. And yet as time goes on, our relationship with the past is increasingly like that of medieval writers themselves—who did not locate themselves in the middle of anything. In this brief essay, I take the perspective of extreme long-term thinking to reexamine the vexed question of how medieval studies can interact with more contemporary fields. How might we share the "now" not only with each other but with our predecessors from other millennia? And how might this perspective transform racial epistemologies? Our answers might just determine the length and vitality of the future.

Periodization has always been political. The Middle Ages are just one

My thanks to Sierra Lomuto for encouraging me to write this essay and to Sarah Masud Preum who actually made me write it—those three hours made all the difference! My first and last reader remains, as ever, Rebecca Biron.

boundary 2 50:3 (2023) DOI 10.1215/01903659-10472359 © 2023 by Duke University Press

component of the segmentation of history that ends up serving any number of partisan causes—stretching all the way back to so-called prehistoric cultures. To the extent, though, that medieval Europe became a defined period at the turn of the sixteenth century, it grew up with global imperialism. And when empire expanded again in the nineteenth century, the racialization of the Middle Ages expanded with it. When colonizers defined unfamiliar peoples far from Europe as "uncivilized," they also classified them as "medieval" (Fabian 1983; Warren 2011). Any "undoing" of periodization thus directly challenges the colonizing deployment of time itself.

Medievalists have been scrutinizing the politics of time for a while now. These efforts have gone hand in hand with critiques of Eurocentrism and calls to incorporate wider geographies into the field. Inspired in part by Dipesh Chakrabarty's (2000) *Provincializing Europe*, for example, medievalists turned to postcolonial theory to reconsider histories of race and power (Ingham and Warren 2003). In a similar vein, a focus on the Mediterranean has made the multicultural realities of premodern cultures abundantly clear (Catlos and Kinoshita 2017). Meanwhile, a fully global approach to the Middle Ages highlights the surprising breadth of premodern interactions and imaginations (Heng 2021). Despite several decades of this sustained work on how contemporary concerns reveal new truths about the past, medievalists have not always managed to convince modernists that we are living in the same world. Perhaps a little perspective from the tenth millennium will help.

What might happen if humans start planning for a ten-thousand-year future? This question is both philosophical and technological; it goes to the heart of planetary survival through the climate catastrophe that is already upon us. In the 1990s, this question inspired the creation of the Long Now Foundation (LNF), whose members seek to counteract short-term thinking— the kind of thinking that measures social and technological impacts in mere years rather than centuries or millennia. At the time, the most salient example of short-term myopia was computing systems not designed for dates beyond 1999. The LNF founders used the "Y2K" problem to think about the "Y10K" problem. Over the past two decades, the LNF has been developing two major projects, the 10,000-Year Clock and the 10,000-Year Library. The library project includes the Rosetta Disk, which might have been called "the 10,000-Year Book"—a micro-etched disk designed to invite anyone who picks it up to find a microscope and read further.[1] Each of these proj-

1. *The Clock of the Long Now*, Long Now Foundation, https://longnow.org/clock (accessed May 12, 2022); "'10,000 Year Library' Conference," Long Now Foundation, https://longnow

ects asks a cultural question with technological dimensions: What can and should last for ten millennia?

Despite this breadth of temporal scope, LNF founders convey the urgency of their efforts with a medieval trope: the future could bring a new "Dark Ages" when digital culture would be lost due to rapid technological change. The analogy here refers to a reductive if widespread stereotype that the end of the Roman Empire left fifth-century Europe in the dark, deprived of knowledge and culture. The "light" brightened a bit in the twelfth century but did not fully return, so the story goes, until the sixteenth-century Renaissance. The LNF's "digital Dark Ages" implies a "digital Renaissance" guaranteed by the triumph of ingenious new technologies. The "digital Dark Ages" concept is part of the broader practice of "tech medievalism" that began in the 1960s with the invention of the internet (Warren 2022: 10–25). The role of medievalism in technology development creates a retrofuturist framework for "the long now" in which the medieval is both precedent and prediction.

We are still "in the middle" of this Middle Ages—somewhere between the beginning and the possible end of human civilization. At this point in time, both the 10,000-Year Clock and the 10,000-Year Library have several material expressions, including websites. In what follows, I wind my way from the clock to that near future called the "digital Dark Ages," to the poet T. S. Eliot, who features on the clock's website, to one of the most creative millennial thinkers of medieval Europe, Henry of Huntingdon (ca. 1088–1157), and back to the clock. From these vantage points, Henry from the twelfth century provides a recent antecedent for imagining the "long now." My method is as much poetic as historical, as much evocation as argument. This story is both narrowly English and broadly global—even postplanetary. It can only be told right now.

The Digital Dark Ages

The clock and the library are explained in detail by Stewart Brand (1999a) in the essay collection *The Clock of the Long Now: Time and Responsibility*. Brand is an eclectic and energetic cultural agitator, best known for creating the *Whole Earth Catalog* (1968–71) but active in many

---

.org/events/02000/jul/30/10000-year-library-conference (accessed May 12, 2022); *The Rosetta Project*, Long Now Foundation, https://rosettaproject.org (accessed May 20, 2022).

pursuits at the intersection of "counterculture and cyberculture" (Turner 2006). *The Clock of the Long Now* is an extended concept pitch—a fantasy in search of engineers, financing, and land. The clock is meant to be "the world's slowest computer"—a mechanical structure designed to "tell time" for ten thousand years.[2] The library, imagined as an adjacent structure, tells a different kind of time by preserving written culture, using denser and denser storage methods to convey accumulated knowledge across the millennia (Brand 1999a: 00:47–48).[3] This curated collection would "reboot" civilization should global society experience a catastrophic loss. With durable, nonelectric storage devices, the library would provide a canon of essential historical, technical, and cultural knowledge to connect postapocalyptic survivors to the long history of human civilizations. The restoration of society will proceed more quickly and smoothly, so the thinking goes, if our descendants do not have to create from scratch.

The clock and the library are designed to avoid "future dark ages" (Brand 1999a: 00:52)—that is, the loss of information through societal collapse. Brand adopts this notion of medieval history from Edward Gibbon's (1776–89) *Decline and Fall of the Roman Empire* (Brand 1999a: 01:46). The distant future, in other words, is framed by the British imperial agenda of the eighteenth century, modeled on Rome as cautionary precedent, and reduced to twentieth-century aphorisms (e.g., "bad things happen fast . . . good things happen slow") (01:56). In this view, the early Middle Ages arrived in an instant:

> Cities emptied; literacy vanished. All the Roman achievements of engineering, culture, and government simply ceased to be. Population in some areas dropped by nine-tenths. Even with the heroic continuity of the Catholic Church, the skein of culture was reduced to fragile wisps: Only one copy of Lucretius made it through the Dark Ages, only one copy of the five books of Livy, one copy of the nine plays of Euripides, one copy of Tacitus, one copy of *Beowulf*. (01:01; see also 00:52)

The end of empire sounds like a catastrophic plague. The drama here is defined by the destruction of books—cultural storage devices that cannot survive without environmental protection or periodic replacement. The texts

2. Long Now Foundation (website), https://longnow.org (accessed May 8, 2022).
3. Brand's book is paginated on the model of a digital clock, beginning with 00:00. This article preserves that pagination when citing the book.

in this case are all notorious companions of empire: they represent how the preservation and promotion of Greek and Roman antiquity served to justify the values and actions of modern imperialism (Warren 2012). The medieval text here, the Old English poem *Beowulf*, became identified with a specifically racialized understanding of English literature as an expression of white supremacy (Rambaran-Olm 2021: 391–93).

In the 1990s, *Beowulf* was also a key component of tech medievalism, with medievalists and technologists alike hailing the triumphant recovery of the text from the fire-damaged manuscript via advanced techniques of computer imaging (Kiernan 1991; Lesk 1997). This kind of digital copying echoes the monk-copyists who produced what Brand calls "heroic continuity" for the Catholic Church. Indeed, monk-copyists are another element of tech medievalism, touted as the quintessential guardians of knowledge (Warren 2022: 15). According to Brand, they alone maintained the "fragile wisps" that eventually brought back culture. In the LNF conception, the clock and the library would be the secular monasteries of the future. The fear of a "future dark ages" thus rests on a convoluted imperial nostalgia laced with white supremacy.

One of the great threats to cultural preservation in the 1990s, as now, is the fragility of digital information. Accordingly, one of the longest chapters in *The Clock of the Long Now* is "Ending the Digital Dark Age" (Brand 1999a: 00:81–92; fig. 1), based on a 1998 LNF conference that convened librarians, archivists, and technologists. They sought ways to "shorten the digital dark age" (00:86), and their solution models were drawn in part from the global Middle Ages. On the one hand, digital archivists would be the new monks: "Digital archivists thus join an ancient lineage of copyists and translators reaching back through European monastic scribes to the Hellenistic scholars at the Library of Alexandria" (00:89). In this lineage, medieval Christian Europe provides the hinge between the oldest and newest libraries. On the other hand, the written record of a Chinese mechanical clock from circa 1090 CE illustrates the kind of technical revival that the library will enable. This water-wheel clock from a millennium ago lasted only ten years but was rebuilt in England in the nineteenth century from a detailed description: "The material clock lasted only a decade; the informational clock, indefinitely" (Brand 1999a: 00:86; Landes 1983: 17–36). Today, this same preservation dream is cast as another medieval icon: as technologists continue seeking solutions to the "digital Dark Ages," some call the solution "digital vellum"—a metaphor based on the durable animal skin used to make most medieval books (Warren 2022: 20–21). This retrofutur-

Figure 1 Title page for chapter 14, "Ending the Digital Dark Age," in *The Clock of the Long Now*, by Stewart Brand, p. 00:81 (https://archive.org /details/clockoflongnow00bran). Each chapter title is presented with a similar analog clock face, with the two hands indicating the chapter number as an "hour"; page numbers are shown as digital "minutes." The book thus has the format of a stopwatch that counts up to twenty-five hours, 190 minutes. This conceit makes the printed book a small-scale model of the long-term timekeeping described across its pages. Source: iMac screenshot, March 12, 2022.

ism resurfaces in the latest update at the LNF website, where "Digital Dark Age" is one of eight concept tags organizing decades of blog posts. In the book chapter, then, Brand gathers medieval precedents to promote a more stable future that remains elusive to this day.

The clock is now being built in the Sierra Diablo mountains near the town of Van Horn in West Texas. The clock's technical development has been led from the beginning by Danny Hillis—prolific inventor, LNF cofounder, and coiner of the term "digital Dark Ages" (Hillis 2017; Brand 1999b). Construction is now underwritten by Jeff Bezos (2011), founder of Amazon.com—a major commercial provider of cloud computing services that began as an online bookstore. Many libraries rely on Amazon for at least some of their off-site digital storage, making Amazon Web Services (AWS) a crucial component of today's bookshelves. In part from these profits, Bezos is building the clock near the facilities of his spacecraft company Blue Origin (Schiller 2013). For an endeavor devoted to long-term thinking, however, the LNF has a selective sense of history: neither the Texas site nor another in Nevada purchased earlier by LNF with other tech patrons recognizes the human history of these lands before the arrival of white colonists in the nineteenth century.[4] The most recent Indigenous stewards include the Shoshone, Paiute, and Apache peoples, among others.[5] The rapid erasure of their memory and the lack of relation with their descendants exemplify the settler-colonialist infrastructure that defines the United States and supports fantasies of temporal mastery. In many ways, the clock materializes the westward drift of empire since the so-called fall of Rome.

The Clock on the Internet

The clock's current setting is remarkably consistent with Brand's (1999a: 00:46–48) description. Given its remote and access-restricted location, for the time being most people will only encounter the clock on the internet. Some version of the clock has been online since the LNF website opened in 1998; Hillis first wrote about it in 1993 as the Millennium Clock.[6] I turn here, though, to the new website launched in June 2011 to highlight Bezos's new role as project patron. At first, the site marked its LNF relationship with two quotes by Brand on the landing page: "We are as gods and we might as well get good at it" (from the 1968 *Whole Earth Catalogue*); "We are as gods and HAVE to get good at it" (from the 2009 *Whole Earth Discipline*).[7] These lines are superimposed on a photo that offers a "gods' eye view" of the drilling rig on the mountain top. On this website, the digital signatures of Brand and Bezos cast the clock into a techno-utopia that projects itself not only to the distant future but beyond Earth—the sky depicted in the distance beyond the mountain and behind Brand's outlandish quotes.

Very quickly, the website's tone shifted to a subtler expression of omniscience (fig. 2). Since at least April 24, 2012, the website's epigraph has been by the English American poet T. S. Eliot (1888–1965):

4. See, for instance, "Nevada," Long Now Foundation (website), https://longnow.org/clock /nevada (accessed May 20, 2022).
5. See Native Land Digital, https://www.native-land.ca (accessed May 20, 2022).
6. Long Now Foundation (website), archived January 25, 1999, Internet Archive, https:// web.archive.org/web/19990125090645/http://longnow.org.
7. "10,000 Year Clock," archived June 20, 2011, Internet Archive, http://web.archive.org /web/20110620083149/http://www.10000yearclock.net.

> We shall not cease from exploration
> And the end of all our exploring
> Will be to arrive where we started
> And know the place for the first time.[8]

These lines are widely quoted for all kinds of inspirational and aspirational purposes, as I learned after a few hours of browsing on Google. Shorn of context, they express a genial optimism in the certainty of wisdom. Taken at face value, they affirm the loftiest ideals of invention and a dedication to sustained effort—ceaseless exploration. The sentiment is entirely appropriate to the endeavor to build a clock that ticks for ten thousand years. Eliot's lines are also a literal description of a clock—the most common analog kind depicted throughout Brand's book (fig. 1): a circular face and two hands cycling through the hours, over and over, yet each minute a "first time" in the ceaseless forward movement of time. The rhythm in these lines of poetry also marks time: although each line has a similar length, the stress pattern varies and accelerates toward a unique double stress at the end, "the first time." Relatedly, the final word gets shorter line by line, descending from four syllables to one (exploration, exploring, started, time). This linear countdown contradicts the semantic message of circular return. Together, the two modes cohere to perform the nature of time itself—a measured repetition that goes round and round, day after day, year after year. If the 10,000-Year Clock ever works, this is precisely what it will do.

The website does not identify the epigraph's source, but a brief internet search located the lines in "Little Gidding" (Eliot [1942] 1971: 49–59). In that context, these four lines are framed by Eliot's particular assimilation of the European Middle Ages. On the clock website, then, Eliot's name turns time back in another direction, joining up with Brand's tech medievalism. "Little Gidding" is the last section of *Four Quartets*, a work dedicated to the nature of time—and known as an astoundingly complex metrical performance (Perloff 2021). The title "Little Gidding" refers to an English village, famous as the home of a seventeenth-century Anglican community much admired by Eliot. "Little Gidding" begins in "Midwinter spring"—an indeterminate season that is "suspended in time" yet very precisely "now and in England" (Eliot [1942] 1971, lines 1, 3, 39). Welcome to Eliot's long now.

As a dizzying array of circular images unfold, we land "Here, the

---

8. "10,000 Year Clock," archived April 24, 2012, Internet Archive, http://web.archive.org /web/20120424230523/http://www.10000yearclock.net.

10,000 YEAR CLOCK | Sierra Diablo Mountain Range

LEARN MORE

We shall not cease from exploration
And the end of all our exploring
Will be to arrive where we started
And know the place for the first time.

T. S. Eliot

UPDATES

Figure 2 Home page of 10,000-Year Clock (https://www.10000yearclock .net). The page features a photo of the Sierra Diablo Mountain Range, two navigation buttons, four lines of poetry by T. S. Eliot, and an overlay of faint dots forming concentric circles. Source: iMac screenshot, March 12, 2022.

intersection of the timeless moment / . . . England and nowhere. Never and always" (lines 52–53). Eliot answers the ten-thousand-year question before it has been asked: "This is the death of earth" (line 69). Gradually, reading through the fog of centuries of literary history, it becomes clear that Eliot's long now, like Brand's, includes the Middle Ages. The details of Eliot's medi-evalism would be long to tell, but medievalist Barbara Newman (2011) has well defined them: they include thematic and formal invocations of Dante Alighieri's *Divine Comedy*, a line from the anonymous fourteenth-century

English poem *The Cloud of Unknowing*, and adaptations from Julian of Norwich's fourteenth-century *Revelation of Love*. Eliot's medievalism lends the poem its specifically Christian sense of time as a linear transcendence: between an absolute beginning and an absolute end, everything is now.

The lines cited for the clock come in the fifth and final section of "Little Gidding." They return us to the now of England—the long now of permanent Christianity:

> A people without history
> Is not redeemed from time, for history is a pattern
> Of timeless moments. So, while the light fails
> On a winter's afternoon, in a secluded chapel
> History is now and England.
>
> With the drawing of this Love and the voice of this Calling.
>
> We shall not cease from exploration
> And the end of all our exploring
> Will be to arrive where we started
> And know the place for the first time.
> (lines 233–42)

The line offset by spaces derives from *The Cloud of Unknowing*, the fourteenth-century poem of Christian mysticism (Newman 2011: 460–61). This line places the fourteenth century between the "now" of the previous line and the "ceaseless exploration" of the following line—only to arrive at a "first time" a few lines later (line 242). The medieval insertion is thus part of every other moment in time—part of the "pattern / Of timeless moments" (lines 233–34). Similarly, the "secluded chapel" (line 236) folds medieval time into centuries of accumulated English afternoons: the chapel at Little Gidding is medieval in origin, restored in the seventeenth century, rebuilt in the eighteenth century, and restored again in the nineteenth century, before receiving Eliot's visit in the twentieth century.[9] At this point, the poem has just a few lines left and rushes through an "unknown, remembered gate" (line 243) toward a final medieval memory:

> Quick now, here, now, always—
> A condition of complete simplicity

---

9. See Little Gidding Church (website), https://littlegiddingchurch.org.uk (accessed May 20, 2022).

(Costing not less than everything)
And all shall be well and
All manner of thing shall be well
When the tongues of flame are in-folded
Into the crowned knot of fire
And the fire and the rose are one.
(lines 252–59; emphasis mine)

These lines echo again Julian of Norwich, speaking once again from the fourteenth century to voice a transcendent resolution at the end of time—a promise of wellness (Newman 2011: 454–61; A. Smith 2022). In the end, the poem, like the chapel, both accumulates and suspends time. Eliot composes these effects by borrowing centuries-old lines of English mystical poetry.

Back on the internet, Eliot's four lines cross the boundary of land and sky. His name marks the location of the drilling rig for the 10,000-Year Clock. Just below, the rock faces tell another scale of time, well beyond ten millennia—an even longer now of geological time to contemplate, the opposite of the "quick now." Centuries of erosion peel away years by the millions. This image is overlaid with a faint pattern of dots in concentric circles, with the epicenter off center to the right (fig. 2). The circular, radiating pattern evokes a ceaseless movement from this place to the infinite beyond. A clock awaiting its hands. The specificity of the literary reference to Eliot belies the other timescales represented on this page—from the million-year-old rocks to the millisecond of pixel renderings. Why remember Eliot, here, now, always? The gesture seeks to lodge the poet in the canon of future knowledge. Will his name be known in the tenth millennium? Will the *Four Quartets* make it into a 10,000-Year Book, one of the disks designed for "very long-term backup" for the world's essential information (Kelly 2008)? Only time will tell.

Remembering the Third Millennium

The techno-utopians are not the first to position themselves between millennia. Back in the second millennium, the English writer Henry, the Archdeacon of Huntingdon, also hoped to communicate across the millennia. Not far from Little Gidding, he wrote a *History of the English People* that includes an epilogue addressed to future readers. He begins by defining himself as a moment in time: "This is the year which contains the writer" (Henry 1996: 494–95; Hic est annus qui comprehendit scriptorem). He then defines the year through a series of historical calculations measuring various distances from the present, until at last he states that "now" is the "1135th year of grace" (495). This date prompts Henry to continue with a millennial reflection: "Already one millennium has passed since the Lord's incarnation. We are leading our lives, or—to put it more appropriately—we are holding back death, in what is evidently the 135th year of the second millennium" (495). The "writer" is thus contained not just by a year but by a millennium of Christian time.

At this scale, "now" expands to the length of Christianity, which Henry believes will last much longer than predicted by the "millenarists" of his day who believed that the earthly world would end after a thousand years. Their later counterparts predicted global catastrophe at the end of 1999. Henry, for his part, rejects the idea that "the conclusion of time will come in our own epoch" (497). He presents his belief in a longer earthly existence as a more accurate interpretation of Christian doctrine. Of course, by 1135 the evidence was plainly on his side. With these arguments and calculations, Henry extends "now" back to the Crucifixion and forward to a much distant future. In this sense, we are still in Henry's "now." This imperium is global and all encompassing, regardless of whether we share Henry's beliefs.

Indeed, in an oft-quoted passage, Henry directly addresses readers of the third millennium—which is to say, readers "now" who may encounter his text in surviving manuscripts, printed editions, or even this article:

> Now I speak to you who will be living in the third millennium, around the 135th year [2135]. Consider us, who at this moment seem to be renowned, because, miserable creatures, we think highly of ourselves. Reflect, I say, on what has become of us. Tell me, I pray, what gain has it been to us to have been great and famous? We had no fame at all, except in God. For if we are famed now in Him, we shall still be famed in your time, lords of heaven and earth, worthy of praise, without Lord God, by the thousands of thousands who are in the heavens. Now, however, I, who will already be dust by your time, have made mention of you in this book, so long before you are to be born, so that if—as my soul strongly desires—it shall come about that this book comes into your hands, I beg you, in the incomprehensible mercy of God, to pray for me, poor wretch. In the same way, may those who will walk with God in the fourth and fifth millennia pray and petition for you, if indeed mortal man survives so long. (497)

As I type out this quote in 2022, the year 2135 still lies in the future beyond my lifetime. A cataclysm may yet interrupt the communication that Henry imagined. Nonetheless, he has already come close to the projected anniversary of his writing. Henry's reputation does endure, at least in some circles. His direct address and request for prayers are already unnerving in 2022 and will only be more so in 2135, when he imagines a memory transfer: that those who are famous in the third millennium will be remembered in the fourth, if indeed those of the third manage to remember the second. Henry considers the possibility that the earthly era of "mortal man" may have ended by the fifth millennium—that it will no longer be "now." And indeed, in 2022 the lifespan of the earth has started to feel more finite. In the context of the climate catastrophe, Henry's "now" stretches to Eliot's ([1942] 1971, line 69) "death of earth."

Time preoccupies Henry, as it does Eliot, in relation to Christian transcendence. And like Eliot, he keeps death close at hand, combining pessimism with hope. The shock of corporal decay is, in the words of Nancy Partner (1997: 32), "the anxious heart of Henry's book." And so he ends the epilogue in "our" tombs:

> I have dwelt at some length on the question of the extent of time. This was because we shall lie decaying in our tombs for such a long time that we shall necessarily lose the memory of all bodily activities, and therefore we should think about it in advance, in order to work hard at seeking the glory, honour, goodness, wealth, dignity, and fame of name that are in God. When you have gained this [glory], you have it and will always have it. When you have gained worldly [glory], it will flow away like water from a broken pitcher [*aqua uase terebrato defluit*], and you have nothing. (Henry 1996: 498–501)

With these final words, Henry chastens the "worldly glory" of the 10,000-Year Clock. While the fleeting nature of earthly fame is a well-worn trope for Christian writers, Henry gives it an elegant expression: just as water flows out of a vessel with a hole in it, so memory fades from generation to generation. Everyone's preservation fantasies are doomed to fail. This epilogue itself, as the passage of time brought more "history" and Henry continued to revise his text, slipped from conclusion to internal transition—not the middle, but no longer the end. This change in narrative structure neatly represents the constant slip from now to then. Henry pointedly did not change the date of "now" (1135) even as he continued writing and revising in later years (Otter 2005: 57–79). The future remains hypothetical, memory remains uncertain, and the end keeps receding.

In Henry's day, England did not have any mechanical timepieces. But by the fourteenth century, Richard of Wallingford (1292–1336) had designed the first mechanical clock (North 2005). Around the same time, builders at Strasbourg Cathedral created an astronomical clock; today a third version designed by Jean-Baptiste Schwilgué (1776–1856) has been ticking there since 1842 (Oestmann 2020). This "ecclesiastical computer" calculates the date of Easter into the third millennium; in principle the calculation of equinoxes extends more than twenty-five thousand years (Hayes 1999: 11). It seems that a clock of the pretty long now has existed for a while. And yet, as Brian Hayes pointed out in a review of Brand's book *The Clock of the Long Now*, Brand had no interest in the Strasbourg clock. Inventors prefer to invent, not maintain others' inventions. After assessing Brand's book, Hayes ends *almost precisely* where Henry does, imagining the early 2100s when the myth of Schwilgué's Strasbourg clock repeats at the foot of the Clock of the Long Now: by this time the clock is in ruins and a visiting child declares "I'll make it go!" That child grows up not to repair the clock but to "scrap the whole mess and build a new and better clock" (Hayes 1999: 11, 13). So, it is said, did the young Schwilgué back in the second millennium.

A Medieval Book on the Internet

The long now might also be called the long middle. In this frame, 1135 and 2135 are not so far apart. Indeed, several of Henry's books have made it to the third millennium. Barring a cataclysm, they are quite likely to reach 2135. Just like the clock, though, medieval manuscripts are not easily accessible to the average person; even specialists must make significant efforts to gain access by traveling and proving their credentials. Yet also like the clock, people can easily find versions of them on the internet. Henry's books might well reach "your hands" by touching the keyboard of a networked computer. Similarly, copies of Eliot's and Brand's books have been photographed and stored in networked repositories. In fact, I accessed almost every text I cite in this article in some electronic format—even the first fragment of Henry's text edited by Diana Greenway, scanned by a library worker from a printed tome of 899 pages and sent to me as a PDF. This convergence of books spanning a millennium into the fleeting "now" of digital formats propels my story back to the "digital Dark Ages."

One of the most accessible copies of Henry's text is on a website hosted by Stanford University Library called Parker Library on the Web.[10]

10. See Parker Library on the Web 2.1, Stanford University, https://parker.stanford.edu (accessed May 18, 2022).

The manuscript is known as Cambridge, Corpus Christi College, MS 280. As part of Parker Library on the Web, MS 280 is integral to a digital ecosystem that includes Henry's millennium-old thoughts on millennial preservation, the LNF founders' decades-old thoughts on digital preservation, and today's activities toward a 10,000-Year Library. The twelfth-century MS 280 lies in a vault in Cambridge, UK, along with the rest of the books collected by Archbishop Matthew Parker in the sixteenth century. Parker's library has remained intact for almost five hundred years. The much younger website illustrates the speed with which the "digital Dark Ages" can overtake even carefully tended digital books. Parker Library on the Web 1.0 launched as an expensive subscription resource for libraries in 2009—partly because its creators recognized that digital preservation would not be cheap (Warren 2022: 181). In 2018, the site relaunched as Parker Library on the Web 2.0—in an open access format built from open-source tools and integrated into Stanford's larger digital collections. Today, I open Henry's book in an internet browser, clicking through an image gallery to find "the year 1135" (folio 142v; fig. 3). On the next image, Henry addresses the third millennium (folio 143r). Clicking forward to another image, Henry presages today's access standards: information ("noticia") should be open and bright ("pateant et enitescant") to the whole world ("orbem terrarium") (folio 144r; translation mine; see Henry 1996: 502). Brand (1987: 202), too, is famous for declaring: "information wants to be free." Free, open, bright: these are all fragile states. Information also needs enough "fame of name" to attract attention and maintenance.

Just as Henry (1996: 703) may unnerve us with his address to "whoever you are reading this," so Parker Library on the Web startles me with a first-person statement of no obvious origin in the Provenance field for MS 280: "The manuscript is the first of those mentioned by Arnold in his Introduction to his edition, xxxv. He thinks it probable that it belonged to St Augustine's, Canterbury, but I cannot identify it in the catalogue, and no mark survives."[11] This speaker is the early twentieth-century cataloguer, M. R. James. Various technical and human processes have conspired to reproduce this statement but also to strip it of context. On the internet, centuries of cataloguing and copying cycle into new creations that undergo constant epistemological upheaval (Warren 2022: 151–92). Even the most recent rendering is also centuries at once. When a dead catalogu-

11. See Cambridge, Corpus Christi College, MS 280: Henry of Huntingdon, Historia Anglorum, Parker Library on the Web, Stanford University, https://parker.stanford.edu /parker/catalog/qf131kj9626 (accessed May 18, 2022).

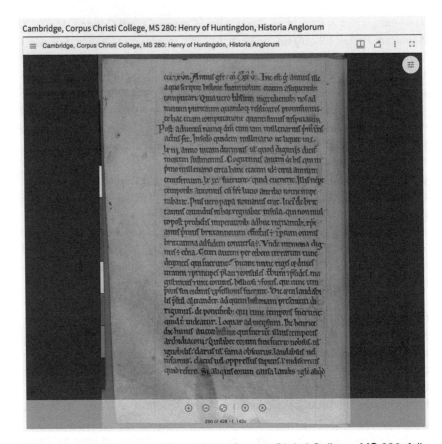

Figure 3 Screen image of Cambridge, Corpus Christi College, MS 280, folio 142v, ca. 1100–1299, on Parker Library on the Web 2.1, with image viewer Mirador 3.0 (https://parker.stanford.edu/parker/catalog/qf131kj9626). The page shows modern titles, navigation and display icons, and a color bar for verification of digital reproduction. Courtesy of Parker Library, Corpus Christi College, Cambridge. Licensed under a Creative Commons Attribution-NonCommercial 4.0 International License. Source: iMac screenshot, March 12, 2022.

er's "I" arrives on a computer screen as if spoken by the internet itself, today may as well be the nineteenth century when "I" first touched a medieval book. When Henry of Huntingdon addresses "you" who are not yet born, he speaks to us. As of now, there is no telling which will last longer, Henry's book in a vault in Cambridge or Henry's book on the internet.

The younger books by Eliot and Brand are more direct products of the "digital Dark Ages." I checked them out from the Internet Archive, a few hours at a time under the borrowing guidelines for copyrighted material. The Internet Archive is fully entangled with the history of the LNF's clock and library. Brewster Kahle and librarian Peter Lyman announced the project in 1997; both attended the 1998 LNF conference that led to Brand's chapter on "Ending the Digital Dark Ages" (Lyman and Kahle 1998). From the time that the Internet Archive began as a library of websites, the "About" page featured Hillis's stark warning about the looming "digital Dark Ages."[12] Although the page has been revised, older versions can still be read thanks to the Internet Archive's own archiving tool, the Wayback Machine. Reading Hillis from 1999 alongside Brand's book about the clock, alongside Eliot's poem about time, draws an information circuit that severs texts from books. Mass digitization of all kinds of books—from medieval manuscripts to cheap paperbacks—has reconfigured both the past and future of books, with far-reaching consequences. The poetry of the twentieth century, the history of the twelfth century—all just so many bits in transit. On the internet, periodization cannot survive the convergence of formats.

Remembering 1881

The dominion of ten thousand years is a dream of occupation, a dream that occupies stolen lands. Just outside the gates that block access to the clock stands a historical marker. It recalls a violent confrontation between Apache warriors and Texas Rangers in 1881—"one of the last battles," the marker says. In these years following the US Civil War and the closing of the so-called frontier, the US government enacted genocidal policies against Indigenous peoples. Apache people defended their lands for as long as they could (Chamberlain 2007). Following their forced removal, occupation of the area passed to a former Confederate turned cattle rancher (Schiller 2013). This local history is briefly summarized on the historical marker from a perspective that celebrates the white European conquerors and enslavers.

The same rhetoric of frontier conquest has framed investments in space travel, now also taking place on these lands at Bezos's Blue Origin facilities. Eliot, remarkably, is part of that story too. When I searched Google

---

12. Internet Archive, "About the Archive," April 13, 2001–February 6, 2017. https://web .archive.org/web/*/https://archive.org/about.

for the epigraph on Bezos's clock website, I found Eliot drafted into the defense of NASA at a 1997 congressional hearing: physics professor Richard Berendzen quoted the same four lines as Bezos to answer the question "Why explore at all?" (US Congress 1998: 72). The rest of the answer is consonant with an imperialist and white supremacist understanding of "America": "because we are the new Columbuses and space is our New World" (70); because in the nineteenth century "as a result of exploration, Americans developed a continental consciousness" (72). This definition of "Americans" requires that the Apache lose the last battle. Eliot becomes the prophet of both space travel and white nationalism.

In this place, the clock manifests as "chronocolonialism" (Hayes 1999: 13). It carries forward a longer history of Indigenous exploitation in tech medievalism. The timekeeping of the long now is a form of time-hoarding—meant to inspire care but shadowed instead by extraction. In the 1960s, when the first internet messages were traveling the continent's furthest edge, Brand developed a multimedia exhibit called "America Needs Indians," in which he sought to bring attention to "forgotten people" (Turner 2006: 66–69; S. Smith 2012: 43–56). He used the exhibit to promote Native American spiritual traditions among white communities. As Lisa Nakamura (2014: 931) has put it, "Stewart Brand viewed Indians as a curative to the anomie and alienation of American corporate culture." Nakamura argues that Brand's efforts were part of the same exploitative ethos that led Fairchild Semiconductor to open a manufacturing plant on the lands of the Navajo (Diné) Nation in the 1960s, where the corporation cast "electronics manufacture as a high-tech version of blanket weaving performed by willing and skillful indigenous women" (931). Fairchild soon moved elsewhere, but settler-colonialist paradigms continue to work their way through computing infrastructure (Warren 2022: 256, 269–70, 279). The clock drilled into unceded Apache lands is the latest component of that infrastructure.

This version of the future may subsume the Middle Ages into a longer now, but it does not promise any undoing of the racial epistemologies that made medieval studies in the nineteenth century. For that, we need to turn elsewhere—or return to the Sierra Diablo landscape with an alternate timeline for the future. We might return with the futurity of what Tarren Andrews (Bitterroot Salish) has called an "Indigenous turn" for medieval studies. In this future, *Beowulf* is counterpoint rather than model: "Unlike the *bēaga bryttan* (ring giver) of Beowulf's world, who gives gifts in exchange for martial loyalty, Indigenous kinship and all other forms of Indigenous relationality are predicated on doing, being, and giving without the expectation of reciprocation" (Andrews 2020: 2). In this future, relations move continuously through time "in a tangibly anticolonial way" (3). In this future, the Apache and the Diné are not forgotten nor commemorated with dusty historical markers but are reweaving their sovereignty, in part by building their own networked technologies (Duarte 2017). In this future, there is no anachronism.

The simple passage of time will never be enough to undo the medieval. If that were so, we would already be well past the mutual defenses that maintain disciplinary boundaries and the exclusionary systems that such boundaries sustain. Even the best efforts to recalibrate the European Middle Ages as postcolonial or global have revealed a tenacious commitment to periodization as a monument worth preserving. I am still pretty attached to the medieval myself. Nonetheless, we need a different kind of long now in order to follow Andrews (2020: 6) and other medievalists of color in understanding "that the contemporary issues of race and racialization illuminated by critical race scholars were not modern in their origins but developed out of premodern thinking about race and identity." In this future, we have all broken with the linear march of periodization and its imperial epistemology—be it Roman, British, or American. Only then can we all relate to Andrews's vital question: "What does it mean for medieval studies to be held accountable by contemporary and ancestral communities of Indigenous peoples whose lives and deaths have created Indigenous studies as we understand it today?" (2). Only then can we remember 1881 as if it were yesterday. What will you do about it now, you who live in the third millennium?

References

Andrews, Tarren. 2020. "Indigenous Futures and Medieval Pasts: An Introduction." *English Language Notes* 58, no. 2: 1–17. https://doi.org/10.1215/00138 282-8557777.

Bezos, Jeff. 2011. "Welcome to the 10,000 Year Clock website." https://www.10000 yearclock.net/learnmore.html.

Brand, Stewart. 1987. *The Media Lab: Inventing the Future at MIT*. New York: Viking.

Brand, Stewart. 1999a. *The Clock of the Long Now: Time and Responsibility*. New York: Basic Books.

Brand, Stewart. 1999b. "Escaping the Digital Dark Age." *Library Journal* 124, no. 2: 46–49.

Catlos, Brian, and Sharon Kinoshita, eds. 2017. *Can We Talk Mediterranean? Conversations on an Emerging Field in Medieval and Early Modern Studies*. New York: Palgrave Macmillan.

Chakrabarty, Dipesh. 2000. *Provincializing Europe: Postcolonial Thought and Historical Difference*. Princeton, NJ: Princeton University Press.

Chamberlain, Kathleen. 2007. *Victorio: Apache Warrior and Chief*. Norman: University of Oklahoma Press.

Duarte, Marisa Elena. 2017. *Network Sovereignty: Building the Internet across Indian Country*. Seattle: University of Washington Press.

Eliot, T. S. (1942) 1971. *Four Quartets*. San Diego: Harcourt, Brace, Jovanovich.

Fabian, Johannes. 1983. *Time and the Other: How Anthropology Makes Its Object*. New York: Columbia University Press.

Gibbon, Edward. 1776–88. *The History of the Decline and Fall of the Roman Empire*. 6 vols. London: W. Strahan and T. Cadell.

Hayes, Brian. 1999. "Clock of Ages." *Sciences* 39, no. 6: 9–13.

Heng, Geraldine. 2021. *The Global Middle Ages: An Introduction*. Cambridge: Cambridge University Press. https://doi.org/10.1017/9781009161176.

Henry, Archdean of Huntingdon. 1996. *Historia Anglorum: The History of the English People*. Edited and translated by Diana Greenway. Oxford: Clarendon Press.

Hillis, Danny. 2017. "Long-Term Timekeeping in the Clock of the Long Now." In *The Science of Time 2016*, edited by Elisa Felicitas Arias, Ludwig Combrinck, Pavel Gabor, Catherine Hohenkerk, and P. Kenneth Seidelmann, 331–36. Cham, Switzerland: Springer. https://doi.org/10.1007/978-3-319-59909-0_37.

Ingham, Patricia Clare, and Michelle R. Warren, eds. 2003. *Postcolonial Moves: Medieval through Modern*. New York: Palgrave Macmillan.

Kelly, Kevin. 2008. "Very Long-Term Backup." *The Rosetta Project*. Long Now Foundation. https://rosettaproject.org/disk/essays.

Kiernan, Kevin S. 1991. "Digital Image Processing and the *Beowulf* Manuscript." *Literary and Linguistic Computing* 6, no. 1: 20–27. https://doi.org/10.1093/llc/6.1.20.

Landes, David. 1983. *Revolution in Time: Clocks and the Making of the Modern World*. Cambridge, MA: Harvard University Press.

Lesk, Michael. 1997. "Going Digital." *Scientific American* 276, no. 3: 58–60. https://www.scientificamerican.com/article/going-digital/.

Lyman, Peter, and Brewster Kahle. 1998. "Archiving Digital Cultural Artifacts." *D-Lib Magazine*, July/August. http://www.dlib.org:80/dlib/july98/07lyman.html.

Oestmann, Günther. 2020. *The Astronomical Clock of Strasbourg Cathedral: Function and Significance*. Translated by Bruce W. Irwin. Leiden, Netherlands: Brill.

Otter, Monika. 2005. "Prolixitas Temporum: Futurity in Medieval Historical Narratives." In *Reading Medieval Culture: Essays in Honor of Robert W. Hanning*, edited by Robert M. Stein and Sandra Pierson Prior, 45–67. Notre Dame, IN: University of Notre Dame Press.

Nakamura, Lisa. 2014. "Indigenous Circuits: Navajo Women and the Racialization of Early Electronic Manufacture." *American Quarterly* 66, no. 4: 919–41. https://www.jstor.org/stable/43823177.

Newman, Barbara. 2011. "Eliot's Affirmative Way: Julian of Norwich, Charles, and *Little Gidding*." *Modern Philology* 108, no. 3: 427–61. https://doi.org/10.1086/658355.

North, John. 2005. *God's Clockmaker: Richard of Wallingford and the Invention of Time*. London: Bloomsbury.

Partner, Nancy. 1977. *Serious Entertainments: The Writing of History in Twelfth-Century England*. Chicago: University of Chicago Press.

Perloff, Marjorie. 2021. "Eliot's Auditory Imagination: A Rehearsal for Concrete Poetry." In *Infrathin: An Experiment in Micropoetics*, 65–90. Chicago: University of Chicago Press. EBSCOhost eBooks.

Rambaran-Olm, Mary. 2021. "A Wrinkle in Medieval Time: Ironing Out Issues regarding Race, Temporality, and the Early English." *New Literary History* 52, no. 3: 385–406. https://doi.org/10.1353/nlh.2021.0019.

Schiller, Dane. 2013. "Amazon.com Founder Has Plans for Massive Clock in West Texas." *Houston Chronicle*, August 19. https://www.mrt.com/news/article/Amazon-com-founder-has-plans-for-massive-clock-in-7442783.php.

Smith, Alicia. 2022. "'Each Way Means Loneliness—and Communion': Reading Anchoritic Literature with T. S. Eliot." *postmedieval* 13: 29–53. https://doi.org/10.1057/s41280-022-00221-7.

Smith, Sherry L. 2012. *Hippies, Indians, and the Fight for Red Power*. Oxford: Oxford University Press.

Thylstrup, Nanna Bode. 2018. *The Politics of Mass Digitization*. Cambridge, MA: MIT Press.

Turner, Fred. 2006. *From Counterculture to Cyberculture: Stewart Brand, the Whole Earth Network, and the Rise of Digital Utopianism*. Chicago: University of Chicago Press.

US Congress. 1998. *Defining NASA's Mission and America's Vision for the Future of Space Exploration: Hearings Before the Subcommittee on National Security, International Affairs, and Criminal Justice of the Committee on Government Reform and Oversight, House of Representatives, One Hundred Fifth Congress, First Session, May 9 and 19, 1997*. Serial Number 105–84. Washington, DC: US Government Printing Office. https://www.google.com/books/edition/Defining_NASA_s_Mission_and_America_s_Vi/HQ8td0Er49IC.

Warren, Michelle R. 2011. *Creole Medievalism: Colonial France and Joseph Bédier's Middle Ages*. Minneapolis: University of Minnesota Press. ProQuest Ebook Central.

Warren, Michelle R. 2012. "Classicism, Medievalism, and the Postcolonial." *Exemplaria* 24, no. 3: 282–92. https://doi.org/10.1179/1041257312Z.00000000017.

Warren, Michelle R. 2022. *Holy Digital Grail: A Medieval Book on the Internet*. Stanford, CA: Stanford University Press. https://doi.org/10.1515/9781503631175.

Part 2. Disciplinary Dilemmas

Race, Medieval Studies, and Disciplinary Boundaries

Adam Miyashiro

The recent disciplinary debates about antiracist and anticolonial medieval studies within national language fields have rekindled debates about how to frame race in the premodern periods. These debates mirror earlier methodological questions in the field of comparative literature about the relationship between globalization and world literature. On the one hand, comparatists across periods and geographical areas have produced interesting work problematizing race within a global and internationalist context, using sociological and critical race theory and studies to foreground how race operates in the literary humanities. On the other hand, medievalists in various national language departments, such as English, French, and Spanish departments, have for the past few years begun to address how race operates in premodern contexts (see Ramey 2016; Whitaker 2019). Earlier work on medieval constructions of race frequently employed postcolonial theory as a way of framing racializations in texts such as Wolfram von Eschenbach's thirteenth-century Middle High German *Parzival*, for example (Lampert 2004). These studies, instrumental as they are, have not

boundary 2 50:3 (2023)   DOI 10.1215/01903659-10472401   © 2023 by Duke University Press

fully considered comparative approaches and have instead focalized along English or foreign language disciplinary boundaries. Given that the premodern world existed before the advent of modern nation-states, national language boundaries circumscribing race in premodernity face two fundamental problems: First, that European notions of race during the *longue durée* of the medieval period of one thousand years went through many changes and often differed based on specific periods, geographies, and socioeconomic circumstances. Second, that European constructions of race were often influenced by texts written in antiquity and traveled across linguistic and cultural boundaries. Depictions of racialized others in the twelfth-century chanson de geste, for example, influenced later medieval English texts two centuries later (see, for example, Heng 2003).

Medieval studies' debates about race and the "global Middle Ages" have taken on the contours of previous debates about "world literature," globalization, and comparative racializations in comparative literature and ethnic studies but have not directly drawn from them or learned from the lessons they offer. The rise of "world literature" has impacted not only the shrinking of comparative literature departments in the United States but also how national language departments (such as English and French) have attempted to globalize their curricula through the "global Anglophone" or "Francophone" models. Given that much of the global Anglophone or Francophone literatures have been produced in the Global South, the co-opting of world literature to national language departments served to erase Indigenous literatures, to focus on literatures not written in English or French, and to excise literary traditions not falling into national boundaries. Just as scholars a decade ago asked how national language disciplines impacted the presentation of world or global literature, medievalists would benefit from comparable questions about the role of national language disciplines in discussing race or the global Middle Ages: What are the stakes of a "medieval" period that is anchored to European timelines and periodizations? This essay argues that previous debates held within comparative literature can shed light on current debates in medieval studies about its Eurocentric and US-centric ideas of racism and antiracism, and the way DEI frameworks have deployed the terms "decolonization" and "antiracism." This article takes a distinctly comparative angle and argues that the comparative methodology of tributary empires offers a productive guide for navigating the global turn in medieval studies.

Comparative Literature, World Literature, and the Globe

Gayatri Spivak posited the "death" of comparative literature in 2004 by claiming that the Old Philology—that is, the Indo-European philologies that dominated the field of comparative literature in the nineteenth and early twentieth centuries and subsequently gave rise to the central disciplines that founded medieval studies—had now died out in favor of a "planetary" view of global literature. One example of this early philological enunciation of comparative literature in the United States occurred when Charles Chauncey Shackford (1815–1895), professor of English at Cornell University, gave a lecture on the discipline in 1871 and already gestured toward a so-called "universal literature" (Shackford, quoted in in Schulz and Rhein 1973). However, this "universal literature" was confined to European literatures exclusively. For René Wellek (1959: 22), a century later, comparative literature came to mean "an international perspective which envisages a distant ideal of universal literary history and scholarship" that could "overcome national prejudices and provincialisms" without undermining the "vitality of the different national traditions." In this estimation, Wellek proposes something of a Eurocentric conundrum: how can we as comparatists on the one hand deconstruct nationalism while also retaining the concept of national traditions? David Damrosch answers with a particularly damning statement about why medievalists were the crux of this problem. In his view, even though medievalists were aware that the national language model did not work in premodern Europe and that linguistic diversity in medieval Europe countered hegemonic linguistic-national formations like "English," "medievalists simply hadn't the *time* to learn those languages [Welsh, Irish] along with everything else they were studying. . . . Deconstructing nationalism in theory, these medievalists had succumbed to it in practice" (Damrosch 2003: 285). Likewise, other comparative literature theorists critiqued the construction of a new "world literature" canon, in essence replicating an already existing literary canon, as a measure to remediate the Eurocentrism of literary studies. Rey Chow's (1994) warning in the Bernheimer Report to resist the impulse of extending the canon of world literature, to supplant or complement the European canon (as constructed along similar nationalist/imperial lines), still resonates in the twenty-first century.

This disciplinary history from comparative literature studies contextualizes recent critiques of the "global Middle Ages" in medieval studies, which have raised the issue with broadening out Eurocentric, and Christian, timelines to the rest of the "world," specifically in the African and Asian continents (Lomuto 2020). Medieval and early modern studies, as constituted in national language departments, have ignored significant interventions that comp lit theorists have made toward globalization, especially as it relates to the Global South. Medieval studies' turn to the "global" has aligned with the post–Cold War divisions of the world, evidenced by the Global Middle Ages Project's description of their geographical trajectory: "Europe to Dar al-Islam, Sub-Saharan Africa to India, Eurasia, China, and the many Asias."[1] Aside from the obvious problem that the "Middle Ages" is a specifically western European temporality overwriting African and Asian temporalities, it structures the global order into "area studies." As Janet Abu-Lughod (2008: 185) has cautioned, *no system is fully global in the sense that all parts articulate evenly with one another, regardless of whether the role they play is central or peripheral.* Spivak's notion of "planetarity," as a mode that supplants the "global," therefore offers a way to avoid the trap of area studies. She asks:

> Can the foothold for planetarity be located in the texts of these spread-out sectors of the world's literatures and cultures? Perhaps. The new comparativist is not obliged to look for them, of course. One cannot adjudicate the task of an entire discipline, in spite of efforts of the world literaturists, the Encyclopedists. I think this drastic epistemic change must be imagined by Comparative Literature. But I cannot will everyone to think so. (Spivak 2003: 87)

Since for Spivak the "death" of comparative literature is the death of what she considers the "old" comparative literature, she is speaking of a comparative literature that is founded on "national-philological" lines, and envisioning a new version.

The response to Gayatri Spivak's *Death of a Discipline* from world literature and comparative literature circles shows just where medievalist criticism can potentially stand to buttress both a rethinking of world literature (for example, where does medieval world literature exist?) and a reenergizing debate about the situation of medieval studies within a broader premodern network. The disciplinary boundaries of comparative literature, as of yet, have not cast off the Eurocentric roots that Spivak has critiqued, even as she points toward a new comparatism that is not beholden to European temporalities and geographies. As Spivak (2003: 8) states, "Area Studies

1. See "About GMAP," Global Middle Ages (website), http://globalmiddleages.org/about (accessed August 25, 2022).

related to foreign 'areas.' Comparative Literature was made up of Western European 'nations.' This distinction, between 'areas' and 'nations,' infected Comparative Literature from the start." However, Spivak acknowledges, "Comparative Literature can also find its own unacknowledged prehistory in this [Islamic diaspora] sector, and thus do a long-range historical revision of the record of its apparently European provenance" (87). Spivak's critique of comparative literature has applicability to medieval studies: since no "nations" were in existence in the period, the field is put into a conundrum that pits modern national-linguistic departmental silos of the modern neoliberal university, with the monolithic and politicized views of areas and religious identities such as "Europe" and "Islam" (or even worse, "Islamicate").[2]

Since comparative racializations take into account a multipolar and ever-shifting view on the relationship between race and comparativity, it is crucial to understand how the ideas of globalization, comparative literature, and critical race studies form within specific geotemporalities. Shu-Mei Shih (2008: 1350), writing in *PMLA*'s special issue on "Comparative Racializations," explains that racialization is a process of relationality between centers of political and economic power and their peripheries, and that it cannot be understood without the process of comparison (drawing on Franz Fanon):

> First, the differences between the dynamics of racialization in the colony and those in the metropole evince the particularity of each instance as place-based (the colony and the metropole) and time-specific (the before and after of arrival in the metropole), but in each instance, comparison is constitutive of the process of racialization. Second, the black man from the colony is the same man that goes to the metropole, which shows that the two processes of racialization are contiguous. This contiguity is not accidental but is a historical consequence of the colonial turn. Comparison between the colony and the metropole, this case shows, is about relationality, not relativism.

The medievalist debate about race in the premodern period is repeating debates in comparative literature about the relationship between

2. See Ghazoul 2006 on how Palestinian literary historian Ruhi al-Khalidi studied Turkish, Persian, French, and English in addition to Arabic in his book *Tarīkh 'ilm al-adab 'ind al-Ifranj wa'l-'Arab wa-Victor Hugo* (*The History of the Discipline of Literature among Westerners and Arabs and Victor Hugo*), published in Cairo in 1904.

the modern national and disciplinary boundaries—and area studies—and reinscribing their own Eurocentric perspectives: one of the first impulses is to simply add non-Western works onto syllabi in medieval literature courses, without a critical awareness of what that inclusion signifies and without critical knowledge of the traditions non-Western literary texts might carry with them. Medievalists' often eschew nonmedievalist sources, such as Cedric Robinson's (2021) *Black Marxism* or the work of sociologist Johnny Eric Williams (2016), and overlook not only how capitalism operates in racialized formations in the contemporary context but also how it structures our own periodization of race within academic discourse. The citation practices of medievalists have excluded nonmedievalist scholars on race and settler colonialism, and thus the disciplinary histories and debates of Black studies / African American studies, ethnic studies, or Native and Indigenous studies have not influenced discourses of race and globalization in medieval studies.

Similarly, medievalists have not attended to the economic networks that shaped race and global contact in the medieval era, frequently assuming traditional periodizations of the so-called rise of capitalism of the fifteenth century, which I will address below more fully. For example, medievalists point toward fourteenth- and fifteenth-century literary texts produced in Britain as an origin point for race-thinking and as a stand-in for the rest of Europe, which mirrors the periodization narrative that race begins with the colonization of the Americas and the beginning of the early modern period (one where capitalism makes an entrance). However, medieval European texts were neither produced nor circulated within silos of national language boundaries. If medieval literature offers a broad topography for the study of race, it is a multilingual, "transnational" site. National language disciplinary boundaries are ill equipped to carry out these studies, but a reformulated comparative approach, theoretically grounded in critical race studies both inside and outside literary academia, would be more well equipped.

One of the reasons why English departments have been so connected with exploring the ideas of race in the medieval period is because of the legacy of British colonialism in the Global South. Early modern scholars such as Kim Hall, Sujata Iyengar, Julia Schleck, and Ania Loomba have excavated racializing and colonial discourses in early modern English drama and travel narratives. Likewise, medievalists such as Geraldine Heng (2018) and Cord Whitaker (2019) have utilized and expanded upon early modernists' methodologies and analyses to explore earlier periods. Settler-colonial states such as the United States, Canada, Australia, New

Zealand, as well as South and Southeast Asian former British colonies, all point back toward the English late medieval and early modern cultures to understand their own colonial formations.

The dominance of the English department in medieval studies' turn toward race has scholarly viability and importance, as scholars must account for the historical specificities of colonialism in their analyses of literary studies. But the centering of England/Britain excludes southern and central Europe, and most crucially the Mediterranean, where other racializations emerged. The medieval Iberia of Juan Ruiz, for example, and the medieval Holy Roman Empire of Wolfram von Eschenbach, or that of Boccaccio's Italy, or even of Chrétien de Troyes's France, all have different ideas of race in different temporalities of Europe, based on their own political, economic, and sociocultural convergences. Furthermore, the disciplinary centering of the British Isles as the site of origin of medieval racial and colonial discourses reinscribes the "national language" construct of our academic disciplines. Meanwhile, in medieval French or Iberian studies, race and settler colonialism only recently made its entry into the field (Altschul 2012; Ramey 2016). Karla Mallette's (2010) important work on Spanish and Italian Orientalisms makes an important intervention that despite the British and French colonial legacies, Orientalism operated differently in countries that did in fact have Arab/Muslim pasts unlike most parts of northern Europe. Nadia Altshul's work in Latin American medievalisms, which she argues descend from Spanish and Portuguese colonialisms, also makes an important contribution to the discussion of race and colonialism as extended to the Americas.

Scholars of premodern Iberia, notably Maria Rosa Menocal, have likewise contributed critiques that should be understood by scholars in the French and English tradition. As Deepa Kumar (2021) has pointed out, the racialized political "blood purity laws" in late fifteenth-century Spain were the earliest racialized biopolitical regime in Europe. But almost a century earlier, in 1402, the Norman Jean de Bethencourt began the conquest of the Canary Islands on behalf of the Kingdom of Castile, leading to one of the earliest settler-colonial projects. It effectively turned the Canary Islands into a one-crop sugar plantation and committed the ethnic cleansing of the Indigenous Guanches islanders, setting the stage for future colonial projects in the Americas.

We can understand the "Middle Ages" to not be "reborn" but to exist as an "afterlife," like the *aptrgangr* (after-walker) of Old Icelandic sagas, a figure who speaks from an afterlife, not in the sense of a place but as a state of re-becoming, un-dead, so to speak. To view the medieval as this "after-life," not as a heavenly bliss or unfathomable hell but as a state of exception, we must understand the "nature" of "nature," or, in other words, how the concept of "natura" inscribes the bare life of comparative medieval studies. I suggest that the medieval can only speak as this prophetic "un-dead" after a death of the (medievalist) discipline.

The Politics of Arabic in Medieval Europe

In 2017, Annika Larsson, a textile archaeologist at Uppsala University in Sweden, announced that they had a "Viking" textile with the Arabic word "Allah" written in Kufic Arabic lettering for an exhibition about early Scandinavian contact with the Muslim world. Mass media outlets like the BBC and the New York Times, among others, immediately reported the story. Another art historian, Stephennie Mulder (University of Texas at Austin) tweeted a critique of what they were calling the "Viking Allah" textile. She debunked Larsson's claim about the presence of the Arabic language on that textile while simultaneously reiterating the larger point that Arab-Muslim society had an influence on northern European cultures (Mulder 2017; Anderson 2017). However, far-right white supremacists used Mulder's careful explanation as an excuse for Islamophobic and racist, anti-immigrant speech, which Mulder and others immediately addressed. Earlier historical objects, such as the famous Viking "Allah" ring found in Birka, Sweden (dated to the ninth century), also indicate that Arabic might have been considered a "prestige" language in Scandinavia at the time. But the use of these material objects has also contributed to forms of Orientalism among early medieval historians, both academic and public. As Paul Edward Montgomery Ramírez (2021) has shown, the famous "Arab" at York's Jorvik Viking Centre in northern England is one such way that Arab "inclusion" into the culture of early medieval Europe, rather than properly contextualizing cultural contact between northern European and western and central Asian populations, reinscribe imperialist and colonialist racialized fantasies of non-Europeans in their modern representations.

One of the most iconic objects that demonstrate this contact between early medieval polities and the Arab-Muslim world is King Offa's Arabic-language dinar, a gold mancus coin associated with the Abbasid dynasty and forged in England. Offa's dinar was struck in the kingdom of Mercia, current-day Staffordshire in the Northwest of England, in roughly 774–75 (near where the largest known gold hoard in an early English burial was

found in 2011, known colloquially as the "Staffordshire hoard"). Offa's mancus is a crude copy of the Abbasid dinar, minted in the reign of al-Manṣūr,
which widely circulated in the Mediterranean. It is imprinted with the name
"Offa Rex" printed upside down (in relation to the Arabic text). On its face,
one can clearly read parts of the *tashahhud*, or part of the Muslim salat
prayer: on the obverse, it reads لا اله الا الله وحده لا شريك له (*lā ilāha illa-llāh waḥ
dahu lā sharīka lahu*; There is no god but Allah alone and He has no equal),
and reverse, مـحـمـد رسـول الله (*Muḥammad rasūl Allāh*; Muhammad is the mes-
senger of Allah). This coin, unique for its inclusion of Latin and Arabic writing in such a stark and contrasting way, troubles prevailing presumptions
about the distance between early England and the Arab Mediterranean in
the early years of the ʿUmayyad Caliphate in the early Middle Ages.[3] King
Offa's dinar evidences the reach of Mediterranean trade networks as far
off as Mercia in northwest England, as the economic power of the Abbasid
Empire impacted all of Europe by the ninth century.

As periodization attempts to chart time and space, the Mediterranean is a geographic area that resists simplistic and reified periodizations but has been subject of one of the most pervasive divides found in
medievalist scholarship. The Belgian historian Henri Pirenne (1862–1935),
known for his "Pirenne Thesis," argued that with the appearance of Islam,
the Western Mediterranean was "closed," forcing Europe to withdraw into
itself, thereby creating a hermetically sealed-off space in order to gener-
ate a sense of itself as distinctly European and Christian. He suggests, in
his final book *Mohammad and Charlemagne*, that "Islam had shattered the
Mediterranean unity which the Germanic invasions left intact. . . . This was
the most essential event of European history which had occurred since the
Punic Wars. It was the end of the classic tradition. It was the beginning of
the Middle Ages, and it happened at the very moment when Europe was
on the way to becoming Byzantinized" (Pirenne 2001: 164). Pirenne calls
the eastern Mediterranean a "Musulman lake," dividing the Mediterranean
into Western and Eastern spheres of power, quoting the fourteenth-century
historian Ibn Khaldūn as saying that "the Christians could no longer float a
plank upon the sea" (164). This is a very selective reading of Ibn Khaldūn,
who goes on to say that control of the Mediterranean ebbed and flowed
between Franks, Byzantines, and Arabs in the following centuries (Ibn
Khaldūn and Rosenthal 1958).

3. See Beckett 2003, which suggests that this coin is evidence that European attitudes
toward the Islamic world were not always pejorative and, if not positive, could be fairly
neutral.

Economic historians of the medieval period have been instrumental in negating much of the Pirenne Thesis, and for this reason, it is important for literary scholars to understand the economic and material contexts for how racial ideologies construct medieval historiographies within which medieval racial ideas flourish. For example, about the break between Germanic culture and the Islamic Mediterranean, historians and archaeologists have followed the gold trade that remained continuous through the seventh and eighth centuries, when we have Frankish and Saxon kings, such as Offa, who were minting imitations of Abbasid dinars, intended for trade in the Mediterranean. There was abundant cultural contact in the early Middle Ages, even in provincial northern Europe. The notion that premodern Europe was a hermetically sealed space falls into a modernist conception of medieval Europe as a mirror for European modernity, but recent archaeological discoveries have gradually worn down this idea, as they have yielded convincing evidence that Muslim presence in the Mediterranean did not end medieval trade routes linking the Mediterranean with Europe. Continuities from the ancient Roman, pre-Islamic, and Islamic Mediterranean persisted throughout the early medieval period. Mediterranean networks complicate our understanding of the category of the medieval. Comparative methodologies that understand the multiple receptions of ancient racializing discourses in the Byzantine, Arab, and North African worlds in addition to southern and eastern Europe, and that contextualize, for example, Arabic geographical descriptions of Africa and Europe, are important for current shifts happening in medieval studies (Chism 2009).

Periodization is a recognized problem with many facets for those working in premodern periods. Jennifer Summit and David Wallace (2007: 447), for example, suggest that periodization "is a template for dividing up not only time but also place." Their primary concern had been the break drawn between the premodern and modern, from the end of the Middle Ages to what we consider to be the early modern periods, suggesting that the categories of medieval, Renaissance, and early modern are "increasingly vexed." Kathleen Davis (2008) has similarly argued that the categories that postcolonial theorists had traditionally taken for granted, such as feudalism and secularism, are bound up with concepts of sovereignty and political theology. The work of Janet Abu-Lughod (2008) has helped reshape the dominant narrative that the West arose from "out of nowhere" around the late fifteenth century—a time, paradoxically, at which both East and West were at their "low ebb" politically and economically.

Medievalist theorizations on the problems of periodization has raised

interesting questions that reach outside of medievalist fields and have generated answers that are insightful and critically engaging regarding the definition of the Middle Ages as a discrete period. Bruce Holsinger (2002: 1196)
has suggested, in his genealogy of neomedievalist critique, that medievalist scholarship stemming from the historiographical practices of the French
Annales school anticipate the subaltern school, suggesting that this postcolonial critique "focused particular attention on the transition from precolonial
feudalism to colonial capitalism on the Indian subcontinent, and its primary
critical debts have been to Marxism, inflected variously through the writings
of thinkers from Antonio Gramsci to Louis Althusser." Postcolonial theory
has influenced medieval studies, as it reveals how the category of "medieval" constitutes an area-studies northwestern European geography. European Marxist discourse sometimes ignores the pluralistic societies that were
present in a premodern world that included Europe but was not confined to
it. The Iberian Peninsula, for example, going through phases of conquest
between Afro-Asiatic (Arab/Berber) and European (Frankish/Byzantine),
having Norman colonies in Tarragona, Sicily, Malta, and the island of Cyprus,
created multiple hybrid cultures that produced at times a vibrant literary culture of Mediterranean combinations (Kinoshita 2009).

Our critiques of the traditional periodizations should not end with
alternative periodizations, but rather, our critiques should make us aware
that periodization itself is as much about geography as it is about temporality; economy and political culture as supercessionary religious ideology;
and most of all, that periodization itself could not happen without some
sense of comparison. Davis (2008) has identified the intersections at which
medieval/modern periodizations and religious/secular categories have
come into existence as a constructed paradigm signaling the transfer of
political authority from ecclesiastical institutions to a secularized state power
in modernity. In such a construct, according to Davis (2008: 77), "Europe's
'medieval' past and cultural others—mainly colonized non-Christians—
were defined as religious, static, and ahistorical—thus open for narrative
and territorial development." In other words, what Davis describes as the
"becoming-feudal" of the European Middle Ages (or how the "fief" becomes
a central narrative category) is how recent modernity achieves the sense of
the epoch of the Middle Ages. This explains, for example, how "feudalism"
describes premodern non-Western colonized groups, even when such a
concept is not found in the local lexicon of colonized peoples. Davis suggests that the "feudality" of the medieval had to be defined in order for a
secular European narrative to be achieved.

The emergent field of "global medieval studies" attempts to challenge Eurocentric definitions of both the medieval period (as feudal) and modernity (as secular). But globalizing the "medieval" also reinscribes traditional narratives of modernity that European colonial encounters in subsequent centuries have defined. How can medievalists break out of the Eurocentrism endemic to the contemporary study of the Middle Ages? The lens of a larger tributary system, which spans antiquity through the early modern period, is a useful methodology (Amin 2010). If we are to truly rethink the Middle Ages from the perspective of postcolonial theoretical models, we must acknowledge the continuing networks that comprise the medieval world, leaving behind attempts to simplify medieval Europe as isolated from its broader contexts.

By considering both the medievalisms of the postcolonial world outside of Europe, as suggested by Kathleen Davis and Nadia Altschul (2009), as well as the margins of medieval Europe itself (in places like al-Andalus, Sicily, and even the early Ottoman Empire), we can come closer to understanding how temporality and its attendant periodizations are shaped by a geopolitical imaginary bound by a long history of tributary empires that have been (mis)taken as examples of medieval European feudalism. Marxist interpretations of feudalism as a category have also had entanglements with periodization of modernity. Samir Amin (2010: 224), in *Eurocentrism*, has suggested that Marxist interpretations of the feudal as a category have been applied unevenly to the premodern, precapitalist societies around the globe—as he says, "reserving the term feudal for Europe (plus the Japanese exception) and refusing to use it in reference to Asia." However, the term "feudal" has recently become attached to both central and western Asian cultures, as well as North African Arab groups. These two "feudalisms"— the European/Japanese model of a feudalism that is generative of capitalist modernity, and the static and permanent feudalism of Muslim Afro-Asia (one which is represented as "degenerative" and out of temporal sync with the modern, secular world)—provides an interesting point of departure into how the secularizing modernity of global capitalism deploys the concept of feudalism. Samir Amin (2010: 2) writes that

> the reproduction of precapitalist social systems rests upon the stability of power . . . and of an ideology that endows it with legitimacy. . . . The mystery that must be elucidated in order to understand the genesis, reproduction, and evolution of these societies and of the contradictions within which they operate is to be found in the area of the political-ideological, not in the realm of the economic. In other

words, what we need here is a genuine theory of culture, capable of accounting for the functioning of social power.

Samir Amin's proposed solution is not to abandon the category of "feudalism" altogether but to understand "feudalism" as a subcategory of a larger system that bound Asian, African, and European cultures in the precapitalist, premodern world: that of the tributary economy.

Resituating Europe within a broader spectrum of premodern tributary economic systems, rather than as an exception to these imperial networks, offers productive methods for literary and historical analysis. For example, the Alexander Romance, from late antiquity to the early modern period, exists in numerous expressions in every major premodern language—Greek, Arabic, Latin, Coptic/Egyptian, Armenian, Hebrew, French, English, Castilian, and Middle Mongolian, to name just a few—and spanned the three Abrahamic religions as well as the three continents. Tributary empires, from Mongolia in the east to Spain, Britain, Iceland, and everywhere in between, were united in a text-network of the Alexander Romance and narrative from the third century BC; it includes Orosius's *Histories* and other ancillary texts, such as *Wonders of the East* and the "Letter of Alexander to Aristotle," that circulated in many languages around Europe. Scholars could also situate the Arthurian and British royal narrative of Geoffrey of Monmouth in relation to the Alexander Romance (Furtado 1995): the Trojan conquest of Britain mirrors Alexander's famous wall, built to contain Gog and Magog. Alexander is the epitome of the tributary system, a figurehead for a vast economic circulation. If we are to read European feudalism as one expression of a tributary system that covered a global expanse, we might arrive at another interpretation of periodicity itself, and, although not perfect, it might help to put European and Mediterranean cultures into context with economic and literary circulations in the wider world.

References

Abu-Lughod, Janet. 2008. "The World System in the Thirteenth Century: Dead-End or Precursor?" In *The Transnational Studies Reader: Intersections and Innovations*, edited by Sanjeev Khagram and Peggy Levitt, 184–95. New York: Routledge.

Altschul, Nadia R. 2012. *Geographies of Philological Knowledge: Postcoloniality and the Transatlantic National Epic*. Chicago: University of Chicago Press.

Amin, Samir. 2010. *Eurocentrism*. 2nd ed. New York: Monthly Review Press.

Anderson, Christina. 2017. "'Allah' Is Found on Viking Funeral Clothes." *New York Times*,

October 14. https://www.nytimes.com/2017/10/14/world/europe/vikings-allah -sweden.html.

Beckett, Katharine Scarfe. 2003. *Anglo-Saxon Perceptions of the Islamic World.* Cambridge: Cambridge University Press.

Chism, Christine. 2009. "Arabic in the Medieval World." *PMLA* 124, no. 2: 624–31.

Chow, Rey. 1994. "In the Name of Comparative Literature." In *Comparative Literature in the Age of Multiculturalism*, edited by Charles Bernheimer, 107–16. Baltimore: Johns Hopkins University Press.

Damrosch, David. 2003. *What Is World Literature?* Princeton, NJ: Princeton University Press.

Davis, Kathleen. 2008. *Periodization and Sovereignty: How Ideas of Feudalism and Secularization Govern the Politics of Time.* Philadelphia: University of Pennsylvania Press.

Davis, Kathleen, and Nadia Altschul, eds. 2009. *Medievalisms in the Postcolonial World: The Idea of "the Middle Ages" outside Europe.* Baltimore: Johns Hopkins University Press.

Furtado, Antonio L. 1995. "From Alexander of Macedonia to Arthur of Britain." *Arthuriana* 5, no. 3: 70–86.

Ghazoul, F. J. 2006. "Comparative Literature in the Arab World." *Comparative Critical Studies* 3, no. 1–2: 113–24.

Heng, Geraldine. 2003. *Empire of Magic.* New York: Columbia University Press.

Heng, Geraldine. 2018. *The Invention of Race in the European Middle Ages.* New York: Cambridge University Press.

Holsinger, B. W. 2002. "Medieval Studies, Postcolonial Studies, and the Genealogies of Critique." *Speculum* 77, no. 4: 1195–227.

Ibn Khaldūn and Franz Rosenthal. 1958. *The Muqaddimah: An Introduction to History.* Princeton, NJ: Princeton University Press.

Kinoshita, Sharon. 2009. "Medieval Mediterranean Literature." *PMLA* 124, no. 2: 600–8.

Kumar, Deepa. 2021. *Islamophobia and the Politics of Empire: Twenty Years after 9/11.* New York: Verso Books.

Lampert, Lisa. 2004. "Race, Periodicity, and the (Neo-) Middle Ages." *Modern Language Quarterly* 65, no. 3: 391–421.

Lomuto, Sierra. 2020. "Becoming Postmedieval: The Stakes of the Global Middle Ages." *postmedieval* 11, no. 4: 503–12.

Mallette, Karla. 2010. *European Modernity and the Arab Mediterranean: Toward a New Philology and a Counter-Orientalism.* Philadelphia: University of Pennsylvania Press.

Montgomery Ramírez, Paul Edward. 2021. "Colonial Representations of Race in Alternative Museums: The 'African' of St Benet's, the 'Arab' of Jorvik, and the 'Black Viking.'" *International Journal of Heritage Studies* 27, no. 9: 937–52.

Mulder, Stephennie. 2017. "The Rise and Fall of the Viking 'Allah' Textile." *Hyper-*

allergic, October 27. https://hyperallergic.com/407746/refuting-viking-allah
-textiles-meaning/.

Pirenne, Henri. 2001. *Mohammed and Charlemagne*. Mineola, NY: Dover Publications.

Ramey, Lynn T. 2016. *Black Legacies: Race and the European Middle Ages*. Gainesville: University Press of Florida.

Robinson, Cedric J. 2021. *Black Marxism: The Making of the Black Radical Tradition*. 3rd ed. Chapel Hill: University of North Carolina Press.

Shih, Shu-Mei. 2008. "Comparative Racialization: An Introduction." *PMLA* 123, no. 5: 1347–62.

Schulz, Hans-Joachim, and Phillip H. Rhein. 1973. *Comparative Literature: The Early Years; an Anthology of Essays*. Chapel Hill: University of North Carolina Press.

Spivak, Gayatri Chakravorty. 2003. *Death of a Discipline*. New York: Columbia University Press.

Summit, Jennifer, and David Wallace. 2007. "Rethinking Periodization." *Journal of Medieval and Early Modern Studies* 37, no. 3: 447–51.

Wellek, René. 1959. "The Crisis of Comparative Literature." In *Proceedings of the Second International Congress of Comparative Literature*, edited by Werner P. Friederich, 148–59. Chapel Hill: University of North Carolina Press.

Whitaker, Cord J. 2019. *Black Metaphors: How Modern Racism Emerged from Medieval Race-Thinking*. Philadelphia: University of Pennsylvania Press.

Williams, Johnny E. 2016. *Decoding Racial Ideology in Genomics*. Lanham, MD: Lexington Books.

Fighting for the Middle:
Medieval Studies Programs and Degrees within Higher Education

Shokoofeh Rajabzadeh

Medieval. Medi. Medium Aevum. The Middle Ages.

A period defined as between the fall of the Roman Empire and the rise of the Renaissance.

Between the classics and the early modern.

To be in the middle, to be in a middle.

To be defined as and by the "middle" is to always be defined by what has passed and what has yet to come. It is to be defined not by what you are made of but by what you are not, by what sits at either periphery or either extreme. To inhabit a space that is defined as a "middle," inflected by a point of origin and a destination, is to constantly negotiate a space defined by anticipation—anticipation of a prehistory *and* a setting-up-for. Or, on the other hand, it is a narrative of revision, reconstruction, deconstruction, a *having-done-with*. It is at once a space of interconnectedness: the middle is a bridge. It survives in the context of other spaces—and yet it can also be a space of extreme isolation, only ever seen when passed over or passed through, and always in service of a different destination.

boundary 2 50:3 (2023)   DOI 10.1215/01903659-10472373   ©2023 by Duke University Press

Medieval studies is the discipline dedicated to the study of the "Middle Ages," the period of years between the fall of the Roman Empire and the Renaissance, the classics and the early modern. There is such generosity in the discipline's temporal scope, a generosity veering toward excess, for how could one thematically organize, much less unify, a period of one thousand years, identified as being in-between? As medievalist Fred Robinson (1984: 750) puts it, the field's temporal parameters are arbitrary: "Our period extends from the close of the classical period to the beginning of the Renaissance. If classicists and Renaissance scholars do not know when their periods begin and end, then that is their problem." As members of an institutionalized community, academic medievalists more or less accept the vastness of our discipline's temporal limits. Though we often focus on and specialize in a specific temporal range (in English studies: Old English, Middle English, late medieval), we recognize that our chosen range is much larger, and that we must be cognizant of setting our selected range into a much broader context of time. And yet, conventionally, medievalists do not apply this framework to other aspects of the discipline's design. For example, they do not extend the same flexibility that they do to temporal scope to geographic scope. Medieval studies is traditionally a "Western European" discipline. When broad, it will also include the Mediterranean. There are also limits on what questions scholars can ask about the materials from this period. Until recently, for example, the methodologies of critical race studies were considered anachronistic, and discussions of race qualified the term with quotations or reframed it as "alterity" or "otherness."

Critical race scholars in medieval studies have extensively discussed what is implicit (and explicit), not just in the history of the construction of the discipline of medieval studies but in the ways that scholars within the discipline often protect the discipline's reach—methodologically and geographically. Adam Miyashiro (2019: 9), for example, has shown how the "field of medieval studies is intertwined with the global colonial project." He has specifically argued that the field's conceptualization of "Anglo-Saxon" relies on Indigenous erasure, genocide, Orientalism, and ethnonationalism. Sierra Lomuto (2019) has discussed how the "temporal construct" of the discipline is "inextricably tied to the spatial construct of Western Europe. And just as Western Europe has been constructed through . . . the imperialist white-supremacist capitalist patriarchy, so too does the 'medieval' carry this valence of power." Her work shows how constructing a discipline in response to desires for "Western" political supremacy (however implicit) "furnishes a heritage site for whiteness" (Lomuto 2016, 2019).

Though scholars who are already qualified as medievalists discuss the disciplinarity of medieval studies in conferences, journals, and blogs, it is not only these spaces that set the boundaries and rules of the discipline. Rather, institutions and faculty design and define the discipline as they design and define graduate programs, degrees, certificates, or undergraduate minors (and though rarer, majors) in medieval studies. Though we think of these programs as training grounds for a profession that already exists beyond them, these programs shape the discipline as they welcome new scholars into it. It is within the process of constructing these qualifying programs that governing bodies determine who—and *what*—a medievalist should be. In deciding what a student must learn in order to qualify as a "medievalist," these governing bodies establish the discipline's identity.

These requirements often suggest that legitimate medievalists are those who work in the service of understanding Europe, even as they are conditioned to do so in an interdisciplinary program that recognizes the necessity of expertise far beyond Europe. For example, the concurrent PhD degree in medieval studies at my alma mater, the University of California, Berkeley, requires "Advanced Competence in Medieval Latin," regardless of specific research interests. It also requires "reading proficiency in a medieval vernacular language."[1] Students can select from any of the following without written permission: courses in Celtic studies, English, French, German, Italian studies, and Scandinavian studies. Arabic, however, requires written permission from the graduate adviser of the degree. Despite the fact that UC Berkeley treats Arabic as a language at the periphery of "medieval studies," a professor from the Near Eastern Studies Department was invited to serve and now serves on the degree's advisory committee. This teetering between inclusion and exclusion exemplifies the way medieval studies as a discipline often claims an interdisciplinarity that performs inclusivity even while it maintains a hierarchy of value.

The issue is that value is inherited and learned. In deciding what a student must learn to qualify as a medievalist, a governing body will inevitably pull from what their own training taught them about what is valuable to learn and master. This process formalizes disciplinarity, and it can be limiting. If a group of scholars are taught that any qualified scholar of the Middle Ages must have full and complete mastery of the Bible above all scriptural texts circulating in the span of a thousand years, then when they

---

1. "Concurrent PhD," Berkeley Medieval Studies (website), https://medieval.berkeley.edu /concurrent-phd (accessed June 10, 2022).

are in a position to design a medieval studies degree, they are more likely to require students to commit to mastering biblical knowledge. For a student who enters the program with an interest in studying translations of the Qur'an in England, the program will require them to prioritize mastery of the Bible, not the Qur'an. And so this program has set a student up for a study of the Qur'an that inflects back on the Bible. In fact, Christopher Livanos and Mohammad Salama's (2023: 145) essay in this issue unpacks the stakes of exactly this kind of disciplinary limitation as they show how "a certain strain of European and American Biblicism continues to impose itself on the field of Qur'anic Studies . . . limiting themes and conclusions" one can derive from Qur'anic studies.

This essay at hand considers the politics of disciplinarity in medieval studies by revisiting my own graduate program at University of California, Berkeley. In 2016, along with a graduate student in the art history department, Jess Bailey, I (myself a student in the English department) took on the role of negotiator and advocated on behalf of a community of graduate students for a more flexible and inclusive conceptualization of the discipline.[2] These efforts were perceived as threatening—and so were we. This essay offers an account of our "diversity work," which I theorize through Sara Ahmed's critical frameworks, in order to share the greatest lesson we learned: aside from the established governing body of the degree program, the fiercest defenders of a conventional, Eurocentric conception of medieval studies were those newest to the discipline—the graduate students.

Though I offer a detailed description of the events that took place before, during, and after our diversity initiative, it is important to acknowledge that this is not a singular experience but one that represents a larger issue within medieval studies and disciplines in general. Sara Ahmed's (2012, 2021) ethnographic research has shown us how often the very people who request and express a commitment to diversity work will reject it. That resistance to diversity and inclusivity is almost inherent to a body once it is institutionalized. Ahmed (2021: 44) further shows us how "institutional racism . . . [is] part of a wider struggle to recognize that all forms of power, inequality, and domination are systemic rather than individual." This essay thus lays bare the events of a single diversity initiative in order to help us understand how medieval studies operates as a discipline.

2. To ensure anonymity as I retell this narrative, I have excluded all names and, as much as possible, identifying markers. (The exception is Jess Bailey, who has given me permission to use her name.)

Middle: The Position of Being among or in the Midst of Something

Five white male professors who each belonged to a different discipline —history, music, German, classics, and art history—founded UC Berkeley's medieval studies program in the 1960s. With the help of the dean of the graduate division at the time, they formalized their shared intellectual, interdisciplinary interests into a degree-granting program. UC Berkeley is one of the few schools where medieval studies is a degree. This means, according to UC Berkeley, that students enrolled have "both a home department and training in the core disciplines of Medieval Studies." In other words, medieval studies at UC Berkeley is a formal discipline, one that "equips graduate students in a variety of disciplines with wide-ranging, rigorous training in the materials and methods necessary for advanced research in the history, languages, culture, and art of medieval Europe."[3] Beyond this brief sentence, there is no other definition or description of the degree. Instead, like other graduate programs, it is the requirements that define it. The following are those requirements: a methods proseminar; a course in medieval history; another course from outside the home department, on a solely medieval topic; advanced competence in medieval Latin; reading proficiency in a medieval vernacular language; working knowledge of the material sources of medieval culture; a field statement; a medieval studies component of the oral qualifying examination; regular participation in the medieval studies colloquium, and one presentation of dissertation work in progress to that colloquium. The website also provides a list of courses one can take to meet the requirements for "medieval history," "a course on a solely medieval topic outside of the home department," and "reading proficiency in a medieval vernacular language." The listed courses that follow these requirements are all conventional courses on European history, and almost all focus on texts (rather than material culture). Though the requirements make space for a student to take other courses that fulfill the requirement, the program does not advertise them and requires students to get permission from the committee chair. Interdisciplinarity is encouraged and appreciated, but also very controlled.

I was admitted to UC Berkeley's English PhD program in 2013, having just finished an MPhil in medieval studies at Oxford University. The

---

3. "Handbook for the Concurrent PhD in Medieval Studies," University of California, Berkeley, 2019, p. 1, https://medieval.berkeley.edu/sites/default/files/ms_handbook_2019.pdf.

concurrent degree's requirements did not serve my research interest, but I felt compelled to consider the degree because of the additional credential it would grant me when entering a competitive job market. I was invested in studying the racialization of Muslims in medieval England. While my Oxford degree had prepared me in paleography, codicology, and medieval history, I still had no background in critical race theory, postcolonial studies, or medieval Arabic. Given that there were no medievalists or early modernists at UC Berkeley who worked on race, I took coursework in nineteenth- and twentieth-century disciplines. Eventually, I communicated that I wanted to opt out of the medieval studies degree, given that I needed to turn my focus during my two years of coursework to topics outside of the scope of medieval studies as UC Berkeley conceived it. I was told I would not be taken seriously as a medievalist if I did not complete the degree. So, I did.

Even while my research focused on Europe, in understanding how English texts in England racialized Muslims, the approved list of courses did not list the ones I needed. So, multiple times, I requested special permission to count courses toward requirements. Having to show advanced competency in Latin meant that I could not strengthen my Arabic with the intensity I needed to in order to consult Arabic texts for my dissertation research. At the same time, in the three years I attended colloquia or lectures by invited scholars, I did not hear from a student or scholar whose work was invested in questions of postcoloniality or race. For a while, I made sense of this by recognizing that the degree's governing body had to make choices that served the bulk of the community. After all, I was a minority, not just racially but in terms of my intellectual interests. I assumed that the committee had to negotiate the needs of a much larger collective community, to which I belonged.

But after witnessing the way the advisory committee managed diversity and equity concerns, I began to wonder whether the committee was disregarding collective community needs rather than negotiating them. For example, I came across a report that the degree's governing body had written to UC Berkeley administration. In it, there was a section that described the degree's diversity and equity efforts. Under this section they celebrated their inclusion of Arabic as an optional language to fulfill requirements. But then they referred to it as an "exotic language." They celebrated that they had recently invited a disabled speaker. But then they did not offer any critical discussion of the degree's diversity health. They did not mention any plans to invite women of color as speakers, nor did they describe any efforts to diversify the program's overwhelmingly white student body. I was serving as the graduate student coordinator at the time and was organizing monthly colloquia. Given how visible I was as a leader in the community who had repeatedly had to request permission to apply outside courses to my requirements, I began to wonder whether the committee understood the ways marginality impacted my work and mental health, much less whether they had a plan to address it. All along, I imagined that the degree's governing body recognized and accepted the responsibility of making this community welcoming to everyone, and that they were weighing the social and intellectual needs of every member against their limited resources. But it started to become apparent to me that there was never any critical inquiry to begin with, that my membership in this community was one-sided: I was welcome to benefit from it, and not the other way around. The report started to circulate among graduate students, and others felt the same. We were all frustrated. And we started to notice other trends that reaffirmed that the advisory committee was not investing in diversity, inclusivity, or equity. For example, we tracked that the committee had given the degree's annual essay prize to men for five years in a row even though nearly half of the graduate students were women.

The new chair of the medieval studies concurrent degree recognized our frustration. In May 2016 she wrote to us that "a good step in sorting issues is having a clear view of what they are" and suggested asking the Graduate Division of Diversity to conduct a survey (pers. comm.). That following fall, graduate students decided to hold a town hall to discuss issues we were whispering about among ourselves in small groups. I chose not to attend. My tenure as graduate student coordinator had just finished, and I had started my exam year. I wanted to pull away from medieval studies for a year and focus on research in postcolonial and critical race theory. The most senior graduate student summarized the concerns that students raised in the town hall into a letter addressed to the advisory committee. Before sending it to the committee, he circulated it for feedback.

When I read the letter, I was overcome with respect for my peers and colleagues. In their criticism of the program and suggestions for change, I recognized a genuine commitment to community and inclusivity. They described how the degree's requirements were "Eurocentric" and "text-based." They put into words the discomfort I felt every time I had to ask for an exception to a course requirement: "One can substitute requirements, but that occurs on an ad hoc and sometimes idiosyncratic basis" (pers. comm., September 24, 2016). Their suggestions for changes to the degree made me realize that we shared a vision for an inclusive, dynamic, and exciting medieval studies discipline, one that made room for the world, even as it invested in a study of Europe. For example, the letter suggested that the committee could consider broadening its scope to include buy-in from Byzantinists or students working on medieval China and Japan who had expressed an interest in the program. Including these students could "have the salutary effect of widening the scope of medieval studies out from its Western European focus." The letter suggested that the degree "ask faculty from non-Western fields to present at one of the colloquia and invite someone who works on a non-Western field to give a talk with some regularity." To address diversity, "adding the phrase 'people of color and women are especially encouraged to apply' to calls for committee positions or the Kalamazoo prize is a simple but important reminder." I could tell from these suggestions that I was seen by my peers (as were the other few women of color in the program) *even though* I was not present in the town hall.

Less than a month later, on October 12, 2016, the advisory committee of the degree responded to the graduate students. They did not respond to any of the specific suggestions. In fact, they dismissed them all for the following reason:

> The Medieval Studies faculty have discussed several times in recent years what understanding of the Middle Ages should guide its program, where its chronological, geographical, and linguistic concentration should lie, and each time have firmly concluded that our current, broadly European and circum-Mediterranean definition is the one that best serves its students and best maintains the conditions of its intellectual vitality. At the same time, we welcome interdisciplinary exchange with our colleagues across the university, particularly if students wish to study areas outside the ordinary remit of Medieval Studies. Recent discussions of the Global Middle Ages have not only emerged from, but have depended on, the disciplinary and institutional formations medieval studies has durably assumed; in the same way, insofar as it is true that "medieval" might denote "a set of intellectual skills," it does so only because those skills are established on the material base of a certain historical particularity. These same formations, of course, define the expectations younger scholars face when entering the field; offering training within them therefore ranks high among the responsibilities we owe our students. It might be worth remarking that the Medieval Studies degree program is, on all sides, optional. Students do not need to pursue it to receive

their PhD, so that those whose needs are not met by its scholarly focus lose nothing by putting their effort elsewhere. Faculty undertake this addition to their required teaching and administrative duties as a service to students; they do not gain either institutional or professional rewards for their labors. In the present period, when the Medieval Studies degree program has been threatened with extinction, its success in attracting interested faculty and students and its reputation for rigorous training have been the sources of its strength. (pers. comm.)

This response presented medieval studies as a discipline that needed protecting. Its language suggested that the discipline had survived as long as it had because of active and careful preservation. Its geographic restrictions—Europe and the circum-Mediterranean—"maintain[ed]" its "intellectual vitality." The repeated emphasis of its "formations," both "disciplinary" and "institutional," suggested that it had retained its strength as a discipline because of foundations built in the past. Despite this preservation, the response suggested it was still a vulnerable discipline, "threatened with extinction." It implied that the letter to the committee invited harm to the field: any relationship toward the field that was not invested in protecting and guarding it firmly was a relationship that could cause it harm. The response poised the field's "rigorous training" in opposition to suggestions that would widen the scope of the field and make it more inclusive, not just for those with other intellectual interests, but also for people of color.

Despite the fact that the committee had "discussed several times in recent years what understanding of the Middle Ages should guide its program . . . chronological, geographical, and linguistic," they did not mention anything about their discussions around chronology or temporal limitations. There was no need to protect, define, or limit this boundary despite how ambiguous and vexed the beginnings of an "early modern" period or the ends of a "classic" one may be. The only mention of temporal limits was one that claimed the discipline maintained "historical particularity," which explicitly contradicts the vast historical range we collectively agree the discipline to have.

Instead, the committee seemed to have directed its efforts toward defining the geographic and linguistic boundaries of the discipline: "broadly Europe" and the "circum-Mediterranean." This is the boundary that, if flexible, could welcome a host of "other" intellectual interests and methodologies. Setting aside the fact that it was, in fact, the students of the degree themselves who had proposed suggestions that would make the degree better serve their intellectual needs, the concern for "intellectual vitality" seemed entangled with what shortly followed this part of the letter, the gesture toward the global Middle Ages: "Recent discussions of the Global Middle Ages have not only emerged from, but have depended on, the disciplinary and institutional formations medieval studies has durably assumed." The committee reminded us that there is a newly formed discipline where the kinds of suggestions we were making belonged. That discipline was not medieval studies but the global Middle Ages. Rather than using the existence of the discipline of the global Middle Ages as a way of making flexible or broadening the intellectual pursuits, methodology, and geographic and linguistic work that can be done in the discipline of medieval studies, the response suggested that the presence of the global Middle Ages relies on a narrow construction of the discipline. The global Middle Ages "depend[s]" on the disciplinary limitations of medieval studies, which the committee was committed to fiercely protecting.

But I did not register all of these insights right then. Instead, as an immigrant whose family has been repeatedly told they were welcome to "leave if they don't like it here" by racist students at school, people standing in line at the supermarket, or USCIS employees, the performatively generous statement that students "whose needs are not met by [the degree's] scholarly focus lose nothing by putting their effort elsewhere" was deeply offensive. The advisory committee's response to the town hall letter would ensure that the program would not serve someone like me, with intellectual interests like mine, as much as it served a white man with intellectual interests solely rooted in Europe. I wondered whether this rhetoric was suggesting that the degree would be stronger without a diverse range of interests that pulled resources in different directions. Over conversations with fellow colleagues and peers in the lounge while drinking microwave coffee and eating leftover department hors d'oeuvres, I realized other students were also bewildered and enraged. Most students felt dismissed and invalidated, regardless of their intellectual interests or racial identities. I had not participated in the town hall or in drafting the letter, and yet my peers had still fought for a program with my interests in mind. And now in our communal rage, I understood that we shared the same values. It was empowering, and I was energized to resist how comfortable the advisory committee was with asking the very students who made up my community to leave it. That night, I began a letter in response to the committee's letter.

Just as my colleagues and peers thought of my needs in the town hall, I wanted this letter to reflect theirs. I imagined this letter would build on the one we had all already agreed to send, but this time it would include signatures, and we would send it on behalf of all of us. But, as I would later realize, something changed for the students after the committee's dismissive response, and they became uncomfortable writing, signing, and sending a community letter.

After I wrote an initial draft and circulated it among graduate students suggesting making it a community letter, a graduate student from the History of Art Department, Jess Bailey, whom I had not yet met, responded immediately and expressed how offended she was at the response to the town hall letter. It had given her even more reason to fight for a more equitable and inclusive conceptualization of medieval studies. We began to work via email and Google Docs. We set the letter generated from the town hall as the base and framed it by discussing the ways in which the committee's response was dismissive and problematic. And then we revised and expanded the list of suggestions. We suggested that the committee invite graduate students to make a list of speakers they would like to see invited to UC Berkeley, so that when the committee invites its two speakers every year, they could pull one from the graduate students' list and another from the faculty's. We suggested that faculty work *with* the graduate students enrolled in the methods proseminar to produce a syllabus. This way students can spend time studying the methods that are pertinent to their research interests, such as postcoloniality. Given the limited focus of the faculty associated with the degree, the methods proseminar could include guest lecturers from fields well beyond Europe. Though we may not be studying the same material, we could learn new methodological approaches from them. Recognizing that those whose research interests fall outside the scope of medievalist faculty will be far less prepared to write a dissertation by their fourth year than those whose research interests fall inside that scope, we also asked that the program leave some of the coursework requirements flexible so that students could choose courses they found useful to their particular dissertation questions.

Jess and I finally met for the first time in a small, windowless office space she had reserved in Dwinelle Hall, with hard copies of the letter draft in hand. She was a petite white woman with an edgy pixie cut. We hugged, somehow already close friends even though we had never met. We were meeting the first group of graduate students regarding the letter. This group was made up of predominantly white women whom I had shared rage with just a week before. I expected our conversation to be about how we were going to develop the letter and was surprised that, instead, the conversation focused on whether we should even write the letter. It began with peers expressing concern over jeopardizing recommendation letters they would have to ask for in the future on the job market. Jess and I both had members from our dissertation committee on the advisory committee as well, and we empathized. We stressed that if we wrote it collectively, faculty could not blame an individual. That led them to express concerns over whether other members would sign it. "Well, will you?" We asked. Over the course of an hour, no one confirmed they would sign. We proposed that we would not send the letter unless at least half of the graduate students signed it, to protect backlash against a handful. But still they did not commit. We proposed adding an option for an "anonymous signature." But they still did not commit. Finally, they said that if white men from the program signed, they would consider signing as well. But they were not comfortable speaking to white men themselves, since they were not yet committed to the letter. So Jess and I then had to meet with a group of white men.

The only students who agreed to sign, even when they had suggestions to the letter, were the students who already felt marginalized and underserved by a program that had promised interdisciplinary training—the art historians, comparative literature students, the few women of color. When it came to the remaining graduate students, Jess and I were in a negotiating middle ground, a space that held us between every subgroup of the field's student body: white women who needed confirmation from white men; text-based studies students who needed art history students to be more specific about the ways they were marginalized. We scheduled meetings with students whenever we were available, in between classes, when we should have been reading for exams, and late in the evening. We spoke to students by phone.

Every student who would not sign nonetheless had feedback for us. However, writing or sharing their criticism of shortcomings of the letter with us was the extent of the labor they were willing to put into its construction. Most of the students' criticism of the letter fell into two broad categories. First, they felt that we were not giving credit to the committee's expressed commitment to diversity. As examples, they provided the fact that the new chair met with graduate students previously in the spring and had written an email to us acknowledging there were issues of equity and diversity, that she was looking into getting the graduate division to conduct a "climate report," and that recently, the committee had worked with several other schools in the University of California system to secure a UC-wide global Middle Ages grant: Middle Ages in the Wider World. One student even wrote to us that though the essay prize had been awarded to men for years in a row, she herself had been encouraged to apply, but had not done so. She suggested that this is reason enough that there is not gender bias and that the letter dismissed the efforts faculty *had* made. The second set of criticisms repeatedly centered around the fact that the letter discussed both diversity in body and diversity in discipline, a logical connection that at least one-third of the students, all in the history and English departments, thought was confusing. This criticism was always in response to the following paragraphs in the letter:

> The letter we received repeatedly sets the academic quality of the degree against our call for more inclusivity, diversity, and equity. It describes the degree as it is as having a "scholarly focus," "intellectual vitality," "rigorous training," and suggests that the changes we propose would jeopardize these valuable qualities. However, we believe that a more inclusive and diverse program would only strengthen the scholarly focus, intellectual vitality, and training of the concurrent degree.
>
> We think it is important that all involved in Medieval Studies affirm that diversity is not just the presence of female, queer, or POC bodies in the room, in the program, on committees, etc. It is the active fostering of an environment that allows everyone to feel valued and respected. It is not enough to simply concede seats at the table so that a minority will be represented. Nor is it enough to acknowledge that there are people who "study areas outside the ordinary remit" and that they are allowed to ask for "exceptions." In fact, it is worth mentioning that marginalization is itself the process of making students feel like exceptions, and this process only reinforces the problem.

Students took issue with this part of the letter. They argued that we cannot critique the makeup of the students in the programs and the intellectual fields of study in the same section. They found it vague to refer to the two as if they are entangled. I will return to the question of diversity disciplinarity below but want to note here that while the criticisms offered were valid, often the suggestions that followed were not. They asked that we find specific anecdotes and offer specific examples of how students felt marginalized. "Specific is better," one student wrote. While these students were explicit that their suggestions, pages and pages in length, were "not a signature" and that we should "check back in" once we had addressed their suggestions, they insisted that we do the work of making explicit the particulars of the ways the program excluded and marginalized students, individually. While they were not comfortable putting forward their names even as anonymous signatures, they were comfortable in asking that students make details regarding their exclusion—emotional and logistic—explicit in the very body of the letter.

We thought, then, that students were expressing genuine concerns about the letter. We thought they were being critical because, in being overly cautious, we might be able to condition the committee to be receptive to the letter's critiques. We never assumed that students might be using feedback as a distraction, as a way of preventing things from moving forward. So, every day, Jess and I met with students, and every night we stayed up revising the letter to include what students said they needed in order to sign. In the middle of the night, we would redistribute the letter, and then come morning, we would check in with students to see if they had further suggestions, if they felt comfortable signing anonymously or by name. In every email, we added the following lines:

> I hope you agree that our requests and suggestions are reasonable, respectful, and direct. We seek, above all, to hold our mentors and ourselves to a greater standard of awareness for the diversity of our program. If you would like to sign the letter, please give me written and documented permission (in writing) to add your name. We will not send the letter unless we have at least half of the concurrent degree students, since it is crucial that we do not alienate or isolate a handful of students.

But every day, we would receive a new set of suggestions or criticisms. And one by one, Jess and I chipped away at the list of suggestions. We removed the suggestion for graduate students to propose speakers because one student felt that it was unhelpful given that the majority of students will cater their interests to western Europe anyway. We removed the suggestion for faculty to develop the methods proseminar syllabus with graduate students because one student felt that this was dismissive of the labor faculty put into developing this course. We removed the suggestion that a number of courses remain flexible. Students, mainly in the English and history departments, argued that the requirements were flexible enough since they allowed you to petition for permission. They even wrote that if Jess and I were claiming that the study of the Middle Ages should include courses beyond Europe, this was too provocative and that it might cause the committee to invalidate the letter as a whole.

It is obvious now, only years later, that this barrage of feedback was not designed to strengthen the letter we were going to put forward but to post obstacles big enough to halt it. Although Jess and I thought we were responding to student needs, we were in fact working through a new set of obstacles. Though we were emotionally overwhelmed, we were committed to taking the suggestions seriously, not only because we thought that these were conditions for them to sign but also because we had shared such deep disappointment with these students after reading the committee's letter. More importantly, we were committed to community and believed, at the time, that other students were too.

So, to ameliorate students' concerns that we were not recognizing the work the committee had already done, we opened the letter with an effusive declaration of appreciation. To mitigate the risks students felt as they signed the letter, we informed the faculty that the students who had signed (anonymously or by name) were taking this risk because they were committed to the degree. And only after this scaffolding did we start to discuss our concerns with the language in the committee's letter, which reminded students that "the degree was optional and that students are welcome to leave if they do not find it useful." "In every way," we stated, "this sentiment places a burden on those students who are marginalized as opposed to the cultures and structural priorities that marginalize them. Students have chosen this degree because they find it valuable. . . . By asking students to revisit a decision they've already made, this statement suggests that the marginalization a student may be experiencing is the result of the student's poor decision making. It is worth noting that this is the only solution the committee has provided us in this letter."

Finally, broken up into two sections—"Intellectual Diversity" and "Increasing Diversity"—we offered a list of suggestions in the letter and provided explanations and justifications for each. Given that prizes were awarded to white men in the program for years, we asked that all calls for applications include the phrase, "People of color and women are especially encouraged to apply." While this was a simple remedy, the next set of suggestions required more substantial action, such as a revision to the program requirements. For example, we asked for a more substantial inclusion of language requirements by suggesting that "each student could be expected to fulfill one core language of their choice and two other medieval languages." Given that the program had repeatedly expressed a commitment to interdisciplinarity, we asked that specific course numbers be removed from the list of requirements. If that was not possible, we proposed instead that the list be expanded to include all courses taught by faculty affiliated with the degree. We suggested something similar for the Material Culture requirement. As it stood, the list that describes material culture privileged text-based studies (paleography, diplomatics, codicology). We suggested that the language in this requirement could be more inclusive either by removing the specific examples of material culture or by adding more, such as art history, architectural studies, and archaeology.

Middle: To Be Equally Distant from the Extremes

The letter was finished. Our deadline to submit had arrived. The night we were wrapping up the letter and sending it off, a small group of graduate students ran into each other at an event on campus. They decided collectively that they were not comfortable signing their names to the letter. And that night, one by one they texted or called us. First, they asked whether we would hold off sending the letter for two weeks. They wanted more time to consider signing it. We said no. We were tired. We had done our best to respond to every student's concern. They were welcome not to sign. Half of them removed their names. The other half changed their signature from named to anonymous. On October 25, 2016, at 12:15 a.m., we sent the letter to the degree's committee.

The next day the committee chair sent the only response we would ever receive:

Dear Shokoofeh,

My thanks to you and your fellow students for sharing your views as we work together to continue to improve the Program.

Yours sincerely,
XXXXXXXX

Though two faculty members wrote to us individually and acknowledged our labor and our commitment to improving the program, they neither rejected the suggestions nor accepted them.

Instead, the following semester, we received notice that the advisory committee had asked the graduate diversity director to conduct a climate report. Here we were, once again, being asked to communicate what we thought were the strengths and weaknesses with the program's diversity, equity, and inclusivity culture. It was not enough that we had conducted our own town hall, that we had summarized our thoughts in a letter, that we had worked as a community to write and submit another letter that made the shortcomings of the degree explicit. "A good step in sorting issues," the chair of the concurrent degree had said in May, was "having a clear view of what they are." Nearly half a year later, hundreds of words later, hours of discussion later, and the advisory committee was still trying to understand what the issues were. They claimed an interest in hearing from us, even after they had dismissed and then ignored the thoughts we had, with painstaking care, delivered to them. They wanted to conduct a survey, to collect data, and to decide whether a majority were in the margins: Is there statistically enough marginalization in the program for the committee to consider it significant?

So, we all filled out a survey titled "MedSt Anonymous Survey about Program's Climate for Diversity." It took most students ten minutes to complete the survey. It took me days. It was too difficult to revisit the events of the past year. Five months later, we all sat in the room where medieval studies colloquia are held and received a summary of the report: 70 percent felt that the program was actively committed to diversity and sensed that it was improving over the previous year. Seventy-eight percent felt comfortable discussing equity and diversity issues with advisers. The facilitator continued to report on statistics that contradicted a year's worth of the conversations I had had with students. Then the report moved away from numbers to a summary of the qualitative responses. In the excerpted quotations that they read to us from long-form reflections, students consistently raised issues with "implicit biases" and "macroaggressions." They said explicitly that faculty knew harassment was happening and yet did not do anything about it. They wrote of toxic gender dynamics among peers. The long-form responses belied the statistics. The summary of the report ended with these micronarratives, and the energy in the room was uneasy. Did it matter that three-quarters of the student body felt that the program was committed to diversity if there were faculty who were explicitly aware of harassment but disregarded it? Can percentages and graphs justify these stories?

We transitioned into an open discussion, moderated by the graduate diversity director. Faculty spoke, both those on the advisory committee and those affiliated with the program. They repeatedly stressed that if harassment—sexual or otherwise—was occurring, we needed to let them know. They reminded us that they were committed to diversity and that they wanted us to experience graduate school in an environment different from the hostile, sexist environments where they themselves had earned degrees. So, we need to speak up, they urged us. All the while, not a single graduate student or faculty from the advisory committee mentioned the letter that included half of the graduate students' signatures. In fact, aside from that single-sentence email response I had received over seven months prior, the committee had not yet addressed the letter. They did not even use the diversity initiatives of the past year as a frame for the graduate diversity survey. But particularly, in this discussion, the repeated insistence that graduate students must speak without any reference to the letter was bewildering. Revisiting its erasure during this town hall while writing this essay years later still sends a chill down my spine.

At some point, Jess and I, who were sitting side by side in the town hall circle, looked at one another. I raised my hand and said, "Faculty keep asking us why there is a culture of silence. But there is not. We spoke up months ago when we sent you a letter. They know what we are upset about. They know what we would like to see happen. But they never responded. We are not the ones who are silent. I am just wondering how they think students can come to them when they cannot even draft a response or engage with what has already been said?" The chair of the medieval studies program immediately jumped in. She said to the diversity director that she wanted to make a brief comment, that the committee received the letter but learned from fellow students that the organizers of the letter (she did not refer to us by name) had pressured students into signing the letter, that there were complaints that students had even felt "bullied" (she used this exact word). Given that there were concerns over this, they had decided not to respond.

I was stunned. There was silence. Nearly all the graduate students were there. And yet they sat in silence. I said, this time as my voice shook and my lips started to quiver, "How could you dismiss every part of that letter for the reasons you have just laid out? If there were concerns over bullying how could you not reach out to us and ask us about our process? You never even asked to have a discussion." There was more silence. Then a different faculty member from the committee said that in listening to this conversation he was realizing that they should have replied. He apologized. The chair did not respond.

Jess and I walked to the bus stop together after the town hall. At first, we were enraged. We yelled—the very fact that the director received reports of bullying and then decided to do absolutely nothing. Is this not evidence of the very culture the letter is criticizing? And then we wanted so badly to know which students had told the chair that we had bullied them and what evidence had they provided. Did the chair even ask for evidence? Was it her? Or was it him? No, it could not be him, because he ended up not even signing, so why would he report it? Maybe it was a group of them? It was a futile conversation. It did not matter. I realize now we were coping with the shock of realizing that now (and for a long while before) we were no longer part of a student community. How wrong we were to think that this was a community letter, that we were coming together as students to discuss and shape the discipline we were working toward entering for the remainder of our intellectual lives. We were, in fact, set in opposition to faculty and students, neither here nor there. We were not of the discipline but positioned against it.

Middle: An Extremely Remote and Isolated Place—i.e., Middle of Nowhere

In her book *On Being Included: Racism and Diversity in Institutional Life*, Sara Ahmed (2012) repeatedly likens the institutional rejection of diversity work to hitting a brick wall. She develops this metaphor because so many of the diversity practitioners she interviews describe the experience of diversity work in the institution as "a banging-your-head-on-a-brick-wall-job." "The feeling of doing diversity work," Ahmed (2012: 26) interprets, "is the feeling of coming up against something that does not move, something solid and tangible." She writes that it is this process of coming up against this wall, however, that makes the wall explicit: "Perhaps the habits of the institutions are not revealed unless you come up against them."

What came of all of our diversity work? The medieval studies advisory committee appointed a faculty member as equity adviser. In a colloquium, they introduced her and encouraged us to make an appointment if we would like to raise any issues or make any suggestions. "A good step in sorting issues is having a clear view of what they are."

Over the years, as I've tried to process this experience, I've returned to the same set of questions: Why didn't the very students who were willing to attend a town hall in order to express their concerns, who had also agreed to have their criticisms of the program forwarded to the governing body, sign *this* letter that Jess and I so painstakingly composed as a communal document? Why did I invest so much into this, even after I removed the suggestions I personally cared about the most? Students' fears, cowardice, white fragility, my own deep sense of impostor syndrome all had a role to play. However, by retelling the narrative of this diversity initiative in the context of medieval studies' disciplinarity, I have come away with a new understanding of these events.

When the chair wrote to the graduate students and described medieval studies as "threatened with extinction," she was invoking not just the crisis in humanities but also the crisis of public higher education. At this point at UC Berkeley, graduate students had already all participated in a union strike both for graduate student negotiations and for workers' rights. We had also witnessed and protested the increasing privatization of the school.[4] The language that medieval studies could only survive by finding "success in attracting interested faculty and students" is itself the language of privatization and the commodification of education that is threatening public education nationally. This was exceptionally strategic even as it was manipulative, because it automatically instilled in graduate students a heightened sense of urgency. The question that the students who constantly critiqued the letter grappled with was no longer about how we can improve the degree but about whether the degree was worth saving. And the answer for half of the graduate students was yes. Those students also happened to be the students safest in the discipline as it is conceived: students in text-based disciplines, particularly those in the English and history departments.

And this is where disciplinarity matters. As scholars Ellen Messer-Davidow, David R. Shumway, and David Sylvan (1993: vii) elucidate, "Socially and conceptually, we are disciplined by our disciplines." Disciplines discipline. There is considerable power in disciplinarity, as it takes a group's shared values and interests and institutionalizes them into a set of practices, through which a group can resist or fortify established intellectual power. In other words, disciplinarity is determined by *who*, not *what*.

Medieval studies at UC Berkeley was established because five professors wanted to formalize talking about the intellectual interests they shared. There are reasons why, in the 1960s, these professors were who they were: five white men from history, music, German, classics, and art history. Title IX was not passed in the United States until 1972, and it was not

4. In 2014, the UC Student Workers and United Auto Workers Local 2865 held a strike to protest unfair labor conditions, class sizes, and wages. In 2015, there were UC-wide protests opposing the regents' proposed tuition hikes. In December 2015, UC Berkeley students protested the wages and working conditions of custodial and parking attendant staff on campus.

until 1980 that women and men were enrolled in American colleges in equal numbers for the first time. It was not until 1919 that the first cohort of Black women was even admitted to UC Berkeley. Barbara Christian, who was the first Black woman granted tenure at UC Berkeley, did not get tenure until 1978. In the words of scholars Bryan J. McCann, Ashley Noel Mack, and Rico Self (2020: 244), "Disciplinary histories are unavoidably entrenched in national histories, they cannot help but enact the nation's racial logics." This degree at UC Berkeley was founded based on the interests and passions of five specific scholars: medieval studies at UC Berkeley as a discipline was shaped by the embodied composition of its founders, which was in turn made possible by a history of racist and sexist exclusionary practices.

When students themselves repeatedly took issue with the fact that the letter spoke of inclusivity of discipline and body in one stroke, they misunderstood the way disciplines create spaces of belonging for some over others. When the advisory committee responded to the town hall letter to say that they had "discussed... what understanding of the Middle Ages should guide its program... and each time have firmly concluded" that its current version "best serves its students and best maintains the conditions of its intellectual vitality," it became evident that they, too, were overlooking the exclusionary practices that made this particular characterization of the discipline possible.

It is in graduate programs where this disciplining begins. Graduate programs define the field as they train people to defend it. It is there where power hierarchies are unmistakable, where there are gatekeepers, where the culture of the field is set. It is in that *middle* space, where students are not yet professionals but also no longer strictly students, where the disciplining of the "middle" is determined. And yet, it is also here where those who are not yet qualified as medievalists are willing to interrogate and resist these boundaries, not having yet fully conformed to them. Often, they are dismissed. Always, they are unknown.

References

Ahmed, Sara. 2012. *On Being Included: Racism and Diversity in Institutional Life.* Durham, NC: Duke University Press.

Ahmed, Sara. 2021. *Complaint.* Durham, NC: Duke University Press.

Livanos, Christopher, and Mohammad Salama. 2023. "A Bridge Too Far? Ludovico Marracci's Translation of the Qur'an and the Persistence of Medieval Biblicism." In "The 'Medieval' Undone: Imagining a New Global Past," edited by Sierra Lomuto. Special issue, *boundary 2* 50, no. 3: 145–69.

Lomuto, Sierra. 2016. "White Nationalism and the Ethics of Medieval Studies." *In the Middle*, December 5. https://www.inthemedievalmiddle.com/2016/12/white-nationalism-and-ethics-of.html.

Lomuto, Sierra. 2019. "Public Medievalism and the Rigor of Anti-racist Critique." *In the Middle*, April 4. https://www.inthemedievalmiddle.com/2019/04/public-medievalism-and-rigor-of-anti.html.

McCann, Bryan J., Ashley Noel Mack, and Rico Self. 2020. "Communication's Quest for Whiteness: The Racial Politics of Disciplinary Legitimacy." *Communication and Critical/Cultural Studies* 17, no. 2: 243–52. https://doi.org/10.1080/14791420.2020.1770822.

Messer-Davidow, Ellen, David R. Shumway, and David Sylvan. 1993. *Knowledges: Historical and Critical Studies in Disciplinarity*. Charlottesville: University Press of Virginia.

Miyashiro, Adam. 2019. "Our Deeper Past: Race, Settler Colonialism, and Medieval Heritage Politics." *Literature Compass* 16, no. 9–10. https://doi.org/10.1111/lic3.12550.

Robinson, Fred C. 1984. "Medieval, the Middle Ages." *Speculum* 59, no. 4: 745–56.

A Bridge Too Far? Ludovico Marracci's Translation of the Qur'an and the Persistence of Medieval Biblicism

Christopher Livanos and Mohammad Salama

The tendency to compare the Bible to the Qur'an has remarkable merits and has occupied the minds of Muslims and Christians throughout significant periods in European history since the Middle Ages. Not only has this comparative tendency been instrumental in informing acts of translations of the Qur'an into European languages since Robert of Ketton's translation of the Qur'an into Latin in 1143, but it has also reemerged on the contemporary scene of Qur'anic Studies with extraordinary force. Although this "return to the Bible"—or to biblical and Syriac traditions both inside and outside the Arabian Peninsula—to study the text of the Qur'an conflicts with the Qur'an's self-interpretation and its immediate context of *asbāb al-nuzūl* (historical contexts/occasions of revelation), a closer look at Latin translations of the Qur'an, and in particular Ludovico Marracci's 1698 work, reveals that early linguistic encounters with the Qur'an in Europe may have set the tone for a long and protracted religio-political cycle of Biblicism and neo-Biblicism. A certain strain of European and American Biblicism continues to impose itself on the field of Qur'anic studies today, repeating the same lim-

boundary 2 50:3 (2023)   DOI 10.1215/01903659-10472387   ©2023 by Duke University Press

iting themes and conclusions. Our reference here is not to biblical scholarship on the Qur'an per se but to biblical-based anti-Muslim polemics. While this strain is not representative of the entire field, which includes multiple approaches, its presence cannot be denied.

Research on the Qur'an that cancels its historical world and ignores the entire process of its dynamic cultural contexts has dangerous epistemological implications. Against this disciplinary reification, it is useful to mention that the work of Angelika Neuwirth continues to be visionary and cautionary in this context. Neuwirth (2013: 200) warns that it would be highly problematic to single out the Bible as the subtext of the Qur'an and cancel its emergence as unique event:

> Western scholarship should be more cautious: it should not allow itself to be lured into the historical fallacy of reducing the Qur'an to a mere post-canonical refiguration of the Bible—an assumption that ignores the unique Qur'anic event, its revelation and proclamation. . . . This revisionist rigorous dismissal of the *certum* of the Islamic tradition is a politically dangerous distortion that we need to be alert to counter.

The field of Qur'anic studies remains in disarray because it follows a discourse and methodology whose purpose is less keen on understanding the Qur'an than defending Christianity and whose motive is more apologetic than exegetical. These problems also point to the imperative of opening medieval studies, a traditionally Christian-centric field, to more interdisciplinary approaches that can intervene in the continued influence of medieval anti-Muslim exegesis on current scholarly engagement with the Qur'an.

In a recent survey of the field, Devin Stewart (2017: 24) accurately describes the "return to the Bible" as a form of "Neo-Biblicism," which he contends is "not entirely new" but connected with the earlier work in the tradition of Abraham Geiger, Heinrich Speyer, and others. "It is merely that in the argument over the dominant influence on Islam," continues Stewart, "the pendulum has swung sharply towards the Christian side rather than the Jewish side." For this reason, Stewart effectively labels this camp "as partaking in 'New Biblicism,' [a camp that is] recognizing its relationship to earlier scholarship, rather than Syriacism. The 'New' recognizes that this resumption of research has been taken up after a considerable hiatus" (24).

It is in the spirt of Neuwirth's caution and Stewart's astute observation that we write this article—namely, to draw attention to the epistemological bias that has obscured the Qur'an as a highly original and theological discourse, and to call for a recognition of this historical fact from within the Western academy of Qur'anic studies. Moreover, if an ideology-free comparative study of the Qur'an and the Bible invites itself, as it mostly definitely does, it is regrettable that historical research and Christian interpretations of the Bible have not until now taken the Qur'an into account. Neuwirth (2016: 57), who makes this striking observation, argues that the reasons for this avoidance are historical as well as political and urges that "Christian as well as Jewish interpretation of the Bible, and indeed Western biblical scholarship in general, could benefit substantially from the Qur'an's biblical criticism, let alone its intrinsic challenge it poses to rethink prevailing exclusivist positions."[1]

Euro-American Biblicism, the methodology of approaching the Qur'an under scrutiny here, first emerged from medieval Europe's perceptions of Islam as a Christian heresy. In that narrow sense, Christian polemicists applied the methods that were already in place for refuting ideas they considered heretical. Christian heresiologists of antiquity and the Middle Ages were accustomed to disputing with opponents who accepted the primacy of the Bible. Medieval Christians, in particular, thought of Islam less as a new religion than as a heretical version of Christianity. Thus, from the outset, Christian commentators responded to Islam within the established framework of antiheretical polemics that assumed disagreements were based on the distortion of scripture. More specifically, acts of translating and interpreting the Qur'an through the filter of the Bible, which originated in the Middle Ages and continued into the early modern period, have continued to inform academic Qur'anic studies today. An informed reader would assume that Ludovico Marracci, whose translation dates to 1698, should not be judged by the standards of modern Qur'anic studies and that the problems his translation demonstrates are different from the current concerns of Biblicism. The goal of this article, however, is not to show the influence of Marracci or hold him accountable for the genealogy of Biblicism in Qur'anic scholarship. Problematic as it is, Marracci's own scholarship on the Qur'an is innocuous when compared to the crooked line of ideological continuity from seventeenth-century medievalism to modern Qur'anic studies.

Thomas E. Burman (2009: 5) has made the insightful observation that a "built-in deficiency in polemical literature" impeded a proper under-

---

1. Neuwirth (2019) applies the same approach of inclusivity, situating the Qur'an within the shared episteme of late antiquity, in her new study, *The Qur'an and Late Antiquity: A Shared Heritage.*

standing of the Qur'an. We agree with Burman, and we argue that Qur'anic studies must go even further than he and others have in addressing the lingering legacies of this deficiency. Another argument Burman makes is that there is "little evidence that would allow us to reconstruct the chains of scholarly affiliation through which the Qur'an circulated and along which ideas about how it ought to be read were passed" (1). We are, however, more inclined on this matter to agree with Pier Mattia Tommasino (2016: 164), who, with regard to the specific case of the 'Aqīda by Ibn Tūmart, has stated, "I am less pessimistic than Thomas Burman. We do have knowledge of readers, copyists and even translators into vernacular languages of the Latin translation of the 'Aqīda." Our position is that scholars can trace lines of transmission not only concerning specific texts but also regarding a broader methodology that has subverted the Qur'an to the Bible. Doing so reveals that this method originates in the polemical methods of the church fathers who predated Islam and has persisted from the Middle Ages to the present. While it was rarely, if ever, the intent of medieval polemicists to misrepresent Islam purposefully, they did explicitly and deliberately attempt to imitate the apologetic methods of the church fathers. This imitation, we argue, was the origin of the "built-in deficiency" that Burman has rightly observed, and we believe the origins and lasting impact of this deficiency need more attention. Alastair Hamilton (2005: 165) has given an admirable account of the roles of the founding chairs in Arabic studies at various western European institutions. While modern Western Qur'anic scholars are likely to view Islam sympathetically, unlike the scholars who held their professorships centuries ago, institutional deficiencies endure. Despite their more hostile view of Islam, premodern Christian apologists were just as interested as modern scholars in understanding Islam. The present article is our attempt to understand the causes of ongoing shortcomings in Qur'anic studies and to work toward solutions. We focus on Latin Christendom, leaving Eastern Christianities outside the scope of our study, because Western religious institutions are the origin of Western academia.

We argue that the "return to Biblicism" that Qur'anic studies currently issues, such as in the work of authors like Gabriel Said Reynolds (for a recent example, see Reynolds 2018), manifests the worst return of the same: a Biblicism that seeks to assert itself by demonizing the Qur'an text. We offer a close reading of Marracci's work not just to demonstrate the biases of his tunnel-vision approach in translating and commenting on the Qur'an but to show that the specter of Marracci still haunts us today. Yet despite its polemics, Marracci's commentary on the Qur'an text accurately reflects the ideological underpinnings of a post-Reformation Europe publicly at war with Islam. The vexing question now is: If medieval Biblicism informed European scholarship on Islam all the way up to Marracci's seventeenth-century work, of what epistemic realities is the current return of Biblicism indeed the image? In other words, through Marracci, we argue that certain currents in the field of Euro-American scholarship on the Qur'an has not advanced but has, in fact, bridged itself to old and impractical polemics: the denigration of one text for the sake of the other. This strain of Bible-inspired work in the current field of Qur'anic studies is neither new nor creative but is in fact precarious. It epitomizes the vicious return of the same, a descent into the Hades of intolerance and bias.

Our purpose therefore is to demonstrate that misconceptions that hinder a proper understanding of the Qur'an in modern Western scholarship have their roots in medieval heresiology. While this contention goes against the grain of contemporary Qur'anic studies, our conclusions are perfectly logical considering academia's origin as a Christian theological institution. For a discipline to transition beyond outmoded medieval paradigms, it must first recognize how pervasive those paradigms are. Although it is now de rigueur for the scholar of Islam to disavow the Orientalism of the eighteenth and nineteenth centuries, no large-scale reckoning with the legacy of medieval and early modern anti-Islamic prejudices has taken place. Modern Qur'anic criticism exaggerates the Qur'an's degree of engagement with the Bible and underestimates its uniqueness. This misunderstanding of Islam can be concretely traced from the church fathers through the medieval Christian apologists up to Marracci's erudite polemic and into the modern era. It is crucial to emphasize that we do not place one unique origin of Biblicism in Marracci, for that would be unfair and inaccurate, but we see his work as a substantial culmination of a trend that also served as an important bedrock for a continuity thesis of Biblicism in Euro-American academia. While one looks in vain for a direct quotation of the Bible anywhere in the Qur'an, one finds a concrete line of transmission perpetuating this misguided Biblicism originating in the academy's original theological mission and extending into contemporary scholarship. Sidney H. Griffith (2013: 55), who argues that a persistent biblical undercurrent informs the Qur'an, nonetheless states, "For all its obviously high degree of biblical awareness, the Qur'ān virtually never actually quotes the Bible." We would agree with Griffith's statement entirely if the word "virtually" were removed, since the apparent paraphrase of Jesus's saying about the camel and the eye of the needle and a couple of phrases such as "The Lord said to Moses . . ." or statements that God's righteous servants will inherit the earth can hardly be considered quotations at all. The recognition of a lack of direct biblical quotation in the Qur'an is informative, but once we have recognized this, we must reevaluate the whole Biblicist presupposition on which much of Western Qur'anic scholarship is built. This emphasis on biblical primacy has impeded meaningful interfaith dialogue, and we conclude this essay with a suggestion that future dialogues should recognize the shortcomings of the Biblicist method and turn to the rich tradition of theologians who have demonstrated a profound understanding of the different Abrahamic faiths.

Despite the lapse of time, the current scene of Euro-American scholarship on the Qur'an still echoes Marracci's premodern views on the Qur'an and the Marian doctrine. This uncanny continuity shows that internal contradictions have underscored Western scholarship on the Qur'an from the start. These contradictions never ceased to impose on the field of Qur'anic studies, as we continue to see the same debate repeating itself over and over again in contemporary scholarship.[2] Western sources that acknowledge their underlying bias tend to be in the realm of religious apologetics. While not without value, such works have an admittedly dogmatic agenda that limits their use for a scholarly understanding of the Qur'an. The predictable underpinnings of such an approach do not really advance the field or suggest by what these scholastic biases could be replaced, except by a seismic shift in the culture of Qur'anic studies scholarship in the Euro-American

2. See, for instance, Reynolds 2018. In his review of Reynolds's book, Jack Miles (2018) remarks that readers "may be offended by it and may draw attention, *ad hominem*, to the fact that Reynolds, a Roman Catholic of partly Arab heritage, is professor of Islamic Studies and Theology at Notre Dame University, a Roman Catholic university." Miles then qualifies his remark by adding that "it is academically ill-mannered to mention such a personal and biographical detail, but perhaps politically naïve to omit it." Irrespective of Miles's point, it is clear that Reynolds has no qualms in repeating the same polemics of Marracci: "It is likely," concludes Reynold (2018: 479), "that the Qur'ān's author has confused and conflated the two Biblical figures named 'Mary.'" In general, Reynolds's scholarship echoes Marracci's, excising the Qur'an out of its immediate milieu and omitting all reference to *Asbāb al-nuzūl* (*Circumstances* [or *Occasions*] *for Revelation*). Reynolds belongs to a school of thought that attempts to remove the Qur'an from the local environment of the first Muslim society, ignoring not only the semantic richness, the sociolinguistic contexts, and the historical circumstances and communal dialogues that prompted the revelation of the Qur'an over the period of twenty-three years but also dismissing the significance of pre-Islamic Mecca and assuming false etymologies between Arabic and Syriac lexicons (e.g., *al-furqān*) in order to advance the argument that the Qur'an is a Syrian Christian lectionary.

academy. Contemporary Biblicists of the Qur'an have key characteristics in common. First, they are in favor of dismissing the history of Islamic tradition altogether in approaching the Qur'an. Studies representative of this approach include Andrew Rippin's (1988) John Wansborough–inspired article "The Function of Asbāb al-nuzūl in Qur'ānic Exegesis"; Stephen J. Shoemaker's *The Death of A Prophet: The End of Muhammad's Life and the Beginning of Islam* (2011); and Gabriel S. Reynolds's *The Qur'ān and Its Biblical Subtext* (2010); among others (see also Witztum 2011; Badawi 2014; Segovia 2015; Azaiez 2015; Zellentin 2013). It is easy to see why this is the case. It will simply dismantle the Biblicist argument if the Western academy were to examine the Qur'an as a spontaneous and organic dialogue with the first Muslim community. A historically interactive text that is heavily and directly engaged with the events of its own community will simply give the Qur'an a formative substance, thus making it original and not derivative of older texts. That is precisely why a historical work like al-Wāḥidī's *Asbāb al-nuzūl*, which runs counter to the Biblicist derivation theory, is summarily ignored, at times even with inexplicable conviction, and dismissed as "suspicious," "presumptive," or "problematic." For instance, in his promulgation of a "conspiracy theory" that seems to appeal to certain readers, Rippin (1988: 2) denigrates al-Wāḥidī's reports in *Asbāb al-nuzūl* and gives them a new ulterior motive as "cited out of a general desire to historicize the text of the Qur'an in order to be able to prove constantly that God really did reveal his book to humanity on earth." Similarly, and predictably, Reynolds (2018: 4) makes an identical disclaimer in the Introduction to *The Qur'ān and the Bible: Text and Commentary*:

> My concern to read the Qur'ān independent of medieval traditions leads me to avoid a "chronological" approach to the text, that is, an approach which assumes that certain passages can be assigned to certain moments in Muhammad's life.... The question of a "chronological" reading of the Qur'ān is in part a larger problem of whether the medieval stories known as "Occasions of Revelation," which are meant to provide the historical context of Qur'ānic passages, in fact do so. It is my conviction that they do not, that these traditions are later efforts to provide a narrative context for Qur'ānic material.

Second, Biblicists approach the Qur'an with a decided theological authority, assuming mastery of Semitic languages while committing serious philological extrapolations and writing with envious confidence and expertise, as if all Christian biblical and Jewish traditions were uniform and historically indisputable. And while one has to approach all religious sources carefully, this particular brand of scholars never hesitates in disavowing the entire tradition of Islam as unreliable. So this approach systematically removes not only "Occasions of Revelation" but also all reference to *Sīra* (biography of Prophet Muhammad), *Ḥadīth* (Sayings of Prophet Muhammad, especially the ones pertaining to explication of verses), and the long-standing *tafsīr* discourse from scholarly consideration. Its proponents would rather argue for a silent and aloof textuality *sans histoire*; namely, they dwell solely and exclusively on textual similarities between passages in the Qur'an and the preceding biblical tradition, *not* to highlight affinities and differences but to present the Qur'an as a derivative copy that has infringed and appropriated the copyrights of that very tradition.

Manichaeism and the First Latin Translation of the Qur'an

The reading of the Qur'an as a heretical Christian text is readily apparent in Latin Christendom's first systematic scholarly engagement with Islam, which took place in the context of events leading up to the Second Crusade, as Latin outposts established by an earlier generation of crusaders were suffering a series of military defeats at the hands of resurgent Muslim forces. Western officials realized arms alone would not defeat their Muslim rivals and therefore saw the need to enter into theological dialogue with Islam. However admirable the attempt at dialogue rather than sheer brute military force may have been, the dialogue failed to resonate with a Muslim audience, based as it was on inaccurate assumptions about Islam. Whatever success the Western missionary effort had in the Middle East, from the time of the Second Crusade to the modern period, this success limited itself to a westernized proselytism directed at indigenous Middle Eastern Christians. Any inroads among Muslims were negligible at best.

An exchange between two of the most important churchmen of the High Middle Ages, Peter the Venerable of Cluny and Bernard of Clairvaux, explicitly spells out the assumptions underlying the West's engagement with Islam. Peter the Venerable commissioned Robert of Ketton to write the first complete Latin translation of the Qur'an. In his advocacy of the study of logic and philosophy, Peter was influential in the intellectual flourishing that has been called the twelfth-century renaissance. His relationship with Islam is complex. Since ancient Greek philosophy was preserved to a far greater extent in the Islamic world than in the Latin West, his promotion of Greek philosophy was de facto a promotion of Islamic Arabic commentary (Kritzeck 1964). Bernard of Clairvaux, like Peter the Venerable, was a central figure in the intellectual and political life of twelfth-century western Europe. Through the efforts of Peter and Bernard, their respective Cluniac and Cistercian orders came to be among the most prominent institutions of the Middle Ages, whose influence shaped the development of education in western Europe.

In 1144, Peter (1967: 298) sent Bernard Robert of Ketton's translation of the Qur'an, with an accompanying letter containing the following advice:

> Propono inde uobis patres omnes, et praecipue patrem Augustinum. Qui licet Iulianum Pelagianum, licet Faustum Manichaeum uerbis et labore suo ad fidem rectam conuertere nequiuerit, non tamen quin de eorum errore magna contra eos uolumina conderet, omisit. Sic de reliquis sui temporis, et non sui temporis hereticis, sic de Iudaeis, sic de Paganis faciens, non solum contra eos sui temporis nomines armauit, sed etiam ad nos et ad posteros omnes maximae aedificationis et instructionis charisma transmisit.

> I therefore recommend to you all of the Fathers, and especially Father Augustine. He was unable to convert Julian the Pelagian or Faustus the Manichaean by his words and his labor to the right faith, but, nonetheless, he did not shirk from composing great volumes against their errors. He did the same against the other heresies of his time and of other times as well as against the Jews and the pagans. Thus he not only armed against those notable adversaries of his own time but even transmitted a spiritual gift of greatest edification and instruction to us and all who follow.[3]

In the above passage, Peter does not entertain the possibility of addressing a new religion with new counterarguments but assumes that Augustine, who lived two centuries before Muhammad, provided not only the methodology but also the definitive arguments to be used against all non-Christian errors for all time. Christians first encountering Islam viewed the new religion as a Christian heresy. We aim to offer insight into why this misreading of Islam developed and, most importantly, how it persists in the tendency of Western scholars to interpret the Qur'an through the prism of the Bible. As the above passage shows, Peter the Venerable acknowledges three sorts

---

3. Throughout this article, translations from Latin are by Christopher Livanos and translations from Arabic are by Mohammad Salama unless otherwise noted.

of non-Christians: Jews, pagans, and heretics, grouping the Manichaeans into the latter category.

Since this first Latin translation of the Qur'an came with advice to use Augustine as the role model for heresiologists, we should note relevant features of Augustine's anti-Manichaean works. Manichaeism, a major rival to Catholic Christianity in Augustine's time, continued to be a major world religion well past the lifetime of Muhammad. By the twelfth century, Manichaeism in the strict sense was practiced only in parts of Asia far removed from the homes of Peter the Venerable or Robert of Ketton, but the term *Manichaean* was nonetheless indiscriminately applied to the various dualistic heresies that flourished in Europe. A similar blurring of distinction between various categories of others likewise characterizes most Western responses to Islam.

Manichaeism, as a scripturally based religion teaching that the prophet Mani was the last in a succession of prophets including Zarathustra and Jesus, figured prominently in the imagination of medieval Christians like Robert of Ketton and Peter the Venerable, who were thoroughly familiar with Augustine's anti-Manichaean polemics when they undertook what was in their time the most in-depth Western Christian engagement with Islam. To understand what we term "the persistence of Biblicism," we must account for Biblicism's origins in a Catholic tradition that developed in opposition to Christian heretics who all accepted the authority of at least parts of Christian scripture. Augustine, Peter the Venerable's heresiologist par excellence, routinely engages his Manichaean opponents in debates over the canonicity of certain parts of the Bible. Do we accept the Old Testament? Do we accept the Gospel? If so, what exactly does "Gospel" mean? Debates on these topics between Augustine and his heretical opponents were well known to Christians of the High Middle Ages, who found in the Qur'an statements that the Torah, the Psalms, and the Gospel are divine revelations. It is not our purpose in this essay to give an opinion on what the Qur'anic references to the Torah, Psalms, and Gospel mean, but we must acknowledge that the Qur'an does not engage with the Bible in the way that the competing sects of early Christianity did. If we read the antiheretical works of the church fathers upon whom medieval Christian writers like Peter the Venerable modeled their anti-Islamic writing, we will find extensive citations of Christian scripture and debate over its meaning in the Catholic writers as well as in what survives of their opponents' writings. Medieval Christians writers pounced upon the Qur'an as a compendium of prior heresies.

Medieval Residues: The Qur'an and the Enlightenment

This misunderstanding of the Qur'an as heretical, however, has led to the persistence of two paradoxical views that have spread widely in Western approaches to the Qur'an since the Enlightenment. One prevailing view is that the Qur'an's content is familiar, coming from slightly altered biblical narratives or idiosyncratic forms of Christianity. Euro-American scholarship on the Qur'an often held this view in tandem with a second prevailing view, which is that the Qur'an's style is far too unfamiliar ever to make sense to the average Western reader. Twentieth century Orientalist scholarship thus presented the Qur'an as simultaneously trite and exotic. Contemporary Euro-American scholarship on the Qur'an is now attempting to throw out Robert of Ketton's bellicose translation and distance itself from the othering approach to Islam, replacing it with a more open-minded approach. New scholarship is extolling the Enlightenment as a period of shifting attitudes toward Islam.[4] But the reason this idealized view of the Enlightenment is not working is precisely because the Enlightenment itself was a more comprehensively mapped imperialistic project than the crusades ever were. Modern scholarship praises George Sale (1734: iii), whose English translation of the Qur'an views Islam more sympathetically than the polemical Ketton or Marracci, and celebrates Muhammad as the "founder of an empire which in less than a century spread itself over a greater part of the world than the Romans were ever masters of." Though Muhammad expressed no interest in conquering any land outside the Arabian Peninsula, Sale upholds him as a model for imperialism at the time of the British Empire's most rapid expansion. If the long-held agenda of European powers was to conquer the Arab-Islamic world and render the entire Middle East subordinate to Europe, then it would be an understatement to say that the Enlightenment succeeded where the crusades failed.

Given the current turmoil in the field of Qur'anic studies,[5] it is not surprising that the Qur'an has not yet become part of the Western canon of monotheistic theology. A text standing firmly in the Abrahamic tradition, no less compelling than the Jewish and Christian sources, continues to be viewed as controversial precisely because of its relationship to Abrahamic monotheism. Can the Western academy understand the Qur'an, at least more generally, as an authentic confirmation of Abrahamic monotheism?

4. See, for instance, Bevilacqua 2018. For a full and comprehensive account of the Enlightenment's reception of the Qur'an, see Elmarsafy 2009.
5. For more on the turmoil in the field of Qur'anic Studies, see Saleh 2010a, 2010b.

Can it end its disparagement of the Qur'an as a mere copy or a heretical mimicry of the biblical tradition and instead see it as a commentary on and a continuation of that very tradition? While these are not easy questions to answer, it is useful to examine the lingering fallacies of Biblicism and trace them back to Marracci's translation of the Qur'an, its accompanying *Refutatio*, and its ramifications in the contemporary Euro-American scholarship on the Qur'an today.

Ludovico Marracci, a Premodern Guardian of Biblicism

Marracci was one of the first early modern scholars to make systematic use of Muslim commentaries in his translation of the Qur'an (Glei and Tottoli 2016). Yet Marracci's Biblicism provides no method for understanding the parts of the Qur'an that do not refer in any way to the Bible. Holy figures who appear in both the Bible and the Qur'an receive the bulk of Western scholarly attention in a methodology that leaves no way to understand parts of the Qur'an that do not reference the Bible, such as narratives of the prophet Ṣāliḥ. To this effect, Marracci's treatment of Ṣāliḥ, Hūd, and Lot are illustrative of the same medieval tendencies that have endured to our own day, though in less overtly polemical terms. One standard is used when discussing Qur'anic narratives that have biblical parallels and another standard when discussing narratives unique to the Qur'an. It is informative to contrast Marracci's treatment of the Qur'an's accounts of Hūd and Ṣāliḥ with his treatment of the story of Lot in the very next paragraph. In his commentary on Q7:73–79 dealing with the prophets Hūd and Ṣāliḥ's she-camel, Marracci (1698: 285–86) writes:

> Omitto quaerere, unde nam Prophetas illos Hūd, & Saleh Mahumetus eruerit. Quod si primus, ut Mahumetanis placet, fuit Heber: secundus vero, ut quidam coniectant, Phaleg, cur ita eorum nomina depravat? Sed hoc novum non est impostori: videmus enim illum pleraque quae in Sacris Litteris virorum nomina habentur, insana metamorphosi in aliena nomina commutare. Illud porro fide prorsus indignum est, quod de camela illa, eiusque pullo Alcoranus innuit, et interpretes copiosus enarrant. Hujuismodi monstra tam inepta Deus per prophetas facere non consuevit.

> I forebear to ask from where Muhammad dug up these prophets Hūd and Saleh. If the former was Eber, as the Muhammadans would have it—and the second, as some conjecture, was really Peleg, then why

misrepresent their names? But this is not new for the imposter; we see many names of men that are found in Sacred Scripture changed into alien names through a crazy metamorphosis. What the Qur'ān states and the commentators elaborate upon quite copiously about that camel and its calf is utterly unworthy of faith. God is not in the habit of making silly monsters of this sort through prophets.

Very few Muslim commentators have, in fact, attempted to link Hūd or Ṣāliḥ with biblical figures. The equation of Hūd with Eber is at best idiosyncratic, and the equation of Ṣāliḥ with Peleg is unheard of in Muslim *tafsīr* (for the Hūd-Eber equation, see M. 282, Abū'l-Fidā'). Immediately following the above statement, Marracci moves on to the Muslim account of the prophet Lot. Referring to the Islamic tradition that the people of Sodom were destroyed by a rain of stones, Marracci writes, "Fuit enim pluvia illa non lapidum, sed ignis, quo Sodoma ceteraeque civitates confines absumptae sunt" (It was the rain not of stones, but of fire, by which Sodom and certain adjacent cities were laid waste). Reference to Lot's name/story appears twenty-seven times in the Qur'an (see, e.g., Q7:80–82; Q11:77–82; Q15:58–74; Q26:160–69; Q29:28–30; Q51:31–37; Q54:33–36). The bone of contention is Marracci's reference to the Qur'anic word "سِجِّيل" (*sijjīl*), which could mean "clay," "stone," or "hardened fireballs" (Ibn Manẓūr, n.d.: 1945–46). In fact, the Qur'an does not go into minute detail about how Lot's compatriots exactly and specifically perished, yet it is clear Marracci's censorious polemic is based on fault-finding and on his conviction that the Qur'an is a derivative text. Furthermore, Marracci criticizes Islam simultaneously for its lack of reliance on biblical authority (as in the narratives of Ṣāliḥ and Hūd) and for its alleged misinterpretation or mistranslation of the Bible. Ironically enough, he saw no contradiction between saying that the Qur'an contained outright fabrication on the one hand and distortion on the other hand.

To the twenty-first-century reader, though, Marracci seems to level against Muslims two mutually contradictory charges: that they do not use the Bible and that they distort it. His methodology lacks an understanding of how Muslims view their own scripture. By writing in Latin, he ensured that a Muslim audience would not read his work:

> Videbor aliquibus in refutandis Adversariorum, et praesertim Mahumeti erroribus, aliquanto acrior, et intemperantior in conviciis fuisse. Neque ego id negabo; et certe improbarem, si haec quae scribo, a Mahumetanis essent legenda. Non enim ignoro sedatis, modestisque verbis Auctori Christiano, et praesertim religioso, etiam cum

extraneis a Religione, esse disceptandum: hac enim ratione facilius ad veritatem alliciuntur. (Marracci 1698: 16)

It will seem to some that I am rather harsh in refuting the errors of adversaries and especially of Muhammad and intemperate in my rebukes. I will not deny this, and I would surely disapprove if what I write is to be read by Muhammadans. I am not unaware that a Christian author, and especially a member of an Order, ought to write for strangers to the Christian religion with calm and modest words, for in such a way they are more easily won over to the truth.[6]

Marracci's wish was to inform Christians, who would then communicate with Muslims in a more diplomatic tone. However, such an exchange of ideas was precluded by the Biblicist assumptions he brought to his analysis, having inherited them from the medieval polemicists with Peter the Venerable at their forefront.[7]

We turn now to close readings of two Qur'anic passages, from Q3 and Q57, respectively. In both cases, we will study how Marracci's commentary, despite his vast erudition, does not address the Qur'an's literary impact and the rhetorical tropes common to the Arabic language. We have chosen passages on the Virgin Mary and Christian monasticism that we find especially pertinent to Christian-Muslim relations. There are other passages from the Qur'an that could be studied in this way, and we hope Qur'anic studies in the future will be enriched by further studies that examine the origins of biases inherent in the Christian polemical tradition and the immense richness of Arabic literary exegesis.

Marracci, the Qur'an, and the Marian Doctrine

We find in the Qur'an's reference to Mary as "sister of Aaron" a good example of a passage where familiarity with Christian traditions and with Arabic rhetorical conventions are both important. Too much exegesis—and Marracci is a prime example—focuses on either defending the passage's plausibility or pouncing on its perceived inaccuracy. The literary impact is thus lost. To briefly deal with matters of the passage's accuracy, we will simply say it is consistent with the Qur'an's overall view of People of the Book to say that

---

6. The translation is partly from Bevilacqua 2013: 96, with spelling regularized to fit our article.
7. For more extensive treatment of Peter the Venerable's relationship with Islam, see Kritzeck 1964. James Kritzeck's work remains one of the most thorough treatments of the subject.

Christians were correct about Mary having been a temple virgin but wrong about the name of her father,[8] which is not even mentioned in the Bible.[9]

As we begin our close readings of the Qur'an and our engagement with Western and Arabic modes of reading, we will juxtapose Marracci's readings of two Qur'anic verses that have long provided fodder for anti-Islamic writers. One is the passage that refers to Mary as "sister of Aaron," and the other is the so-called sword verse—namely, Q9:5, which has been interpreted as an incitement to religious violence and even an abrogation of the Qur'an's calls to spread the faith by peaceful means. We will bring the "sword verse" into our discussion of the "sister of Aaron" passage to highlight how a dismissiveness of the rich traditions of Arabic philology and Muslim exegesis underscore Marracci's learned commentary.

Medieval and pre-Reformation Christians were understandably both impressed and bewildered by the references to Mary in the Qur'an. Since Marian doctrine was one of the pivotal points of disagreement between Protestant and Catholic Christians, it is indeed fascinating to see how Europeans read Qur'anic passages on Mary as the Reformation developed. Marracci's text offers an excellent example of this variation on the Marian doctrine. In his translation of the Qur'an he constantly invokes the Bible and assumes a readership familiar with those biblical figures referenced in the Qur'an. This explains why, in his commentary, Marracci refers to the Bible and uses it as his main source to refute the Qur'an. Marracci's Biblicism is especially abundant in references to Mary. He tends to engage in extensive commentaries on those references, which often lead to lengthy discussions of the Trinity and the divinity of Christ. While Marracci takes Muslim critiques of trinitarianism quite seriously, he remains dismissive of notions such as Mary being "sister of Aaron"[10] and Gabriel being the "spirit of God." To this effect, his comment on Q9 is revealing: "Totum fere alcora-

8. Marracci says that Mary's father was named Joachim, although neither of Mary's parents is named in the Bible (see, for instance, Marracci 1698: 107). While, as a Catholic theologian, he was not bound by *sola scriptura*, it is nonetheless striking to see his rebuke of the Qur'an for differing with Christian tradition regarding a name that is never mentioned in the Bible.

9. It is not our intention here to address controversies regarding what role, if any, young girls had in first-century Temple Judaism but rather to state that the Qur'anic references to Mary are best understood in this light. For the topic of the religious roles of young girls in Temple Judaism, see Nutzman 2013.

10. Before Marracci, Nicetas Byzantius was one of the earliest European polemicists to use the Bible to accuse the Qur'an of errancy in the Marian passage. Nicetas's work is also known as *Refutation of the Qur'an* or *Anatropē*. See Byzantius 1912: 24.

num destruit Mahumetus hac Sura" (Marracci 1698: 306; With this sura, Muhammad destroys almost the entire Qur'an). The commentary sources Marracci relies on took an extreme version of the abrogation interpretation while not acknowledging that exegetes disagree on how much of previous revelation, if any, is abrogated by this sura. However, Marracci seems determined in his stand that Q9 is where Muhammad switched from persuasion to force. Keeping in mind his eagerness to use the "sword verse" as a reason to dismiss the entire Qur'an, we may see how in Q3 he treats the matter of Mary with the same dismissive lens:

> Ex ipso Surae hujus titulo, crassimus Mahumeti error ostenditur, dum Mariam Deiparam filiam Joachim confundit cum Maria filia Amran & sorore Moysis & Aaron. Id vero infra clarius patet, ubi vocat Mariam Deiparam Sororem Aaron. Distorqueant quantum volent Mahumetani expositiores verba Alcorani, nunquam Prophetum suum ab hoc errore poterunt vindicare. (107)

> With the very title of this sura, Muhammad's quite crass error is shown, whereby he confuses Mary, the Mother of God and daughter of Joachim, with Miriam the daughter of Amram and sister of Moses and Aaron. Later this becomes even more clear, where he calls Mary (the Mother of God) "sister of Aaron." However much the Muhammadan commentators may try to distort the words of the Qur'an, they can never absolve their prophet of this error.

It is hard to see the logic in Marracci's criticism of Muhammad in the passage above. The notion that Mary was a temple virgin was common in Muhammad's time; therefore she was a "sister" of the House of Aaron—the temple priests—in a sense that would have been immediately recognizable in her culture. This emphasis on virginity in relation to the Temple should self-evidently explain the context of the Qur'anic passage. She was supposed to be a temple *virgin*, so people were wondering where the baby came from (Q19:28). The contended translations/interpretations of the "يا أخت هارون" construction in this verse (including the various interpretations listed in Ṭabarī 1994 and Ibn Kathīr 2000) have led both Christian and Muslim apologists to be stuck in a vapid hermeneutical circle. Without exception, looking at the sources from before 1700, Christian commentators say that Muslims attempt to defend a clear blunder, and Muslim commentators say that Christians attempt to find problems in a clear, unproblematic passage. This itself is credible evidence of how premodern patterns of thought reproduce themselves in contemporary discourses.

The only way out of this unproductive circle, in addition to identifying it, is to read this phrase and the entire episode from the sura in a manner that recognizes the Qur'an's narrative, its linguistic reference and rhetorical purpose—that is, to bypass the conventional Christian-Muslim apologetics and simply examine the linguistic practices of the Arabic language in the Qur'an text itself and its relation to the context of first-century Temple Judaism. أخت هارون, or "sister of Aaron," is a reference to Mary's role as a consecrated temple virgin. The Jewish priests were the descendants of Aaron, so the كُنية (*kunya*, "nomenclature") is a reference to her close relationship with the priesthood. We hardly ever hear this reading offered in modern scholarship, but it seems quite straightforward. Classical Arabic poetry includes examples of references using the vocative *iḍāfa* construction of "أخت يا" to distinguish a free, unadulterous woman from a "slave" woman who does not own her own body. This reference is key in emphasizing the honorable and free status of Mary included in the vocative "يا أخت هارون." The following line from a love poem by al-Farazdaq shows this connotation clearly:

يا أُختَ ناجِيَةَ بنِ سامَةَ إِنَّني أَخشى عَلَيكِ بَنِيَّ إِن طَلَبوا دَمي
لَن يَقبَلوا دِيَةً وَلَيسوا أَو يَرَوا مِنّي الوَفاةَ وَلَن يَرَوهُ بِنُوُّم
(Farazdaq 1983: 123–24)

Oh Sister of Nājiyya ibn Sāma (tribe) / I worry for you of my sons who would seek revenge
They won't accept a compensation nor will they / Even if they see a fulfillment from me (and they won't) let it sleep

According to the Qur'an, Mary was an orphan whose father عمران (Amram) died before she was born, and that is why her mother (Anna, who is mentioned but not named in the Qur'an) "gifted" her to God while she was still a fetus and upon her birth gave her the name Maryam (Q3:34–37). Because she was an orphan "daughter" (the Qur'an emphasizes the importance of this reference: "I have given birth to a female, and a female is not like a male"; Q3: 36), reference to the culture, which celebrates males more than females—hence Anna's supplication for God to protect her—is more compelling. She was for that reason adopted by Zechariah (Zakariya), father of John the Baptist (Q19:7), also a priest of the sons of Aaron according to Luke 1:67–79. The reference to Mary as "sister of Aaron" thus makes perfect sense within the context of stories of Mary being a temple virgin, which were well known in Muhammad's time. We need not concern ourselves with whether or not there were consecrated virgins in first-century Temple Judaism. The point here is that, given the traditions current in Muhammad's time, there is no need to suppose he conflated the biological sister of Moses and Aaron with the mother of Jesus.

Reference to Aaron in Q19:18 is thus at the level of the reminder for Mary (a woman carrying the trust of Aaronian consecration of the Temple) to remember who she is and what she represents. Aesthetically, the verse builds up a stark contradiction between Mary and members of her small community, or a dramatic irony, between what Mary represents and what in their minds they perceive she has committed. This unspeakable shock is intensified by the trope of irony as a drama of an almost scandalous moment in the public confrontation between Mary and her people. When they saw her carrying a baby in her hands, and when "she brought him to her people, carrying him," they said, "'Oh Mary, you definitely have brought about something novel'" (Q19:27). Mary's people were completely dismayed, wondering how Mary could have done such a thing, especially when she is from "the lineage of Aaron," and especially when her "father was not a man of nefarity," nor was her mother "unchaste" (Q19:28).

The issue with Marracci's approach to the Marian doctrine in the Qur'an is twofold. First, Marracci, as well as medieval and Reformation Christian commentators in general, seems convinced that the Qur'an is a heretical text and is therefore overly eager to find fault with it. Most Muslim commentators, from the other side of the equation, have not been sufficiently familiar with non-Muslim traditions about Mary's life. If one takes "sister of Aaron" to mean "sister with a close, spiritual relationship with the house of Aaron," then we have a reading that is consistent with classical Arabic usage and that would not have been at all jarring to someone in seventh-century Arabia who was familiar with traditions about Mary's life.

Second, Mary is highly revered in the Qur'an, and reference to her is ubiquitous and consistent. She is the one and only woman mentioned by name in the whole Qur'an, and her name is sometimes mentioned in relationship to her son, the Messiah who is often referred to in the Qur'an appositively as "المسيح عيسى بن مريم" (the Messiah, Jesus the Son of Mary), a testimony to her venerable status in the Qur'an. Even without reference to Jesus, the name Mary still appears fifteen times in the Qur'an with consistent accuracy (see Q3:36; Q3:37; Q3:42; Q3:43; Q3:44; Q3:45 (twice); Q4:156; Q4:157; Q4:171; Q5:17; Q5:110; Q19:16; Q19:27; and Q66:12).

To conclude our discussion of Mary as a focus of religious controversy and the persistent allegation that Muhammad conflated Mary the Mother of Jesus with Miriam the sister of Moses and Aaron, we refer once more to the construction "Oh Sister of Nājiyya ibn Sāma" in the poetry of al-Farazdaq. It is analogous to the Qur'anic "sister of Aaron" passage in that Nājiya bin Sāma was the eponymous founder of a tribe, and members of the tribe could be referred to figuratively as his "brothers and sisters" although they were, in fact, his descendants. We do not need to solve complex and controversial issues of biblical genealogy or of the ancestry and tribal affiliation of Jesus's relatives to say that classical Arabic often used *sister* in a figurative sense. For our purposes, it is most instructive to concentrate on Marracci's method of dismissing all but the crudest literal interpretations of the Qur'an. Indeed, it would make little sense in the passage in question (Q19:27–28) for Mary's people to refer to her biological brother. It fits perfectly into the context of the passage, however, to refer to her role in the Temple and her relationship with the priesthood in order to contrast her reputation for chastity with the alleged indiscretion they falsely conclude must have preceded the birth of her child. An interpretation that makes sense theologically, philologically, and rhetorically would be to understand "sister of Aaron" as "temple virgin." The passage is not about Mary's sibling but about the perceived scandal of a temple virgin having a child. Reference to "brothers and sisters" in a spiritual sense has been ubiquitous in Christianity from its inception, as it has become in Islam. Marracci, as a Catholic priest, dealt on a constant daily basis with people referred to as "brothers and sisters" although they were not biologically related, and his refusal to recognize the possibility of such a figurative meaning in the Qur'an is typical of his overall polemical methodology. We will now turn to the Qur'an's discussion of monks, who, as Marracci intimately knew, called one another "brother" in a spiritual sense.

Monasticism and Marracci's Attack on Sura al-Ḥadīd (Q57)

A methodology rooted in Arabic philology and Muslim exegesis provides an escape from the morass of biblical primacy. In his treatment of the Qur'anic passage on monasticism in Sura al-Ḥadīd (Q57), Marracci must contend with a topic not specifically addressed in the Bible. Indeed, the absence of a biblical mandate for monasticism was central to Protestant apologetics. Discussions of monasticism and Marian doctrine were therefore related in that both topics were pertinent to intra-Christian debates as well as to Christianity's encounter with Islam. Unable to use his familiar methodology of citing scripture, Marracci relies instead on an ad hominem attack on Muhammad's character.

Marracci's commentary on Q57 is one of the harshest polemics one could come across in his Qur'an commentary. He starts out by saying that Muhammad was out to defraud people of their money. His commentary on the sura begins: "Mirum est Mahumeti ingenium ad pecuniarum aucupium. Primum enim captat popularem auram ex laudibus Dei: ut ex concepta de illius pietate opinione, nemo posset in illo fraudem suspicari" (Marracci 1698: 705; Muhammad's ingenuity for hunting after money is remarkable. First, he captures the breath of popular favor by the praise of God so that, by reason of the belief about his piety, no one could suspect him of fraud). Then he immediately moves on to discuss monasticism, contending that, while admittedly not instituted by Jesus Christ, it is still a valid way of worshipping God. Marracci acknowledges that monasticism is in many cases corrupt, but he attributes the degeneration to human frailty rather than to any inherent flaw in monasticism. There is a clearly defensive tone throughout Marracci's commentary on Q57, since this is the sura where monasticism is specifically mentioned, and charges against the financial corruption of monastic institutions had been commonplace since long before Marracci's time. Marracci thus begins his defense with a timely offense, launching his commentary on the sura with an attack on Muhammad as a greedy manipulator. The placing of the polemic is jarring, since little at the outset of Q57 has to do with calls for money, nor is it one of the suras normally cited in relation to the zakat tax or other almsgiving duties in Islam. It is therefore hard to understand what purpose Marracci's polemic serves other than as a preemptive attack before bringing up the sensitive subject of monasticism and the charges of corruption that inevitably ensue.

Marracci responds to the Qur'an's mention of monasticism by saying that there are good monks and bad monks. The Qur'anic verse in question does not contradict Marracci's position. We see a pronounced dialectic of continuity and discontinuity in this verse. For the continuity thesis, Q57:27 and Q57:28 are built on Q57:26: Jesus is presented as a historical continuity, a variation on the theme of calling for the one God, and an extension of the line of prophets from Noah to Abraham to Moses to Jesus to Muhammad. The Arabic particle "ثم" (then / after that) denotes continuity over time. The transitive verb(al) sentence "أرسلنا" (We sent X) in Q27:26 correlates with the transitive verb(al) sentence "قفينا" in verse 27 (we continued, in their footsteps, to send prophets), creating a syntactic parallelism and a thematic continuity. The expression "قفينا على آثارهم" is unique in Arabic, meaning literally "to send forth in their footsteps," thus interweaving a thread or a concatenation of prophethood across human time.

What is clear, based on the simple past verbal construction "ابتدعوها" (they devised it) is that the Qur'an presents monasticism (in Q57:27) as an exception or a contingency plan in a long and extensive line of the monotheistic tradition, and not necessarily as a formative principle of Christian dogma. Thematically as well as stylistically, monasticism stands out in Q57:27 as a discontinuity, if not an aberration, in relation to the concatenation of prophethood outlined in Q57:26 and the beginning of Q57:27. This Qur'anic version of monasticism must not have settled well with Marracci, who, in his commentary, acknowledges that monasticism was not directly ordained in scripture but still regards it as a valid devotional practice.

Biblicism, the Vicious Return

We now return to our claim that there appears to be a compulsive return of a certain strand of Biblicism in the field of Qur'anic Studies among European and American scholars. This is not to say that a comparative approach to the Qur'an via the Bible or vice versa is untenable. On the contrary, the Bible remains a significant part of Islamic religious heritage, and comparative approaches undoubtedly have the appeal of enriching one's understanding of both texts and connecting the epistemological dots in Abrahamic monotheism, especially by putting these texts in a larger context and casting a different light on their subject matter. Additionally, as a third variation on the theme of Abrahamic scripture, the Qur'an often and self-evidently invites comparison with the Torah and Gospels, and at times even compels these comparisons to take place as a way of understanding and interpreting the text.

However, the biblical primacy model for Qur'anic exegesis, in place in the West from the time of Peter the Venerable till today, has proven unproductive in advancing the field, understanding Islam, or entering into a constructive dialogue with Muslims. We therefore propose another model, also grounded in medieval Christianity, with a parallel if less academically prominent history. We propose a shift from Peter the Venerable's search for heresy and distortion to an approach to the Qur'an in the tradition of Giovanni Boccaccio's famous parable of the three rings from day 1 of the *Decameron*. In this fourteenth-century story, Saladin puts a Jew named Melchisedech on the spot by asking him which of the three Abrahamic faiths is true. Melchisedech prudently responds with a parable in which a wealthy man separately told each of his three sons that he was giving them his precious ring as a sign that he was the father's true, beloved heir. The wealthy man then had a master goldsmith make two exact replicas of the ring. Thus the three sons were each left believing themselves to be the one true heir. Boccaccio provides us with a pluralistic framework for interfaith dialogue that, far from requiring us to reject the West, has roots in one of the central masterpieces of Italian and world literature.

Qur'anic scholars can benefit from Boccaccio's tale for Melchisedech's emphasis on God's love for all humanity. Divine affection is a theme pervasive throughout the Qur'an yet understudied in Western Qur'anic scholarship. Melchisedech tells Saladin that the father's equal love for each of his children is what prompted him to give each an artfully crafted ring and to lead each to believe he was uniquely favored. While the story prioritizes the universality of God's love, it does not demand a facile relativism. Read carefully, the story has Melchisedech affirming the primacy of Judaism while recognizing that other faiths are not crass distortions but genuine expressions of love.

It is instructive to trace the parallel reception histories of the Qur'an and of Boccaccio's tale in early modern Europe. Counter-Reformation editions of the *Decameron* bowdlerized Boccaccio's pluralistic tale. Editions of the Qur'an published in the Counter-Reformation era were uniformly polemical in scope, and the polemical focus culminated in Marracci's commentary, which is monumentally erudite yet completely inconducive to meaningful understanding between Christians and Muslims. The whole Western missionary effort toward Islam failed to convert Muslims and succeeded only in bringing eastern Christians into Western forms of Christianity. The eighteenth century marked a shift in Western outlooks toward the Qur'an, and it was likewise during the Enlightenment that Boccaccio's tale of the three rings was promoted with renewed energy as a model for interfaith relations. Most notably, Boccaccio's story serves as the basis for Gottholt Lessing's 1779 play *Nathan der Weise*, with its appeal for religious tolerance.[11] As we have noted, we find fault with certain approaches taken toward the Qur'an during the European Enlightenment. While we reject Marracci's treatment of the Qur'an as an act of plagiarism and Sale's idea of Islam as a blueprint for Imperial dominion, we equally reject the nitpickings of today's Biblicism and insist on a reinfusion into Qur'anic studies of the tradition found in Boccaccio and Lessing, where the search for religious copying is less important

11. See P. Stewart 2004 for a discussion of Boccaccio's three rings tale, its antecedents, and its reception.

than the appreciation of each religion's basis in God's love. The Qur'an has a mesmerizing tendency to resolve centuries-old biblical quarrels by deferring them to God's mercy and the day of reckoning, a much-needed affirmation and acknowledgment that disagreements and differences among humans need not lead to animosities and textual anxieties about which one got it first or who got it right:

$$\text{إِنَّ الَّذِينَ آمَنُوا وَالَّذِينَ هَادُوا وَالصَّابِئِينَ وَالنَّصَارَى وَالْمَجُوسَ وَالَّذِينَ أَشْرَكُوا إِنَّ اللَّهَ يَفْصِلُ بَيْنَهُمْ يَوْمَ الْقِيَامَةِ ۚ إِنَّ اللَّهَ عَلَى كُلِّ شَيْءٍ شَهِيدٌ}$$

(Q22:17)

Those who have believed and those who are Jews and the Sabeans and the Christians and the Magians and those who have associated others with God—God will decide among them on the Day of Judgment. God is a Witness to everything.

And like the Bible, the Qur'an invites us to accept and transcend all our differences. To be sure, the Qur'an does not contain a single quotation from the Bible. Yet, like the Bible, it contains endless affirmations of God's love for humanity. We will thus understand the Qur'an better if less attention is given to its biblical sources and more is given to neglected topics such as divine affection and epistemic humility.

References

Azaiez, Mehdi. 2015. *Le contre-discours coranique*. Berlin: De Gruyter.

Badawi, Emran Iqbal El-. 2014. *The Qur'ān and the Aramaic Gospel Traditions*. New York: Routledge.

Bevilacqua, Alexander. 2013. "The Qur'an Translations of Marracci and Sale." *Journal of the Warburg and Courtauld Institutes* 76: 93–130.

Bevilacqua, Alexander. 2018. *The Republic of Arabic Letters: Islam and the European Enlightenment*. Cambridge, MA: Harvard University Press.

Burman, Thomas E. 2009. *Reading the Qur'ān in Latin Christendom, 1140–1560*. Philadelphia: University of Pennsylvania Press.

Elmarsafy, Ziad. 2009. *The Enlightenment Qur'ān: The Politics of Translation and the Construction of Islam*. Oxford: Oneworld.

Farazdaq, al-. 1983. *Dīwān al-Farazdaq*. Edited by Illiyā al-Ḥāwī. Beirut: Dār al-Kitāb al-Lubnānī.

Glei, Reinhold F., and Roberto Tottoli. 2016. *Ludovico Marracci at Work: The Evolution of His Latin Translation of the Qur'ān in the Light of His Newly Discovered Manuscripts; With an Edition and a Comparative Linguistic Analysis of Sura 18*. Wiesbaden: Harrassowitz Verlag.

Griffith, Sidney H. 2013. *The Bible in Arabic: The Scriptures of the "People of the Book" in the Language of Islam*. Jews, Christians, and Muslims from the Ancient to the Modern World 48. Princeton, NJ: Princeton University Press.

Hamilton, Alastair. 2005. "The Quran in Early Modern Europe." In *Oostersche weelde: De Oriënt in westerse kunst en cultuur; Met een keuze uit de verzamelingen van de Leidse Universiteitsbibliotheek*, edited by Jef Schaeps, Kasper van Ommen, and Arnoud Vroljik, 131–43. Leiden, Netherlands: Primavera Pers.

Ibn Kathīr. 2000. *Tafsīr al-Qurʾān al-ʿaẓīm, 1184–1185*. Beirut: Dār Ibn Ḥazm.

Ibn Manẓūr. n.d. *Lisān al-ʿArab*. Edited by ʿAbdullāh ʿAlī al-Kabīr, Muḥammad Aḥmad Ḥasaballāh, and Hāshim Muḥammad al-Shādhlī. Cairo: Dār al-Maʿārif. https://www.baheth.info/find/web/%D8%B3%D8%AC%D9%8A%D9%84 (accessed April 17, 2023).

Kritzeck, James. 1964. *Peter the Venerable and Islam*. Princeton, NJ: Princeton University Press.

Marracci, Ludovico. 1698. *Alcorani textus universus ex correctioribus Arabum exemplaribus summa fideatque pulcherrimis characteribus descriptus*. Padua, Italy: Typographia Seminarii. https://archive.org/details/AlcoranusTextusMaracci.

Miles, Jack. 2018. "A Feast for the Polymath: Jack Miles on Gabriel Said Reynolds's 'The Qurʾan and the Bible.'" *Los Angeles Review of Books*, December 17. https://lareviewofbooks.org/article/a-feast-for-polymaths-jack-miles-on-gabriel-said-reynoldss-the-quran-and-the-bible/.

Neuwirth, Angelika. 2013. "Locating the Qurʾan in the Epistemic Space of Late Antiquity." *Ankara Üniversitesi İlahiyat Fakültesi Dergisi* 54, no. 2: 189–203.

Neuwirth, Angelika. 2016. "Qurʾanic Studies and Historical-Critical Philology." *Philological Encounters* 1: 31–60.

Neuwirth, Angelika. 2019. *The Qurʾan and Late Antiquity: A Shared Heritage*. Translated by Samuel Wilder. New York: Oxford University Press.

Nicetas Byzantius. 1912. "Refutatio Mohamedis." In *Patrologia Graeca*, vol. 105, chap. 36, Coll. 720, edited by J. P. Migne.

Nutzman, Megan. 2013. "Mary in *The Protevangelium of James*: A Jewish Woman in the Temple." *Greek, Roman, and Byzantine Studies* 53: 551–78.

Peter the Venerable. 1967. *The Letters of Peter the Venerable*. Edited by Giles Constable. 2 vols. Cambridge, MA: Harvard University Press.

Reynolds, Gabriel S. 2018. *The Qurʾān and the Bible: Text and Commentary*. New Haven, CT: Yale University Press.

Rippin, Andrew. 1988. "The Function of Asbāb al-nuzūl in Qurʾānic Exegesis." *Bulletin of the School of Oriental and African Studies* 51, no. 1: 1–20.

Sale, George. 1734. "To the Right Honorable John Lord Carteret." In *Koran, Commonly Called the Alcoran of Mohammed, Translated into English Immediately from the Arabic, with Explanatory Notes, Taken from the Most*

Approved Commentators, to Which is Prefixed, A Preliminary Discourse. London.

Saleh, Walid A. 2010a. "The Etymological Fallacy and Qur'ānic Studies: Muḥammad, Paradise, and Late Antiquity." In *The Qur'ān in Context: Historical and Literary Investigations into the Qur'ānic Milieu,* edited by Angelika Neuwirth, Nicolai Sinai, and Michael Marx, 649–98. Leiden, Netherlands: Brill.

Saleh, Walid A. 2010b. "Ibn Taymiyya and the Rise of Radical Hermeneutics: An Analysis of *An Introduction to the Foundations of Qur'ānic Exegesis.*" In *Ibn Taymiyya and His Times,* edited by Yossef Rapoport and Shahab Ahmed, 123–62. Oxford: Oxford University Press.

Segovia, Carlos. 2015. *The Qur'ānic Noah and the Making of the Islamic Prophet: Study of Intertextuality and Religious Identity Formation in Late Antiquity.* Berlin: De Gruyter.

Stewart, Devin. 2017. "Reflections on the State of the Art in Western Qur'anic Studies." In *Islam and its Past: Jahiliyya, Late Antiquity, and the Qur'an,* edited by Carol Bakhos and Michael Cook, 4–68. Oxford: Oxford University Press.

Stewart, Pamela D. 2004. "The Tale of the Three Rings." In *The Decameron First Day in Perspective,* edited by Elissa B. Weaver, 89–112. Toronto: University of Toronto Press.

Ṭabarī, Ibn Jarīr al-. 1994. *Jāmiʿ al-bayān ʿan taʾwīl āy al-Qurʾān.* Vol. 5. Edited by Bashshār ʿAwwād Maʿrūf and ʿIṣām Fāris al-Ḥirastāni. Beirut: Muʾassasat al-Risāla.

Tommasino, Pier Mattia. 2016. "Textual Agnogenesis and the Polysemy of the Reader: Early Modern European Readings of Qur'ānic Embryology." In *After Conversion: Iberia and the Emergence of Modernity,* edited by Mercedes García-Arenal, 155–73. Leiden, Netherlands: Brill.

Witztum, Joseph. 2011. "The Syriac Milieu of the Qur'an: The Recasting of Biblical Narratives." PhD diss., Princeton University.

Zellentin, Holger Michael. 2013. *The Qur'ān's Legal Culture: The Didascalia Apostolorum as a Point of Departure.* Tübingen, Germany: Mohr Siebeck.

Part 3. Critical Possibilities

Undoing Medieval Race Studies

Mariah Min

1. "It's Not about Race"

On January 31, 2022, ABC's morning talk show *The View* featured a segment in which the hosts discussed instances of book banning in schools. In her capacity as moderator, Whoopi Goldberg outlined the contours of a recent case: "A Tennessee school pulled the graphic novel *Maus* out of their lessons on the Holocaust, because it contained some nudity and some bad language" (*View* 2022). Both she and cohost Joy Behar then observed the discrepancy between the harrowing subject matter of *Maus* and the focus on social niceties in these stated objections to the book, with Behar wondering if the flagging of nudity might actually be "a canard, to throw you off from the fact that [the objectors] don't like history that makes white people look bad." Goldberg responded: "Well, this is white people doing it to white people." The conversation continued, the room coalescing around a general agreement that book banning is a disservice to students because it fails to challenge their viewpoints or foster their inherent empathy. At this juncture, Goldberg stepped in to extend her previous point. There is a fair bit of over-

boundary 2 50:3 (2023)   DOI 10.1215/01903659-10472415   © 2023 by Duke University Press

lapping dialogue in the subsequent exchange, but the thread that I can pick up (involving Goldberg, Behar, and cohosts Ana Navarro and Sara Haines) is as follows:

> *Goldberg*: Well also, if you're going to do this, then let's be truthful about it. Because the Holocaust isn't about race. No. It's not about race.
> *Behar*: They considered Jews a different race.
> *Goldberg*: But it's not about race. It's not about race. Because—
> *Behar*: What is it about?
> *Goldberg*: It's about man's inhumanity to man. That's what it's about.
> *Navarro*: But it's about white supremacy. It's about going after Jews, and gypsies, and—
> *Goldberg*: But these are two white groups of people.
> *Haines*: They didn't see them as white, though.

The blowback was immediate. Among others, Jonathan Greenblatt (2022)—CEO of the Anti-Defamation League—tweeted the following: "No @Whoopi-Goldberg, the #Holocaust was about the Nazi's [*sic*] systematic annihilation of the Jewish people—who they deemed to be an inferior race." Later that day, Goldberg taped an episode of *The Late Show with Stephen Colbert*, where she was asked to address her comments from earlier that day and the ensuing fallout. She explained that her point of view stemmed from an understanding of race that was rooted in her own experience: "As a Black person, I think of race as being something that I can see. So—I see you and I know what race you are. . . . You can't tell who's Jewish. It's not something people say, 'Oh, that person is Jewish,' or, 'This person is Jewish'" (*Late Show* 2022). Before the show cuts to commercial, Colbert and Goldberg have this final exchange:

> *Colbert*: Have you come to understand that the Nazis saw it as race? Because asking the Nazis, they would say, "Yes, it's a racial issue."
> *Goldberg*: Well, see, this is what's interesting to me. Because the Nazis lied. It wasn't. They had issues with ethnicity, not with race, because most of the Nazis were white people, and most of the people they were attacking were white people. So to me, I'm thinking—how can you say it's about race, if you are fighting each other?

That evening, Goldberg (2022) tweeted an apology that quoted Greenblatt and read in part: "On today's show, I said the Holocaust 'is not about race, but about man's inhumanity to man.' I should have said it is about both... I stand corrected." She apologized once more on the February 1 episode of *The View*, and ABC placed her on a two-week suspension, from which she returned as scheduled.

The incident, like so many others, faded quickly from public consciousness. It was neither the most controversial moment of Goldberg's career, nor in the broadcast history of *The View*. I state this not to argue for a continued censure of Goldberg based on her remarks but to underscore the lack of sustained impact this event had on popular discourses of race despite directly shedding light on widespread misconceptions about how race comes into being and functions in the world. From Goldberg's position that skin color exists as a self-evident racial marker to her use of "ethnicity" as a distinct category severable from race, to the US Holocaust Museum's (2022) subtweet correction that "Jews were not defined by religion, but by race," this fleeting but illustrative dispute demonstrates the extent to which *mobility* is the most underacknowledged aspect of race in contemporary thought.

By *mobility*, I refer to the ability of race to take shape and become salient alongside multiple different axes of varying ontologies.[1] Some axes are somatic, such as skin color or shape of facial feature; some are customs performed by the body, such as language or diet; at times race is abstract, as in our "expectations for how the world operates" (Jerng 2017: 2); at times it is experienced as the ramifications of unequal power structures, a "state-sanctioned or extralegal production and exploitation of group-differentiated vulnerability to premature death" (Gilmore 2007: 28). These various ways of conceptualizing race, when considered together in their heterogeneity, can all contribute to our understanding of the multifaceted workings of race; their plurality is vitally instructive. However, as borne out in the anecdote above, race is more often misconstrued as static across time, space, and local context, something that stands categorically apart from "ethnicity" and "religion," equated with its visible signs.

This overprivileging of the visuality of race is, in fact, not limited to popular misapprehension. Mark Jerng (2017: 2, 7) points out that even "race critique has overemphasized the visual epistemology of race" at the

---

1. Not to be confused with *changeability*—the phenomenon of someone's racial identity changing from one group to another—which is discussed later in this essay.

expense of "the often nonvisual ways in which race is 'noticed,'" citing the work of Osagie Obasogie (2014: 18) on "how social forces ... produce the very ability to see race." Sierra Lomuto (2019: 174) generatively applies this framework to premodern literature, exhorting medieval studies to "shift our analysis of race away from the point at which it is already visible, and towards the conditions of its production." Thus the saga of Whoopi Goldberg, which might initially appear to be a strange prelude to this essay, turns out—in its staging of how conceptual fixity elides the mobility of race—to be intimately enmeshed with conversations animating the study of race today.

Goldberg's remarks, in their specific assertion that Jews may be an ethnically but not racially distinct group, also unexpectedly hearken back to earlier debates about race in medieval studies. The 1990s and early 2000s saw skepticism from many medievalists regarding the use of *race* as a critical term that could be applied to the period, due to their belief that race was solely biological and therefore inapplicable to the culturally conducted group differentiation of the Middle Ages.[2] However, even to these scholars, the experience of medieval Jews stood out as an instance in which cultural factors were imbued with the totality and force of race. One prominent example is William Chester Jordan (2001: 169), who could write in a special issue of the *Journal of Medieval and Early Modern Studies*, "I have my doubts about the utility of 'race' (an allegedly fixed category) as an analytic concept in the modern world. These doubts are compounded when 'race' is applied to the Middle Ages"; but he also laments in the same breath that "medieval Catholic attitudes towards Jews—a perfect laboratory to test theories of medieval racism—largely escapes the notice of the essays assembled here" (166–67). Then as now, racism against Jews becomes the case study for how race is not exclusively the product of a supposedly discernible visual alterity but a mobile notion that attaches to a limitless set of constructed discrepancies. As Geraldine Heng (2018: 3) has influentially formulated, "Race is a structural relationship for the articulation and management of human differences, rather than a substantive content."

Mobility also lies at the heart of what I take to be the affordances and pitfalls of "medieval studies" for the theorization of race. The boundedness of medieval studies as a field is both a condition that can allow for the mobility of race to come into stark focus and a limitation that prevents the fuller comprehension of how race can take a multitude of different forms even within coterminous historical periods and cultural backdrops. Conceptual

2. For accounts of this skepticism, see Heng 2018: 25–26; Kim 2019: 4–7.

fixity precludes Goldberg and her critics from being able to agree that the key terms implicated in their debate—skin color, whiteness, anti-Blackness, culture, religion, ethnicity, systemic power—are *all* potential elements of racialization; the same conceptual fixity is what "medieval race studies" seeks to destabilize yet cannot help but reproduce. The only way out of this bind is to undo the knot of the field, for scholars of the Middle Ages to forge robust intellectual ties with colleagues across the disciplinary silos into which the structure of the academy has placed us.

2. "The Multiplicity of Racial Identities"

In the introduction to this special issue, Lomuto (2023: 8) reminds us of how Kathleen Biddick (1998) has described "pastist" and "presentist" approaches to the Middle Ages as a delimited period. Were the Middle Ages different from us (pastist) or similar to us (presentist)? As Biddick argues, this question is inherently unsound because it fails to interrogate why the Middle Ages exist as a reified comparison point at all. It is also an unanswerable question, because it is built on the assumption that there is a coherent and unified "Middle Ages" that can be compared to a coherent and unified "us." Similarly, medievalists' recent tendency to label "medieval race studies" a subfield unto itself invites an analogous question: Was medieval race different from modern race, or similar to modern race? This counterpart query is just as unsound and unanswerable, although it has hitherto been a central concern for the examination of race in the Middle Ages.

The pastist approach seeks to answer this question by pointing out the centrality of religion to discourses of race in the Middle Ages, concluding that medieval race operates differently from modern race because somatic markers such as skin color were not the primary criteria for group categorization. When somatic markers do surface, they function as offshoots or aftereffects of religious group belonging, as in the spectacular literary scenes of characters' bodies transforming upon conversion. The Muslim Sultan of *The King of Tars*—to zero in on one example among many—is described as "blac and lothely" (Chandler 2015: 922; black and loathly) but becomes, upon his conversion to Christianity, "al white . . . and clere withouten blame" (923–24; all white and clear without blame).[3] Those on the

---

3. Other examples include a group of four Muslims in the *Cursor Mundi* who kiss a blessed branch and turn from black to white, and a kingdom of white knights in the Stricker's "Die Königin von Mohrenland" who turn black when Black Muslim women convert them. For discussions of these texts, see Heng 2018: 16; Tinsley 2011: 921.

far dogmatic end of the pastist scale argue that this disqualifies medieval group categorization based on religion from being a form of race at all; that is, because of the popular conception that race inheres in the unchanging and visible color of the body—a sentiment echoed in Goldberg's remarks about "race as being something that [she] can see"—the physical change-ability of these literary bodies through conversion indicates that the Middle Ages had no notion of race. The differences that medieval people under-stood as separating in-group from out-group were solely those of religion, as opposed to race: ethnicity, at most.

Admittedly, the pastist orientation of "medieval race studies" does underscore the way that race is anything but static. By identifying the mas-ter discourse of race in the Middle Ages as religion, and as somatic color in the contemporary US context, it highlights how racial formations can come into being through different sets of criteria in different historical moments. However, the usefulness of this framework turns out to be a limited one; ultimately it cannot account for the complexity of either "medieval race" or "modern race" and therefore fails to register the mobility of race *within* moments of historical time. Describing the chapter divisions in *The Inven-tion of Race in the European Middle Ages*, Heng (2018: 4) explains that her range of organizing topics addresses "racializing momentum that manifests unevenly, and nonidentically, at different places and at different times" and "the dynamic field of forces within which miscellaneous instances of race-making can occur under varied local conditions." Neither "medieval race" nor "modern race" materializes in any one way, as Heng has shown. The corpus of Middle English literature alone features bodies that change upon conversion (for example, in *The King of Tars* [Chandler 2015]) and bodies that do not (in *The Sultan of Babylon*), Englishmen whose Englishness can be recognized by their complexion (*Richard Coer de Lyon*), Englishmen who are so affected by travel that they cannot recognize England (*The Book of John Mandeville*), white demons (*Richard Coer de Lyon* again), Black saints (*The Three Kings of Cologne*), and cannibalism performed by Chris-tian kings (once more, *Richard Coer de Lyon*), distant marvels (*Mandeville*), and Jewish mothers (*The Siege of Jerusalem*) alike.[4] People in the United States today purchase DNA ancestry tests because race is genealogical; their state bans Muslim travelers because race is religious; municipal gov-ernments implement stop-and-frisk policies because race is ocular; and

4. Where tropes occur across several works, one sample text is listed in the interest of economy.

shopkeepers demand that patrons speak English because race is linguistic. When a person is racialized differently from one day to the next depending on the length of their beard, it is difficult to deny that race is mobile not only *across* time but *within* time.

Lomuto (forthcoming) traces the potentially liberatory aims for dating the invention of race to the early modern period, which would tether the concept to the motivating interests of the transatlantic slave trade and thereby lay bare the artificiality of its construction. Although she grants that this is indeed one way of establishing that there is no biological basis to race, she also points out—following Michelle M. Wright's (2015) work in *Physics of Blackness*—that "locating origins . . . imposes a linear racial epistemology that forecloses the multiplicity of racial identities in the present" (Lomuto forthcoming). As Wright (2015: 25) argues, selecting any single trajectory of racialization to imbue current Blackness with a linear timeline of development—such as "the most frequently discussed, published, and assumed epistemology: Middle Passage Blackness"—runs the risk of exclusion because inevitably, "some Black identities do not fit on the timeline." Similarly, the pastist approach, because it reifies the "past" and the "present" into coherent, homogenous categories that are suited for direct comparison, has difficulty perceiving that multiple axes underlie racialization in both the present and the past.

Although pastism and presentism may appear to be diametrically opposed viewpoints, they are identically limiting in that they share this propensity to flatten. In its essence, presentism is merely a form of pastism keyed to a different calendar; presentism in medieval studies asserts that modernity began in the Middle Ages, whereas pastism asserts that modernity began right after the Middle Ages. The issue of what exactly constitutes modernity is left unquestioned, as is the very premise that modernity has replaced the premodern wholesale. Both pastism and presentism look for race in the Middle Ages by searching for a lucid likeness of "modern race," but race itself resists lucidity because it has no singular form, even within the arbitrary boundaries of a single historical era. Race refracts and reflects itself endlessly throughout history; some mechanics of racialization loom larger in certain times and places, but ultimately race is always multiple because it is mobile. Thus the subfield of "medieval race studies" is conceptually restrictive because it presupposes that there is such a thing as "medieval race," which may or may not resemble "modern race," when the protean nature of race renders such a presupposition farcical. Race-thinking is aporetic at every moment in time, self-contradictory and hydra-headed.

"Medieval race studies" as an isolated area of research is, therefore, a diversion of energy toward the futile attempt to delineate the relationship between two things that never were quantifiable as merely two things. It herds us into modes of thinking that inevitably cleave to pastist or presentist allegiances, neither of which satisfactorily captures the way that race is always on the move. The breaking down of boundaries between medieval studies and nonmedieval disciplines will allow us to redirect this wild-goose chase to more fruitful ends. Scholars have long explored the mobility of race, and for medievalists to study race without availing themselves of such preexisting analysis is to reinvent the wheel only to end up with a shape that clatters awkwardly along the ground. Conversely, contextualizing the lessons of race studies across many fields and through many lenses within a longer history of race helps us sharpen our ideas about how that mobility functions. Medieval examples of race-thinking can better illuminate—for example—the processes through which various registers of race overlap, slide into, and shore up others, or the way that Blackness "shimmer[s]" like a mirage between literality and metaphor (Whitaker 2019: 5). If public understanding has yet to sufficiently incorporate mobility into its perception of race, the task is for scholars all along the historical continuum to amplify one another in order to disseminate and popularize the work that has already been done and will be done. We cannot remain partitioned in our temporal enclosures; if race is mobile, then so must we be.

3. "From the Grime to the Clean-Cut Iambic"

As I have shown, a bounded "medieval race studies"—whether through pastism or presentism—occludes the full mobility of race *within* time and the connections between instances of race-making *across time*. Not only is this a disservice to the task of comprehending race, but it also prevents all readers and teachers of medieval texts from being able to recognize the extent of rhetorical work performed therein. Without an awareness of how race can become salient in diverse ways in different situations, we are liable to inaccurately dismiss texts with deep investments in race-making as being devoid of racial concerns. In this current section, I want to present an indicative case study of one such text. These are the opening lines of Chaucer's (1987: lines 1–12) General Prologue to the *Canterbury Tales*, a passage so fundamental to the constitutive fabric of medieval literary studies and English departments that it has been rendered rote for many:

Whan that Aprill with his shoures soote
The droghte of Marche hath perced to the roote,
And bathed every veyne in swich licour
Of which vertu engendred is the flour;
Whan Zephirus eek with his sweete breeth
Inspired hath in every holt and heeth
The tendre croppes, and the yonge sonne
Hath in the Ram his half cours yronne,
And smale foweles maken melodye,
That slepen al the nyght with open ye
(So priketh hem nature in hir corages),
Thanne longen folk to goon on pilgrimages.

When April, with his sweet showers,
Has pierced the drought of March to the root
And bathed every vein in such liquor
By whose power the flower is engendered,
When Zephyrus, too, with his sweet breath
Has inspired in every wood and heath
The tender sprouts, and the young sun
Has run half his course in the Ram,
And small fowls make melody
That sleep all the night with open eyes
(So nature pricks them in their hearts)—
Then folk long to go on pilgrimages.

The first eleven lines of the General Prologue are lush with vernal flurry. A welcome rain penetrates the parched earth, sap rushes through the unfurling plants, the wind and sun quicken life in everything they touch, and the birds will not stop serenading each other. As a depiction of nature doing what comes naturally to nature, the passage is a touchstone example of the lightly concupiscent buzz that accompanies countless literary accounts of springtime. Even the subsequent shift of focus to people—"Thanne longen folk to goon on pilgrimages" (line 12; Then folk long to go on pilgrimages)— happens fluidly enough that it, too, sounds like just another item on a to-do list of activities for when the weather turns warm. Spring brings with it a restlessness for action, a taste for the excitement of "straunge strondes" (line 13; unfamiliar shores) and "ferne halwes" (line 14; faraway shrines), animating folks just as it animates nature.

This swivel toward humans happens fairly late. After eleven breath-less lines about the landscape, still in the middle of the first protracted sentence, the swivel barely registers as a swivel at all; human beings and their activities are seamlessly incorporated into the blissful admixture of the natural world. Dealing in such large-scale generalities as these lines do, the enormous vastness of the word "folk" (line 12) easily goes unnoticed. But it is not, of course, all "folk" that long to go on pilgrimages. The people referred to here—the only ones that matter enough to mention or are natural enough to be in accordance with the rest of nature—are Christians. That is, anyone whose religious identity does not inculcate the seasonal desire to participate in Christian rituals is construed as functionally unnatural and nonhuman.

A charge of nonhuman (or subhuman) status leveled against out-groups by socially dominant in-groups is a rhetorical mainstay of racialization, burdening its targets with an anomalous identity of incomprehensible, categorical difference. However, the static view of race that many medievalists espouse—which still proliferates in public understanding, as evidenced by the Whoopi Goldberg anecdote—searches for race only where bodies are present (for an overview, see Heng 2018; Kim 2019). Somatic race alone cannot draw out the racializing valence of these lines, because there is no physical body to categorize; without any characters to persecute or be persecuted, even religious race needs to unmoor itself from the anchor of the believing body before it can discern the Christian subject being constructed through this appeal to the natural world. But even in the absence of human bodies, Christianity functions as a racializing heuristic in this passage, pitting the natural world—its veins and hearts suffused by the same immanent principle that manifests as Christian feeling—against its nonbelievers. In the sense that the hegemonic ambitions of medieval Christianity become folded into the self-fashioning of Europe as colonial power, this naturalization of Christianity also adumbrates a longer history of whiteness, a relationship that merits further study. One scholar working at this intersection, Nahir I. Otaño Gracia (2020: 44), diagnoses pilgrimage in particular as a form of "symbolic conquest—a hallmark of settler colonialism"; though the route of pilgrimage in the *Canterbury Tales* remains within England, there is a parallel process of epistemological occupation here, in its writing of Christianity into the landscape.

Naming the work done in this passage as race-making has implications for how we interpret it in the context of the *Canterbury Tales* as a whole and in the context of medieval literature as an archive. As Heng (2018: 23) writes, *"Not* to use the term *race* would be to sustain the reproduction of a certain kind of past, while keeping the door shut to tools, analyses, and resources that can name the past differently." Terminological precision paves the way for analytical possibility. Furthermore, naming race as race also impacts how we think with the texts that remake these lines. Such comparative analysis occurs most frequently in the classroom, as we seek to elicit student interest by highlighting modern cultural output that bridges the perceived gap between students and the Middle Ages. In particular, Patience Agbabi's "Prologue (Grime Mix)" from her collection *Telling Tales* has become the go-to text to place in conversation with the opening of the General Prologue. Through the persona of Harry "Bells" Bailey, bouncer-turned-gastropub-owner, Agbabi (2014: 1–8) undoes and redoes Chaucer's rite of spring:

> When my April showers me with kisses
> I could make her my missus or my mistress
> but I'm happily hitched—sorry home girls—
> said my vows to the sound of the Bow Bells
> yet her breath is as fresh as the west wind,
> when I breathe her, I know we're predestined
> to make music; my muse, she inspires me,
> though my mind's overtaxed, April fires me.

In place of Chaucer's nature, these lines introduce a study of April, someone a bit like a person and a bit like a personification. The remainder of the poem—or, to take "Grime Mix" at its word, the song—continues to paint a portrait of Harry and April as "the Rhyming Couplet" whose electric connection provides the occasion for the piece (42).

This April, halfway between human and elemental force, retains her close ties to the natural world: Her breath like the "west wind," (5) "strong as a ram," (19) she "blooms" (25) and quickens Harry Bailey to ardor. But if this is nature, it is yet a nature distinct from Chaucer's. We are entreated to imagine April in Harry's "jaw-dropping jeans" (20), sharing English space with the urban public transportation system of the "Routemaster bus," (29) borrowing signifiers from the environment and making them hers until *she* is the wind, the rain, the birds, the sun, the spring. Furthermore, what she inspires in her admirers is a pilgrimage that vastly minimizes its potential Christian valences. The tellers of the tales are "poet pilgrims competing for free picks," (31) and Harry takes her as his muse "to make music" (7). Moved to action by what she stirs in him, Harry—instead of kneeling before Becket's shrine—aims to display his devotion by delivering a virtuosic grime verse: "See my jaw dropping neat Anglo-Saxon, / I got ink in my veins more than Caxton / and it flows hand to mouth, here's a mouthfeast / verbal feats from the streets of the South-East" (21–24).

The pilgrimage that this April prompts is, in essence, the very act of literary invention. Or, once again, to heed the subtitle of the poem—the pilgrimage is the creation of this grime track, a piece of Black British music. Agbabi's "Prologue" links nature to Blackness through the transformed figure of April, who here is no longer tasked with promoting the naturalization of Christianity. But without the acknowledgment that Chaucer's General Prologue is performing racial construction, it would be impossible to see what Agbabi's remix achieves, to appreciate the sharpness of its critical teeth. In the absence of race as a central structuring concern of these two texts, all we are left with is a catchy modern poem inspired by a famous old one, and no systematic way of articulating why Agbabi's work matters to medieval literary studies. To include *Telling Tales* on a syllabus without contending with the mobility of race that underlies these texts is to treat it as a paratextual curiosity, valuable solely for the reason that it is a collection by a Black poet that testifies to the enduring appeal of Chaucer. "Medieval race studies," by virtue of its boundedness, gives itself license to regard the nonmedieval (especially the postmedieval) as peripheral; but ironically, our understanding of the medieval can only remain partial if we refrain from engaging seriously with the ways of seeing the past that the present has to offer.

4. "What Happened with Whoopi Goldberg"

On January 31, 2022, I was five days into the spring semester. The course that I was teaching, Medieval Race, had only just met for one class session. It is worth noting that the title of the course reproduces exactly the kind of disciplinary siloing that I have been arguing against in this essay; part of what led me to that name was a desire for succinctness, but I think a larger part was the sheer fact that I had not yet deeply considered the implications of the phrase. "Medieval Race" was—and remains—the shorthand for this area of study, and I adopted what I had heard without thinking much about it. There is an easy allure to exceptionalism, after all; the course title is appealing (to its instructors and students both) for precisely the same reasons that the isolation of the medieval is problematic. *Not just any old race, but medieval race*, is the unspoken promise. *That's what will make it strange and interesting.* I had newly developed the class for the postdoctoral fellowship that I had started the previous fall, a position that had been advertised as being in the field of "medieval studies and race."

Even after catching oblique online references that day to an incident involving Whoopi Goldberg and race, it took me a while to follow the entire sequence of events as they developed, spanning from *The View* to *The Late Show* to the Twitter apology to the suspension. But by the next meeting of the class, I was up-to-date and anxious to talk about it. As I walked into the room, I found myself asking the students: "Have you heard what happened with Whoopi Goldberg?" The alternative, "Have you heard what Whoopi Goldberg did?" sat uneasily in my throat for reasons I could not articulate yet; I needed more time to reflect alongside scholars and frameworks of race theory before I could untangle my hesitation. I did not agree with how Goldberg had defined race in her comments, but neither did I completely subscribe to how her critics were defining it. The issue did not seem to be a simple matter of personal misstep or offense, and to consider Goldberg's position atypical did not capture the differently instantiated but similarly inflexible ideas about race that I had observed elsewhere. Her case was, if anything, where a larger problem came to a head.

Since 2018, Brown University has had a curricular designation titled "Race, Gender, and Inequality" (now "Race, Power, and Privilege") as part of its "Pathways to Diversity and Inclusion: An Action Plan for Brown University" (DIAP). I requested this designation for Medieval Race and was granted it, which meant that students searching for classes could filter the catalog for DIAP courses and see Medieval Race on the list. Consequently, the vast majority of the students who signed up for Medieval Race were those who had never taken a course about the Middle Ages before, and many of them were committed to learning about critical race studies but were stepping into the field for the first time with this class. This was, in many ways, the perfect group of students to have for the initial run of this course; my explicit aim in crafting the syllabus was to take the presence of race throughout time as a given and to place medieval texts in dialogue with modern theoretical frameworks about race in order to examine the resonances and discrepancies we could find. Perhaps because they were coming to the material with a fresh set of eyes, the students were remarkably open-minded about the forms that race could take and ready to explore the mobility of race in both the Middle Ages and in our contemporary contexts.

What we meant to build was not a perimeter dividing the Middle Ages from modernity, nor a straight track of correspondence with no surprises along the way. The goal was to weave multinodal webs, drawing connections among an assortment of racial formations residing in discourses ranging from the concrete to the abstract, from the body to language, waning and waxing in prominence throughout history, but all of them forms of *race*, elusive and chimerical and indubitably real in its effects. As I now take the time to reflect, I newly value the wording of my fellowship position—"medieval studies and race"—how its *and race* provides the space for *medieval studies* to open up into a wider intellectual realm, to take the opportunity to shape a field that confronts its limitations and reaches beyond them, toward the possibilities that other fields can offer.

Toward what we can offer each other. The collaboration I have experienced in the past year has taught me more than I ever could have learned alone. Medievalists from other subfields, scholars of other humanities and social sciences disciplines, experts in Black and Caribbean studies, practicing artists—all have shown me things about race in the Middle Ages where I had not thought to look before. What if this sort of collaborative work were the default mode of scholarship in the academy? If we were structurally encouraged to blur the lines in the sand that sequester us from one another, how might we be able to surprise ourselves? There are mindsets of solitude and individual exceptionalism that we have internalized through the reward structure of the university, and we are hindered as well by the material arm of that reward structure, which neglects to fairly appreciate or compensate communal labor. Truly effective, lasting change can only be achieved when shifts in thought become etched into the ways that groups seek to regulate its members; our piecemeal collaboration can soothe us, but it cannot reverberate outside of ourselves until we reconfigure the institutions to which we belong. The incipient endeavor to undo "medieval race studies"—or "medieval studies" more generally—must culminate in a larger question still: How can we agitate for a systemic recognition of the fact that the only real work is work that is done together?

References

Agbabi, Patience. 2014. "Prologue (Grime Mix)." In *Telling Tales*, 1–2. Edinburgh: Canongate Books.

Biddick, Kathleen. 1998. *The Shock of Medievalism*. Durham, NC: Duke University Press.

Chandler, John H., ed. 2015. *The King of Tars*. Kalamazoo, MI: Medieval Institute Publications.

Chaucer, Geoffrey. 1987. *The Canterbury Tales*. In *The Riverside Chaucer*, edited by Larry D. Benson, 3–328. Oxford: Oxford University Press.

Gilmore, Ruth Wilson. 2007. *Golden Gulag: Prisons, Surplus, Crisis, and Opposition in Globalizing California*. Berkeley: University of California Press.

Goldberg, Whoopi (@WhoopiGoldberg). 2022. "On today's show, I said the Holocaust 'is not about race, but about man's inhumanity to man.'" Twitter, January 31. https://twitter.com/WhoopiGoldberg/status/1488320164517101574.

Greenblatt, Jonathan (@JGreenblattADL). 2022. "No @WhoopiGoldberg, the #Holocaust was about the Nazi's systematic annihilation of the Jewish people." Twitter, January 31, 4:05 p.m. https://twitter.com/jgreenblattadl/status/1488257054582226951.

Heng, Geraldine. 2018. *The Invention of Race in the European Middle Ages*. Cambridge: Cambridge University Press.

Jerng, Mark C. 2017. *Racial Worldmaking: The Power of Popular Fiction*. New York: Fordham University Press.

Jordan, William Chester. 2001. "Why 'Race'?" *Journal of Medieval and Early Modern Studies* 31, no. 1: 165–73.

Kim, Dorothy. 2019. "Introduction to *Literature Compass* Special Cluster: Critical Race and the Middle Ages." *Literature Compass* 16, no. 9–10: 1–16.

The Late Show with Stephen Colbert. 2022. "How Whoopi Became Today's Hot Topic on 'The View.'" YouTube video, 6:54. February 1. https://youtu.be/SdkhVQZGSSU.

Lomuto, Sierra. 2019. "The Mongol Princess of Tars: Global Relations and Racial Formation in *The King of Tars* (c.1330)." *Exemplaria* 31, no. 3: 171–92.

Lomuto, Sierra. 2023. "Belle da Costa Greene and the Undoing of 'Medieval' Studies." In "The 'Medieval' Undone: Imagining a New Global Past," edited by Sierra Lomuto. Special issue, *boundary 2* 50, no. 3: 1–30.

Lomuto, Sierra. Forthcoming. "Race." In *The Chaucer Encyclopedia*, ed. Richard Newhauser. Hoboken, NJ: Wiley.

Obasogie, Osagie. 2014. *Blinded by Sight: Seeing Race through the Eyes of the Blind*. Stanford, CA: Stanford University Press.

Otaño Gracia, Nahir I. 2020. "Borders and the Global North Atlantic: Chaucer, Pilgrimage, and Crusade." *English Language Notes* 58, no. 2: 35–49.

Tinsley, David F. 2011. "Mapping the Muslims: Images of Islam in Middle High German Literature of the Thirteenth Century." In *Contextualizing the Muslim Other in Medieval Christian Discourse*, edited by Jerold C. Frakes, 65–101. New York: Palgrave Macmillan.

US Holocaust Museum (@HolocaustMuseum). 2022. "Racism was central to Nazi ideology." Twitter, January 31, 4:10 p.m. https://twitter.com/HolocaustMuseum/status/1488258287254577153.

View, The. 2022. "'Maus,' 'To Kill a Mockingbird' Removed from Schools." YouTube video, 6:12. January 31. https://youtu.be/AhITfM4bqO8.

Whitaker, Cord J. 2019. *Black Metaphors: How Modern Racism Emerged from Medieval Race-Thinking*. Philadelphia: University of Pennsylvania Press.
Wright, Michelle M. 2015. *Physics of Blackness: Beyond the Middle Passage Epistemology*. Minneapolis: University of Minnesota Press.

Different and Familiar:
Les enfances Renier and the Question of Medieval Orientalism

Anne Le

In a recent conversation about the relevance of Edward Said's (1978) *Orientalism* to premodern studies, scholars Kaya Şahin, Julia Schleck, and Justin Stearns (2021: 197) underscore the need to continue interrogating "the current structures of knowledge production about the 'East' in both European and Near Eastern premodern studies." Their discussion demonstrates how *Orientalism* continues to shape methodologies across disciplines. An enduring trend is the unpacking of the relationship between the Middle Ages—an era that, as scholars point out, Said overlooks in his work—and later centuries, particularly those witness to colonial and postcolonial hegemonies. For instance, Amy Burge (2016: 7) looks at fourteenth- and fifteenth-century Middle English romances alongside twenty-first-century sheikh romances to argue "that romance manipulates hybrid representations of religious and ethnic difference in order to create successful romantic unions." Burge's monograph builds upon seminal research from the first decade of the twenty-first century that demonstrated the importance of postcolonial approaches to medieval studies, resonating par-

boundary 2 50:3 (2023)   DOI 10.1215/01903659-10472429   © 2023 by Duke University Press

ticularly with the work of Kathleen Davis and Nadia Altschul (2009), which brings together postcolonial theory with medievalisms to interrogate legacies of colonial ideologies.[1]

In these considerations of *Orientalism*, medieval studies reckons with identity and race in productive ways. The publication of Geraldine Heng's (2018) *The Invention of Race in the European Middle Ages* and the launch of the "RaceB4Race" conference series supported by the Arizona Center for Medieval and Renaissance Studies mark a watershed moment in the field's theorization of race. More scholars are researching discourses of racialization in the medieval context and how they are related to race and racism in our contemporary time.[2] This wave of scholarship highlights the need to return to and expand foundational theories like Orientalism to account for the richness and specificity of medieval sources.

Despite Said's influence on these developments, his approach to the Middle Ages has been a sticking point for medievalists. Generally, they take issue with his emphasis on binarisms in his analysis, which flattens the heterogeneous nature of the Middle Ages.[3] The term *medieval Orientalism* emerged from these critiques to adapt Said's framework to the Middle Ages. However, I argue that while working to historicize and analyze how Orientalism might or might not translate to pre-(European) colonial cultures, scholars have not critiqued the use of "medieval" in "medieval Orientalism" or considered how it has limited opportunities for medieval literature and culture to enrich studies of Orientalism more broadly. "Medieval Orientalism" reinscribes the medieval-modern divide that shuts out the Middle Ages—as its own type of "Other"—from the development of modern critical theory. The very concept of a "medieval Orientalism" entrenches the medieval-modern divide, an epistemological barrier that hinders the development of post-Saidian Orientalism insofar as it may be cut off from the historically important work done by scholars of premodern texts.

I am not advocating for anachronistic readings wherein context falls to the wayside; to do so would be a disservice to the rich and unique con-

---

1. See, for example, Dagenais and Greer 2000; Cohen 2001; Cohen 2003; Ingham and Warren 2003; Heng 2003; Ganim 2005; Kabir and Williams 2005; Uebel 2005; Gaunt 2009. These works are indebted to the work of Kathleen Biddick (1993, 1998), Kathleen Davis (1998), and Robert Bartlett (1994).
2. Other recent publications include Vernon 2018; Kaplan 2019; Kim 2019; Lomuto 2019; Turner 2019; Whitaker 2019; Betancourt 2020; Black 2020; and Otele 2020.
3. For an overview of critiques of Said's approach to the Middle Ages, see Lampert-Weissig 2010.

tours of texts, be they medieval or not.[4] Rather, I encourage a broadening of Orientalism so that there is room for the Middle Ages to enrich theories of Orientalism and in turn inform theorizations of racializing discourses. Ambivalence is particularly crucial to the deployment of Orientalism as depicted in medieval French literature. By limiting my linguistic and geographic focus, I highlight how Orientalism functions in one particular context. My hope is that this work contributes to more studies about how heterogeneity and ambivalence operate in Orientalisms across other medieval and even early modern contexts.[5] I argue that difference and familiarity work together as tools to produce enigmatic and heterogeneous depictions of otherness, and Latin Christendom triumphs over and subsumes alterity to achieve its goals of conquest and expansion. Yet alterity, even when subsumed, can still influence Latin Christian ideas of self and facilitate transformations in relation to the "other" (Uebel 2005). Locating and analyzing moments of ambivalence in the face of alterity is a productive way of sifting through how Latin Christians reckoned with human difference.

Les enfances Renier (The Childhood of Renier) is a thirteenth-century Old French chanson de geste with a myriad of intercultural encounters and is a compelling case study for thinking through Orientalism and ambivalence. It is part of the Guillaume d'Orange cycle, a collection of over twenty chansons de geste from the twelfth and thirteenth centuries that narrate Frankish Latin Christian battles against Muslims, particularly those from the Iberian Peninsula. Les enfances Renier acts as the cycle's epilogue by recounting the adventures of a younger generation of warriors. By the same token, the text's setting and references to the First and Fourth Crusades link it to the Crusade cycle, which recounts events of the First Crusade and its aftermath. The titular Renier's adventures involve encountering a variety of people from different areas of the Mediterranean. This range of contact and relationships highlights the need for theorizing Orientalism in a way that accounts for ambivalence toward those deemed familiar but ultimately different throughout the medieval Mediterranean.

4. For an example of how to respect context and the specificities of time periods and places when reading medieval literature through a postcolonial lens, see Kinoshita 2007.
5. For other potential avenues of exploration for medievalists and early modernists when it comes to postcolonial approaches, see Kinoshita 2007, 2009; Lampert-Weissig 2010; Şahin, Schleck, and Stearns 2021.

Medievalists and Orientalism

Medieval Orientalism emerged from medievalists' engagement with frameworks from postcolonial studies throughout the first decade or so of the twenty-first century. Suzanne Conklin Akbari (2012: 2) has unpacked Orientalist stereotypes in Latin and English works from the twelfth through fifteenth centuries by revealing "how Western discourses concerning Islam and the Orient developed and how they mutually reinforced one another." Akbari's work is as much about "the nature of premodern efforts to understand difference and identity as it is about the specific figure of the Muslim in the medieval imagination" (2). Akbari's analysis teases apart religious and geographical differences because a wide variety of medieval texts articulate separate discourses regarding Islam and the Orient. In other words, she cautions against the conflation of "Islam" and the "Orient," which she identifies as a shortcoming of Said's analysis (12). Yet, what is unclear is Akbari's consistent use of the qualifier "medieval" in front of Orientalism and the insistence on separating Orientalism during the Middle Ages from later forms—a convention that continues in medieval studies. While Akbari rightfully acknowledges the varied factors at play and the need to respect historical context, there is a risk of sequestering the Middle Ages and its deployment of Orientalism from contributing meaningfully to understandings of later European colonial studies. By tracing these emergent discourses, does Akbari not also contribute to the theorization of Orientalism at large? Is it not possible to point out this medieval era of Orientalist discourse while also expanding the broader theoretical framework? How can scholars who wish to push Orientalism beyond its initial parameters avoid reifying the medieval-modern divide?

There is also the problem of an overselective corpus even across medieval Europe. While Akbari draws important distinctions between religious and geographical alterity, her corpus of study overlooks a wealth of Old French literature from the twelfth and thirteenth centuries that also features depictions of interfaith encounters as well as travel around the Mediterranean. These texts reflect medieval French attitudes vis-à-vis neighboring Iberia and the other spaces around the Mediterranean Sea that were hubs for intercultural exchange and commerce; France's historical relationship to these areas is more intimate than that of England in major part because of its geographical proximity. As Sharon Kinoshita (2006: 3) has argued, taking a global approach to medieval French literature allows for an examination of histories of political accommodation, commercial exchange, and cultural negotiation throughout the Mediterranean across religious lines: "Medieval French speakers had a much greater degree of involvement and knowledge of the cultures of the Iberian Peninsula and the Mediterranean than modern readers generally credit." Medieval French literature reflects these experiences; exploring these representations of cross-cultural encounter can reveal a great deal about the array of attitudes regarding different types of contact (Kinoshita 2010).

This essay builds upon Kinoshita's work to highlight how the medieval complexities she sheds light upon can indeed be part of an Orientalist discourse, particularly when we look at post-Saidian developments. Kinoshita (2006) has laid out the problematics of Orientalism in the context of the Middle Ages. While acknowledging that discourses in the Middle Ages may resemble Saidian Orientalism, Kinoshita argues that Latin Christians' interactions with Muslims and the Islamic world were in fact more complex than the term "Orientalism" suggests. She has also argued that "acknowledging the historical complexity of the Middle Ages—examining its political, economic, and cultural practices as well as its ideological pronouncements—unsettles the picture of its monolithic and monologic orientalism" (Kinoshita 2007: 80). The Middle Ages is a "heterogeneous and contestatory period" that takes place "before European hegemony, before nation-states and before national vernaculars," and it challenges us "to put into practice our avowed critical desire to see beyond the binary, to encounter an 'Other' whose alterity may reside precisely in its different conception of difference" (89). Kinoshita's analyses echo that of postcolonial scholars who have developed Said's critique beyond his original scope.[6]

Indeed, the work done by medievalists resembles post-Saidian developments in postcolonial studies. For instance, Lisa Lowe (1991) and Ali Behdad (1994) have built upon Said's critique regarding European knowledge of the Middle East and its relationship to the history of Western colonialism via studies of French and British Orientalists from the eighteenth through twentieth centuries and their objects of representation. Behdad (2020), upon reflection, writes that he and Lowe have "independently argued that difference, ambivalence, and heterogeneity are the fundamental attri-

6. Kinoshita indeed engages with contemporary postcolonial studies and even references contemporary historical fiction as rich sites for expanding our theoretical approaches. She demonstrates how to appreciate these developments yet heed the importance of context (Kinoshita 2007: 88).

butes of Orientalist discourse that have ensured its cultural hegemony and political longevity." This comment resonates with the work done by Sharon Kinoshita and other medievalists like Marianne Ailes and Lynn Ramey; they all note how ambivalence permeates medieval French romances and epics and their depictions of interfaith difference. These scholars have written extensively about texts that feature contact between Latin Christians and characters known by the exonym *Saracens*—who happen to be fictionalized, distorted stand-ins for Muslims—to reveal how interfaith relationships come in numerous configurations.[7] Their work on ambivalence bridges the medieval-modern divide when it comes to theorizing how literature represents human difference.

The Dynamic Mediterranean Sea

Old French romances and chansons de geste contain numerous examples of representations of peoples and relationships across different spaces, genders, languages, and faiths. Cross-cultural contact drives much of these texts. Though texts may be steeped in the crusading ethos that upholds Latin Christian superiority, they can (and often do) contain depictions of cross-cultural romantic relationships, alliances, and accommodation (Ramey 2019: 137). In other words, narratives of conquest are not monolithic in nature, nor do they trade in strict binaries of good and bad. Rather, interpersonal relationships are dynamic and multifaceted.

Les enfances Renier relentlessly represents via its setting the heterogeneity of the southern Mediterranean and the Holy Land (corresponding to modern-day Palestine, Israel, western Jordan, and areas of southern Lebanon and southwestern Syria) in the decades leading to the First Crusade (1096–99). Heterogeneity generates ambivalence even as it invites recognition, marking, and policing of cultural—specifically, religious—differences. *Les enfances Renier* reveals the way that Latin Christian ambivalence

---

7. *Saracen* was a term used throughout Latin and Byzantine Christendom from the seventh through sixteenth centuries to refer to Muslims primarily of Arab origin (though often those of Turkic and Persian origin as well). For the rest of the article, I will use the term *Muslim* in lieu of *Saracen* unless quoting directly from source material or other scholarship. This practice follows the work of scholars such as Shokoofeh Rajabzadeh (2019) and Hélène Sirantoine (2019), who note the epistemological violence that the term *Saracen* carries. However, the term does not always necessarily refer to fictionalized adherents of Islam. Sometimes writers used the term when discussing pagans from northern Europe.

toward Muslims can be negotiated through a complex management of difference; in turn, the text expands our understanding of Orientalism and its deployment in medieval French literature. Orientalism functions through the ambivalent treatment of the Muslim characters, and the most exceptional Muslim allies act in ways that serve the aims of Latin Christian expansion. Ambivalence oscillates between what is different and familiar throughout *Les enfances Renier* to construct an Orientalist discourse that works to maintain Latin Christian superiority. The text seizes upon the glimmers of familiarity among what is foreign to the benefit of the Latin Christian characters and their goals. Renier, the titular hero, encounters scenarios and people who are simultaneously different and familiar.

Les enfances Renier recounts Renier's journey, as the "enfances" (childhood) in the text suggest, from infancy to young adulthood. The text traces his adventure, which begins from his birth to a noble family in the medieval French city of Pourpaillart. Renier comes from a long line of warriors: his father, Maillefer, is a powerful noble whose father, Rainouart, fought with Guillaume d'Orange throughout the Iberian Peninsula to maintain Frankish territory. Criminals kidnap him and take him to Muslim-controlled Venice, where he spends his childhood under the care of the young Muslim princess Ydoine. He becomes a formidable young man who embarks on a quest to find his birth parents.[8] The text foretells his rule over Constantinople, an oblique reference to the Latin Empire of Constantinople (1204–61) founded in the wake of the Fourth Crusade (1202–4), and his son will go on to be a great knight and leader as well.

Renier's upbringing under Ydoine's care looks syncretic, yet things familiar to a Latinate Christian audience appear transposed onto his education in this fantastical version of Venice. Though he thrives in this milieu, his status as a Latin Christian and foundling mark him as an outsider and prevent total integration. He decides to leave and crisscross the southern Mediterranean in search of his Latin Christian birth family. Renier also must protect his beloved Ydoine and her lands from invading rival Muslim forces. In his travels, he helps a young Byzantine ruler secure the throne in Greece,

8. Venice was never under Muslim rule. The Republic of Venice (697–1797) was a sovereign state and maritime republic encompassing the northeastern parts of modern-day Italy. It enjoyed an advantageous location along the Mediterranean Sea that allowed it to flourish into a trading power in a commercial network connecting Europe, North Africa, and Asia. Though the Venetian navy participated in the Crusades (most notably during the Fourth Crusade), Venice maintained a fraught relationship with the papacy. See Lane 1973; Norwich 1982.

vanquishes Muslim foes in Sicily, and even forms alliances with Muslims in the Holy Land. Renier and Ydoine—who eventually converts to Latin Christianity—marry and have a son by the name of Tancred, who becomes a major leader of the First Crusade. The Tancred of the text corresponds to Tancred of Hauteville (1075–1112), who was an Italo-Norman leader of the First Crusade.[9] In this way, *Les enfances Renier* constructs a genealogy for the actual crusader, Tancred, that provides Muslim ancestry.[10] Renier's adventures pave the way for the next generation—the Latin Christian heroes of the First Crusade—to claim the Holy Land. *Les enfances Renier* reconfigures history and genealogy to create connections across different spaces and peoples. The results of the disastrous Fourth Crusade, more contemporary to the text's date of composition, mingles with histories and memories of the First Crusade to produce a narrative that renders the Mediterranean a playground of adventure wherein Latin Christendom's great young warrior, Renier, does what actual crusaders failed to do, simultaneously bridging religious and imperial divides while upholding Latin Christian supremacy.

An Orientalist discourse built upon ambivalence becomes visible upon a closer look at the interpersonal relationships that Renier cultivates. Renier demonstrates a mastery of knowledge and power over his Muslim peers, whom the text makes implicitly inferior because of their faith. Marriage to Ydoine, a convert, allows for a shift in their dynamic from that of foster mother and son to wife and husband; tension between acceptance and subsumption undergird their relationship, which bears a son who goes on to one day wage battles of conquest over land that could be considered rightfully his thanks to matrilineal connections.[11] Renier's alliance with a Muslim guide who escorts him to the Holy Sepulchre in Jerusalem illustrates the need to depend on someone else's deep knowledge of a treacherous land.

9. The historical Tancred eventually became the Prince of Galilee as well as the regent of the Principality of Antioch because of the campaigns of the First Crusade. For a study of his real family tree that does not include a converted mother, see Petrizzo 2019.
10. Tancred is not the only medieval Christian historical figure to be given fictional Muslim ancestors. *Le conte de Floire et Blanchefleur* gives Charlemagne a Muslim grandfather, Floire, who converts to Christianity to marry Blanchefleur (D'Orbigny 2003). According to the *South English Legendary*, Thomas of Becket has a Muslim mother (Mills 2011).
11. I interpret Ydoine's position as his mother and her relationship to Venice as a means of connecting Tancred to the land. In reality, Muslim kinship and systems during the Middle Ages and beyond varied. See Kooria 2021 for an overview of the scholarship surrounding Muslim matrilineal systems. For the mixing of cultures and kinship systems, particularly in the Arab-Muslim spaces, see Mateo Dieste 2012.

Throughout these different configurations of interfaith and intercultural relations, ambivalence abounds to the benefit of the Latin Christian who seeks
to navigate, conquer, and know the Muslim Mediterranean.

An Education Abroad

Renier receives an education in a foreign land, yet the text's description of the school setting and curriculum looks familiar to a Latin Christian
audience. As the text recounts Renier's early years, ambivalence in the
classroom operates in ways that ultimately underscore his unique situation
as a young Latin Christian foundling growing up among Muslims. Ydoine
entrusts Renier to male Muslim teachers for his education, all while allowing
him to maintain his own faith. This formal schooling steered by Muslim men
offers Renier firsthand experiences with Islamic Venice's expectations for
young boys of the aristocracy. The text provides ample detail about Renier's
education and emphasizes how "de son aage ne trovast on son per" (Dalens-
Marekovic 2009, line 1570; among his age group he had no peer).[12] Renier's education looks like what is expected of Latinate Christian boys of the
aristocracy: he masters rhetoric, board games, equitation, swordsmanship,
archery, and more (lines 1563–88). Renier is the best student in his class,
and the text relishes in his exceptionality. The text explains that "nul Sarra-
zin ne peut a lui riber, / Luitier, saillir qu'il ne face mater. / Touz les enfanz le
prennent a blasmer / Et a hair et moult fort cueriner / Pour ce qu'il veut touz
les autres passer. / Plus avoit force Renier le bacheler / A ses .X. anz et plus
peut endure / Que n'ont .II. autres ou trois, c'est sanz douter" (lines 1581–88;
No Saracen could fight him without getting defeated. Since Renier surpasses
his peers in everything, they take to criticizing and detesting him. At the age
of ten, the young Renier is stronger than them. He is undeniably stronger
than two or three of his peers combined).[13] School is a space for Renier's
growth and development despite the religious differences between him, his
instructors, and his peers. In fact, religious difference does not appear to be a
hindrance to Renier's educational achievement, and courses about the local
faith are absent from the text's account of the curriculum. Despite forgoing
the typical educational environment for boys of his stature and background,
Renier receives a robust education from the Muslims that would prime him

12. Translations from Old French to modern English are my own.
13. The text expresses numbers as roman numerals preceded and followed by a period
(e.g., .I.).

to be a worthy and just knight in the eyes of a reader familiar with the expectations placed upon aristocratic Latin Christian boys.

Education in *Les enfances Renier* plays with the categories of difference and familiarity to the benefit of the lone Latin Christian character. Since the students all share the same space, Renier's Muslim peers also receive an education expected of aristocratic Latin Christian boys in lieu of the contemporary madrasa system.[14] However, the other boys' non-Christian status impedes them from achieving the levels of mastery that Renier attains. Renier's environment does not preclude him from tapping into his knightly and courtly potential. The Muslim-dominated milieu only highlights how exceptional he is, and the text delights in his ability to flourish in this foreign yet familiar context. The boys all receive an education befitting a noble youth, but the best student is particularly exceptional thanks to what implicitly makes him different: his faith.

It is tempting to point out binary Orientalist tropes here—a "Western" boy thrives and out-performs his "Eastern" peers in their "Eastern" space, thereby stoking their resentment and jealousy. Yet, the transposition of a familiar "Western" education onto the text's setting disrupts the trope of the "East" as an exotic space. Renier's education is indistinguishable from an ideal education that a noble boy in medieval France would receive. Orientalism here plays with difference and familiarity to recast religious conflict in unexpected ways. His academic excellence reflects Latin Christian superiority over Muslims in a manner that de-emphasizes physical conflict and high-stakes war between differing cultures. Strife between Renier and the Muslim boys does not take place on the battlefield, which would be the typical setting for conflict between Latin Christian and Muslim men. Rather, the classroom is the site of jealousy and tension. In other words, educational spaces are not neutral, and this is evident in how the text simultaneously depicts the classroom as an interfaith space of growth as well as a space where differences are reinforced given Renier's academic achievements. While Renier thrives, his peers grow jealous of his success. When tensions finally erupt and the Muslim boys attack Renier and he retaliates, the classroom setting makes it seem more like a squabble between schoolboys than a dramatic "clash of civilizations" between warring factions.[15] Cries of

14. For the madrasa and historical Islamic education, see Berkey 1992; Lapidus 2002; Hussain 2013.
15. "Clash of civilizations" comes from Huntington 1996. Medievalists overwhelmingly take issue with the phrase as a reductive and misleading analysis of Christian-Muslim relations during the Middle Ages.

"bastart trouvé" (line 1652; found bastard) punctuate the blows the boys deal to Renier. They insult not his religion but his status as a foundling, thereby decentering religious conflict despite his faith being the source of his excellence and the real reason for their jealousy. Religious difference does not operate as an overt cause of antagonism between Renier and Muslims during his time in Venice, but it does play a large part—in conjunction with his status as a foundling—in marking him as different from everyone else.

Historical and Genealogical Refashioning

Les enfances Renier presents an instance of imperial and genealogical self-fashioning that connects Latin Christian and Muslim lineages by claiming that some leaders of the First Crusade have converts as their mothers. These genealogies that the text constructs serve to present the First Crusade as a project that involves crusaders taking what is rightfully theirs thanks to matrilineal ties. *Les enfances Renier* presents these genealogies as the result of marriages between Christian (Latin and Byzantine) men and Muslim women who convert to Christianity. Close consideration of the genealogical maneuvers at play in the text can reveal valuable insights into attitudes toward exogamy wherein taking a foreign spouse is advantageous to larger projects of proselytization and conquest. In Shirin Khanmohamadi's (2019: 19) work on the twelfth-century *Mainet*, a chanson de geste that presents Charlemagne's childhood spent among Muslims at the Andalusian court and his eventual marriage to a Muslim royal, she writes that "genealogical innovations of epics . . . in which we find Muslim lineage grafted with European ones . . . suggest that the Saracen-filled *chansons de geste* have more to tell us about the cultural plurality of medieval European imperial self-definition and translatio/n than critics have to date appreciated." Literary depictions of genealogies for real historical figures can reveal ideological preoccupations regarding land and power throughout the contentious areas of the eastern Mediterranean. This historiographical work allows for conquest and control in ways that de-emphasize conflict on the battlefield. A fruitful exogamous marriage is a way to extend power and authority, especially throughout the lands of one's spouse.

The most notable marriage in the text is the one between Renier and Ydoine. The two lovers bear a son named Tancred, and the text foretells his achievements during the First Crusade. In addition to Tancred, the text mentions the conception of other men and references their roles during the First Crusade. This is all historiographically significant, particularly because it renders the historical capture of Jerusalem and the establishment of the crusader states as a meaningful project not just of religious but familial reclamation as well. The lands at stake are different in that they must be taken from foreign rule, but they are familiar thanks to maternal connections.

Ydoine's conversion allows her to marry Renier, and their union has major consequences for the genealogical and imperial concerns of the text. Her conversion and marriage place her in the company of other Muslim noblewoman throughout Old French romances and chansons de geste who convert out of love, yet what sets Ydoine apart from the rest of her cohort is the shift in her role from foster mother to bride. Conversion ushers in a change in religion *and* in relationship; this transformative process inextricably links love and religion. The conversion scene, despite how crucial it is to the ideological investments of the text, is rather short: "Avoec Renier ot .I. prestre ordené; / Enz el pales sont les fons apresté, / La ot Ydoine son cors regeneré, / Mes ne li fu onc son non remué, / Ydoine ot non touz jours en son aé. / Ceuls de la vile sont tuit crestïané, / Qui le refuse si ot le chief copé" (Dalens-Marekovic 2009, lines 5875–81; Renier had a priest with him, and the baptismal font was prepared in the upper room. Ydoine's body was regenerated there. Her name, however, did not change. She kept the name Ydoine for the rest of her life. All the townspeople converted. Anyone who refused lost their head). Baptism allows her to be born anew and provide a fundamental change in her relationship to Renier (Le 2022). She must convert so that she can be a good wife to Renier and mother to Tancred. No longer is Ydoine a Muslim princess whose role is to raise and protect the hero: she now is a Latin Christian woman. As an exceptional Muslim woman, it is to the text's ideological advantage to incorporate Ydoine—as well as her forcibly converted subjects—into the Latin Christian fold. Domestication of a foreign woman is crucial to expanding Latin Christian influence throughout the Mediterranean. Orientalism, in conjunction with conversion, operates here to incorporate Ydoine, her lands, and her subjects into the ideological aims of the text. Upon marriage, Renier gains access to her lands—which extend beyond Venice into the eastern Mediterranean—and her subjects. Tancred, as her son, has a connection to this land as well. Love, conversion, and expansion are all intertwined.

Renier's and Ydoine's Sicilian wedding location reflects their love; the history of the island underscores the heterogeneous dynamic of their relationship. The lovers marry in the city of Messina, which Renier had helped Robert Ricard—a fugitive from France and reference to the historic Norman warrior Robert Guiscard (1015–85)—to conquer from its Muslim rulers.[16] In fact, Renier and Ydoine share their wedding day with other couples wherein the male partner is one of Renier's friends from his travels. Robert Ricard marries Ydoine's unnamed mother (who must also convert), Droon de Grèce (a Byzantine warrior) marries Gonsent (Ydoine's governess), and Baudouin (the heir to the Byzantine Empire whose name is a curious reference to the historical Baldwin I, the first emperor of the Latin Empire of Constantinople) marries Gracienne (Renier's younger sister) (Dalens-Marekovic 2009, lines 17873–90).[17] Their unions reflect Sicily's own diverse history, which bore witness to Greek, Roman, and Byzantine Greek rule before the arrival of Muslim Arabs in the ninth century. When the Normans first invaded Sicily in 1038, the island had been subject to Muslim Arab rule for approximately two hundred years. The time of Muslim domination over the island has been described as "turbulent years with some prosperity" that fostered the growth of a "cultural 'golden age'" (Mallette 2005: 4).

Norman conquest of Sicily brought an end to Muslim Arab rule and led to the establishment of the Kingdom of Sicily. In 1072, brothers Robert and Roger Guiscard led Norman forces to overtake the city of Palermo, which was the administrative center of Arab Sicily. Karla Mallette (2005: 5) explains that upon their arrival, the Normans "adopted and adapted the cultural practices they found in Sicily" in lieu of replacing it all with their own. In other words, the Normans maintained Sicily's status as a heterogeneous, multiconfessional, and multilingual space in the middle of the Mediterranean Sea. Muslims comprised much of the island's population until as late as the early thirteenth century, but by the mid-thirteenth century—not too far off from the composition of *Les enfances Renier*—the Normans expelled those who had not already left or converted to Christianity, marking the end of about four centuries of widespread Islamic presence. However, to this day, the centuries of Islamic rule survive via impact on the Sicilian and Maltese languages, toponyms, agriculture, local cuisine, and architecture.

The text, via the weddings, plays with the island's history in a way that reveals how intimate relationships can function in service of conquest,

---

16. In the text, the city is known as Loquiferne prior to its conquest by the Latin Christians, who rename it Messina.

17. Baudouin and Droon de Grèce meet Renier while they are in exile from Byzantium after Pierrus, Baudouin's older brother, seizes the throne. Baudouin's dispossession resembles that of the historical figure Isaac II Angelos, whose elder brother, Alexios III Angelos, usurped him from the Byzantine throne. For more on Isaac II Angelos and the general relationship between Byzantium and the Crusades, see Angold 1997; Harris 2014.

particularly since the Muslim women must convert to Christianity. Muslim identity is subsumed into Christianity—be it Latinate or Byzantine, depending on the spouse. While the realities of the Kingdom of Sicily show preservation of Muslim Sicilian culture, the women in the text must change. *Les enfances Renier* recognizes Sicilian history yet reconfigures it so that the core message of Christian superiority becomes clear through the conversion of the Muslim women. Given the text's possible date of composition being close to the expulsion of Muslims from Sicily, it is not a surprise that the women convert to insure the viability of the marriages.

The historiographical and genealogical interests of the text continue as the married couples have children who become major players in the First Crusade (Le 2022). It is God's plan for Tancred to share the date of conception with other crusaders:

> En cele nuit don't vous parler m'oez
> Que Tancré fu conçut et engendrez
> Et son bon oncle, Buyemons li senez,
> Si con devise la vraie autoritez,
> Par la Dieu grace en maint loi[n]taing regnez.
> Tout ce fist Diex cui il ert pris pitez
> Quar au desouz estoit crestientez:
> Li Apostole iert a Romme enserrez,
> Si le guerroie .I. paien defaez.
> (Dalens-Marekovic 2009, lines 17946–55)

> According to an authoritative source, the night that I just discussed—during which Tancred and his good uncle, the sensible Bohemond, were conceived—many princes of renown were begotten by the grace of God in several lands far apart from each other. God, moved with pity, acted this way because Christendom was in a weak position: the pope was besieged in Rome and a nonbelieving pagan was waging war on him.

The text states that Tancred shares a date of conception several men, notably Bohemond (1054–1111) and Godfrey of Bouillon (1060–1100). References to the First Crusade permeate this textual moment. The men's simultaneous conception is how God shall help the pope defend Christendom—a way to insert divine intervention and intention into the historiography of the First Crusade. The men shall conquer Antioch and Jerusalem by force, which is an explicit reference to the campaigns on the eastern shores of the Mediterranean. The historical Tancred accompanied his uncle, Bohemond, who had joined the Crusade to accompany Godfrey of Bouillon. After extensive military campaigns leading to the conquest of Jerusalem, Tancred became the Prince of Galilee, one of the four major seigneuries of the Kingdom of Jerusalem. Godfrey, a militaristic star of the First Crusade, became the first ruler of the Kingdom of Jerusalem. Bohemond, for his part, conquered Antioch in 1098 and ruled it to the great ire of Alexios, the Byzantine emperor.

In both reality and *Les enfances Renier*, Tancred and Bohemond have an uncle-nephew relationship. They are related via the maternal line: Ydoine and Bohemond are half-siblings thanks to Ydoine's mother's marriage to Robert Ricard. As I mentioned earlier, the text's Robert Ricard is a reference to the historical Norman warrior Robert Guiscard, father to the historical Bohemond. Since Tancred is Ydoine's child, Bohemond is his uncle. The historical Tancred and Bohemond were related via Tancred's mother, Emma of Hauteville (1080–1120), who was Bohemond's sister. Emma and Bohemond were the children that Robert Guiscard had with his first wife, Alberada of Buonalbergo, a duchess from Apulia. The text redraws familial lines and relationships between Tancred and Bohemond and the lands they are said to conquer. The composer of *Les enfances Renier*, the men's connection to the region by way of Alberada's Apulian origins is insufficient.[18] By having mothers—Ydoine and Ydoine's mother—who come from influential and powerful Muslim realms, the texts' Tancred and Bohemond have a connection (albeit a tenuous one) to the lands of their mothers' origin.

This historiographical restructuring demonstrates how converts can oscillate between belonging and estrangement to advance the ideological investments of the text. The text advances a particular genealogy for the crusaders to enable and revitalize the history and memory of the First Crusade. By the mid-thirteenth century, the time of *Les enfances Renier*'s composition, the Crusades throughout the eastern Mediterranean were a series of relative failures (Riley-Smith 1987). Notably, Latin Christian crusaders made the controversial decision to attack Constantinople in 1204 during the Fourth Crusade (1202–4), which greatly damaged the relationship between the Latin and Byzantine churches. The crusaders partitioned the Byzantine Empire, which left it vulnerable to conquest by the Ottomans. Closer to *Les enfances Renier*'s approximate date of composition was the Seventh Cru-

18. Apulia has a history of being under Muslim rule. The Emirate of Bari was an Islamic state during the second half of the ninth century. For more, see Kreutz 1996.

sade (1248–54), which failed to reclaim Jerusalem and surrounding areas. Given these failures, to reflect upon the First Crusade is to recall triumphant times when Latin Christendom waged successful campaigns into the eastern Mediterranean. Connecting Tancred and Bohemond more deeply to the area via their converted mothers is a means to revitalize the historiography of the First Crusades. *Les enfances Renier* rewrites history and genealogical lines to insert the reclamation of heritage to the campaigns of the First Crusade. Though the text portrays Muslim women who convert to Latin Christianity, their Muslim past remains relevant so that a convenient stake to the land exists for their children. One can be simultaneously domesticated and foreign based on the needs of the text, thereby underscoring the potential of ambivalence to be leveraged for ideological gains.

Allies around the Mediterranean

Orientalism operates to Renier's advantage in his friendship with a former Muslim enemy: Grandoce, the emir of Tripoli. Their interactions demonstrate how religious differences do not impede alliances, though they can be constructed in a way that benefits one party more than another. In other words, Renier as a Latin Christian gains a great deal through his friendship with a high-ranking Muslim ruler from the southern Mediterranean. Grandoce possesses an intimate knowledge of the Holy Land, which puts him in a privileged position over Renier. This knowledge—obscure to Renier as an outsider—is valuable for successful travel throughout the region. Renier relies upon Grandoce's familiarity with the land to fulfill his pilgrimage to the Holy Sepulchre in Jerusalem.

Renier and Grandoce meet as adversaries, but mercy and tribute pave the path to friendship. Grandoce, eager to conquer Venice for himself after Ydoine's conversion (as well as that of her subjects), launches a military campaign. Renier, who now controls Venice as Ydoine's husband, rushes to defend the city. After intense combat and Renier's decisive victory, Grandoce begs Renier to spare his life: "Sauvez ma vie, ja n'i serez perdans, / Mes ne serez par moi grevé nul tans, / Si vous donrai mile mars de besans / Et .C. mantiaus de soie traïnans, / .M. espevriers et .M. chevaus courans" (Dalens-Marekovic 2009, lines 19342–46; Spare my life, and you will not lose because I will never harm you again. I will give you a thousand marks of coins, a hundred silk cloaks with trains, a thousand sparrow hawks, and a thousand powerful horses). Unlike other moments in chansons de geste where defeat may inspire a Muslim character to convert to Latin Christianity, neither Grandoce nor Renier mention conversion. Instead, Grandoce negotiates for his life by pledging loyalty and reinforcing his commitment through tribute. Grandoce's extensive riches are no surprise, given the trope of Muslim rulers being in possession of opulent wealth. This reference to great wealth—including gold, textiles, and fine horses, which are associated with the Middle East and North Africa—finds resonances with later depictions of the "Orient" as a space of material wonders to seize. Grandoce's tribute participates in the construction of stereotypes about Muslims of North Africa and the Middle East. This scene has epistemological significance as a medieval example of what later becomes a solidly familiar Orientalist trope.

Despite references to wealth, this interaction reveals a bigger preoccupation with Grandoce's intimate knowledge of the land and political connections as a Muslim ruler. Renier rejects the offered goods and instead asks that Grandoce, who he begins to refer to as "frere" (brother), serve as his guide to the Holy Sepulchre (line 19366). Grandoce honors Renier's request, and they navigate their way eastward from Venice to Tripoli and finally to Jerusalem. Renier receives a particularly warm welcome in Tripoli thanks to Grandoce's connections there. Grandoce's cousin, Corbadas, sees to it that Renier feasts and feels welcome in Tripoli: "Roy Corbadas au courage adurez / A son cousin joï et honourez / Et pour s'amour a Renier moult festez: / Richement furent serviz et conrreez / Jusqu'au demain que li fu ajournez" (line 19684–88; The hard-hearted King Corbadas welcomes his cousin with signs of joy and respect. Out of affection for him, he organizes a feast in honor of Renier. He and his men are served and treated with pomp until the next day). Renier's stay in Tripoli reveals the power of homosociality even in Muslim circles: honoring a cousin's guest as your own and preparing a feast seems familiar to those acquainted with the homosocial networks among Latin Christians in other chansons de geste (Ailes 1998). This warm welcome is possible thanks to the friendship Grandoce has with Renier, which opens many doors for the Latin Christian pilgrim navigating foreign spaces and courts.

However, religious divides remain prevalent and pose real dangers despite moments of meaningful accord and accommodation. Muslim forces led by Corsabrin, one of Grandoce's other cousins, ambush Renier and his party shortly upon arrival to the Holy Sepulchre. Grandoce is unable to reason with his cousin, thereby reminding the audience that not all Muslims are amenable to alliance. Bound by loyalty to Renier, Grandoce retreats to Tripoli to gather reinforcements for Renier's battle against Corsabrin. The unfinished extant text ends as this conflict turns dire for Renier and his men who anxiously await Grandoce's reinforcements. Corsabrin's forces outnumber Renier's. Latin Christian survival is contingent upon a swift response from Muslim allies. The stakes of the bond that Renier and Grandoce share involves life and death. Renier spared Grandoce's life, and he must now rely upon Grandoce to save his. The extant text's missing and unknown ending, however, throws a wrench into Renier's and Grandoce's relationship: Does Grandoce indeed return with reinforcements? Does he betray Renier? The inconclusive nature of the narrative makes the men's interdependence ambiguous, thereby leaving the possibility of violence at the hand of Muslim characters as likely as salvation.

Conclusion

This article presents examples of intercultural interaction from the incredibly rich *Les enfances Renier* with the aim of demonstrating how medieval French literature can represent interpersonal Christian-Muslim relationships with an ambivalence that ultimately serves to uphold Latin Christendom. This ambivalence is key to how Orientalism operates throughout the text. Yet *Les enfances Renier*, despite being a rich case study, is only one text. I invite medievalists and postcolonialists to create a reciprocal flow of work that strengthens and expands existing critical frameworks. As I demonstrate above, *Les enfances Renier* relishes in the complexities of ambivalence: characters and situations move back and forth between what may be "different" and/or "familiar" to a Latin Christian audience. It is precisely this ambivalence—which undergirds the text's ultimate support of Latin Christian supremacy—that needs to be examined further in medieval French literature and beyond. These analyses can offer great insights into representations of human difference, thereby illuminating emergent discourses about inclusion, exclusion, and all the shades of ambivalence in between.

References

Ailes, Marianne. 1998. "The Medieval Male Couple and the Language of Homosociality." In *Masculinity in Medieval Europe*, edited by D. M. Hadley, 214–37. London: Routledge.

Akbari, Suzanne Conklin. 2012. *Idols in the East: European Representations of Islam and the Orient, 1100–1450*. Ithaca, NY: Cornell University Press.

Angold, Michael. 1997. *The Byzantine Empire: A Political History, 1025–1204.* 2nd ed. London: Longman.

Bartlett, Robert. 1994. *The Making of Europe: Conquest, Colonization, and Cultural Change, 950–1350.* Princeton, NJ: Princeton University Press.

Behdad, Ali. 1994. *Belated Travelers: Orientalism in the Age of Colonial Dissolution.* Durham, NC: Duke University Press.

Behdad, Ali. 2020. "The Afterlife of Orientalism." Review of *On the Threshold of Eurasia,* by Leah Feldman. *b2o* (blog), August 25. https://www.boundary2 .org/2020/08/ali-behdad-the-afterlife-of-orientalism-review-of-leah-feldmans -on-the-threshold-of-eurasia/.

Berkey, Jonathan Porter. 1992. *The Transmission of Knowledge in Medieval Cairo: A Social History of Islamic Education.* Princeton, NJ: Princeton University Press.

Betancourt, Roland. 2020. *Byzantine Intersectionality: Sexuality, Gender, and Race in the Middle Ages.* Princeton, NJ: Princeton University Press.

Biddick, Kathleen. 1993. "Decolonizing the English Past: Readings in Medieval Archaeology and History." *Journal of British Studies* 32, no. 1: 1–23.

Biddick, Kathleen. 1998. *The Shock of Medievalism.* Durham, NC: Duke University Press.

Black, Daisy. 2020. *Play Time: Gender, Anti-Semitism, and Temporality in Medieval Biblical Drama.* Manchester: Manchester University Press.

Burge, Amy. 2016. *Representing Difference in the Medieval and Modern Orientalist Romance.* New York: Palgrave Macmillan.

Cohen, Jeffrey Jerome, ed. 2001. *The Postcolonial Middle Ages.* New York: Palgrave Macmillan.

Cohen, Jeffrey Jerome, 2003. *Medieval Identity Machines.* Minneapolis: University of Minnesota Press.

Dagenais, John, and Margaret R. Greer. 2000. "Decolonizing the Middle Ages: Introduction." *Journal of Medieval and Early Modern Studies* 30, no. 3: 431–48.

Dalens-Marekovic, Delphine, ed. 2009. *Enfances Renier: Chanson de geste du XIIIe siècle.* Paris: Honoré Champion.

Davis, Kathleen. 1998. "National Writing in the Ninth Century: A Reminder for Postcolonial Thinking about the Nation." *Journal of Medieval and Early Modern Studies* 28, no. 3: 611–37.

Davis, Kathleen, and Nadia Altschul, eds. 2009. *Medievalisms in the Postcolonial World: The Idea of "the Middle Ages" outside Europe.* Baltimore: Johns Hopkins University Press.

D'Orbigny, Robert. 2003. *Le conte de Floire et Blanchefleur.* Edited and translated by Jean-Luc Leclanche. Paris: Honoré Champion.

Ganim, John M. 2005. *Medievalism and Orientalism: Three Essays on Literature, Architecture, and Cultural Identity.* New York: Palgrave Macmillan.

Gaunt, Simon. 2009. "Can the Middle Ages Be Postcolonial?" *Comparative Literature* 61, no. 2: 160–76.

Harris, Jonathan. 2014. *Byzantium and the Crusades*. 2nd ed. London: Bloomsbury.

Heng, Geraldine. 2003. *Empire of Magic: Medieval Romance and the Politics of Cultural Fantasy*. New York: Columbia University Press.

Heng, Geraldine. 2018. *The Invention of Race in the European Middle Ages*. Cambridge: Cambridge University Press.

Huntington, Samuel P. 1996. *The Clash of Civilizations and the Remaking of World Order*. New York: Simon and Schuster.

Hussain, Amjad M. 2013. *A Social History of Education in the Muslim World: From the Prophetic Era to Ottoman Times*. London: Ta-Ha.

Ingham, Patricia Clare, and Michelle R. Warren, eds. 2003. *Postcolonial Moves: Medieval through Modern*. New York: Palgrave Macmillan.

Kabir, Ananya Jahanara, and Deanne Williams, eds. 2005. *Postcolonial Approaches to the European Middle Ages: Translating Cultures*. Cambridge: Cambridge University Press.

Kaplan, M. Lindsay. 2019. *Figuring Racism in Medieval Christianity*. New York: Oxford University Press.

Khanmohamadi, Shirin. 2019. "Charles in Al-Andalus." *Digital Philology: A Journal of Medieval Cultures* 8, no. 1: 14–28.

Kim, Dorothy. 2019. *Digital Whiteness and Medieval Studies*. Yorkshire: Arc Humanities.

Kinoshita, Sharon. 2006. *Medieval Boundaries: Rethinking Difference in Old French Literature*. Philadelphia: University of Pennsylvania Press.

Kinoshita, Sharon. 2007. "Deprovincializing the Middle Ages." In *The Worlding Project: Doing Cultural Studies in the Era of Globalization*, edited by Rob Wilson and Christopher Leigh Connery, 61–75. Berkeley: North Atlantic Books.

Kinoshita, Sharon. 2009. "What's Up in French Medieval Studies?" *Australian Journal of French Studies* 46, no. 3: 169–77.

Kinoshita, Sharon. 2010. "Worlding Medieval French Literature." In *French Global: A New Approach to Literary History*, edited by Susan Suleiman and Christie McDonald, 3–20. New York: Columbia University Press.

Kooria, Mahmood. 2021. "Matrilineal Negotiations with Islam." *International Feminist Journal of Politics* 23, no. 2: 192–97.

Kreutz, Barbara M. 1996. *Before the Normans: Southern Italy in the Ninth and Tenth Centuries*. Philadelphia: University of Philadelphia Press.

Lampert-Weissig, Lisa. 2010. *Medieval Literature and Postcolonial Studies*. Edinburgh: Edinburgh University Press.

Lane, Frederic C. 1973. *Venice, a Maritime Republic*. Baltimore: Johns Hopkins University Press.

Lapidus, Ira M. 2002. *A History of Islamic Societies*. 2nd ed. Cambridge: Cambridge University Press.

Le, Anne. 2022. "To Have and to Hold: Conversion, Genealogy, and Imperialist Aims in *Les enfances Renier*." *Comitatus*, no. 53: 77–101.

Lomuto, Sierra. 2019. "The Mongol Princess of Tars: Global Relations and Racial Formation in *The King of Tars* (c. 1330)." *Exemplaria* 31, no. 3: 171–92.

Lowe, Lisa. 1991. *Critical Terrains: French and British Orientalisms*. Ithaca, NY: Cornell University Press.

Mallette, Karla. 2005. *The Kingdom of Sicily, 1100–1250: A Literary History*. Philadelphia: University of Pennsylvania Press.

Mateo Dieste, Josep Lluís. 2012. "Are There *'Mestizos'* in the Arab World? A Comparative Survey of Classification Categories and Kinship Systems." *Middle Eastern Studies* 48, no. 1: 125–38.

Mills, Robert. 2011. "Conversion, Translation, and Becket's 'Heathen' Mother." In *Rethinking the South English Legendaries*, edited by Heather Blurton and Jocelyn Wogan-Browne, 381–402. Manchester: Manchester University Press.

Norwich, John Julius. 1982. *A History of Venice*. New York: Vintage Books.

Otele, Olivette. 2020. *African Europeans: An Untold History*. London: Hurst.

Petrizzo, Francesca. 2019. "The Ancestry and Kinship of Tancred, Prince Regent of Antioch." *Medieval Prosopography* 34, no. 1: 41–84.

Rajabzadeh, Shokoofeh. 2019. "The Depoliticized Saracen and Muslim Erasure." *Literature Compass* 16, no. 9–10: 1–8.

Ramey, Lynn T. 2019. "Orientalism and the 'Saracen.'" In *The Cambridge Companion to the Literature of the Crusades*, edited by Anthony Paul Bale, 136–45. Cambridge: Cambridge University Press.

Riley-Smith, Jonathan. 1987. *The Crusades: A Short History*. New Haven, CT: Yale University Press.

Şahin, Kaya, Julia Schleck, and Justin Stearns. 2021. "*Orientalism* Revisited: A Conversation across Disciplines." *Exemplaria* 33, no. 2: 196–207.

Said, Edward W. 1978. *Orientalism*. New York: Vintage Books.

Sirantoine, Hélène. 2019. "What's in a Word? Naming 'Muslims' in Medieval Christian Iberia." In *Making the Medieval Relevant: How Medieval Studies Contribute to Improving Our Understanding of the Present*, edited by Chris Jones, Conor Kostick, and Klaus Oschema, 225–38. Berlin: De Gruyter.

Turner, Victoria. 2019. *Theorizing Medieval Race: Saracen Representations in Old French Literature*. Cambridge: Legenda.

Uebel, Michael. 2005. *Ecstatic Transformation: On the Uses of Alterity in the Middle Ages*. New York: Palgrave Macmillan.

Vernon, Matthew X. 2018. *The Black Middle Ages: Race and the Construction of the Middle Ages*. New York: Palgrave Macmillan.

Whitaker, Cord J. 2019. *Black Metaphors: How Modern Racism Emerged from Medieval Race-Thinking*. Philadelphia: University of Pennsylvania Press.

Spoiled History: Leprosy and the Lessons of Queer Medieval Historiography

Shoshana Adler

White supremacists tend to fetishize the European Middle Ages: recent examples include Celtic crosses at the Unite the Right rally in Charlottesville and the crusader chant "Deus Vult" at the January 6, 2021, riot at the US Capitol. As Sierra Lomuto (2016) has cogently argued, the deployment of this sort of medieval iconography celebrates not a specific ethnic identity but instead whiteness as a "racial category of privileged dominance." These symbols surface a contemporary emotional attachment to the Middle Ages, and specifically to the figure of the medieval crusader. In many ways, such an attachment is easily intelligible: the crusader is a figure of war, one that frames its own aggression and violence as a necessary defense of white Christian supremacy and heritage. American white supremacists' identification with medieval imagery makes a claim about recursive historical continuity. Though its assertions of identification and

I'm indebted to a number of people whose comments, suggestions, and questions radically clarified the shape of this paper: in particular, Melanie Abeygunawardana, Sierra Lomuto, Heather Love, and David Wallace.

boundary 2 50:3 (2023)   DOI 10.1215/01903659-10472443   © 2023 by Duke University Press

attachment are to figures different from the crusader, queer theory has made similar claims about recursive history and the status of transhistorical attachment. This scholarship can help clarify the operations of such emotional attachments to figures from the medieval past. Borrowing from these debates, this essay focuses on histories of emotional attachment to the leper, a medieval figure whose status as ultimate difference helps reconfigure emotional identification across history.

Metahistoriographic descriptions of the Middle Ages promise a reckoning with the white supremacist underpinnings of the very concept of "the medieval." In accounting for the place of the Middle Ages, such descriptions must contend with the contradictions of a medieval past constructed in scholarship as both heady point of origin for a wide variety of modern phenomena *and* as historical difference qua difference. These contradictory historiographic orientations, which Kathleen Biddick (1998: 83) describes in their incarnations in medieval scholarship as "pastism" and "presentism," are not unique to the field of medieval studies, though the Western Middle Ages does occupy a unique position in historiography. Both the racist epistemological procedures bequeathed to medieval studies by Victorian scholars working to shore up the ideological foundations of British Empire and the contemporary availability of the medieval as fantasy fuel for white supremacists are evidence of the racism buttressing the field. Tension between the Middle Ages as marker of absolute difference from modernity and the Middle Ages as genealogical origin point structures the claims of white supremacists who frame the European Middle Ages as white heritage being violently denied to them. Part of what is at stake here is the epistemological status of charged emotional recognition.

The sodomite is an obvious object of investigation for issues of historiographic identification; by contrast, the leper is intractable, less available for emotional connection. The image of the leper, clanging a clapper to warn others of their imminent approach, appears in the contemporary view as indigestible difference, the abject incarnation of the medieval. In medieval literature, however, the leper frequently appears as a metaphor for the holiness of abjection, as when Christ is described as *quasi leprosus* in his suffering and physical degradation.[1] In these treatments, leprosy is a form of penance and rehabilitation. Appearing in the Bible as the pre-

---

1. *Christus quasi leprosus* was a frequent topic for sermons. The idea emerges from Saint Jerome's translation of a verse in Isaiah. For a recent scholarly overview of *quasi leprosus*, see Giles 2018.

eminent embodiment of impurity, frequently associated with sexual per-
versity, deployed as a metaphor for sin in religious commentary, and lav-
ished with terms of the utmost disgust, the leper, as Julie Orlemanski (2012:
144) aptly characterized it, "has come to be the grotesque embodiment of
historical alterity itself." The leper is synonymous with the medieval. This
symbolic centrality is a result of nineteenth-century ideological needs. This
essay proceeds first by exploring attachment genealogies in queer theory
debates, and then by detailing the emotional valences of the medieval leper,
both within medieval literature and in later historiography, as a figure that
marks historical distance. Finally, the essay turns to Robert Henryson's
fifteenth-century poem *The Testament of Cresseid* to investigate attachments to a particular leper. Attention to the circuits of desire that animate
claims to the past on the basis of identification and personal attachment, I
argue, can account for the attraction the Middle Ages exerts on both medievalists and white supremacists.

Spoiled Identification

Medievalist scholars who are not white supremacists have an under-
standable impulse to distinguish between the Middle Ages proper and the
idea of the Middle Ages as it circulates among contemporary racists. Much
excellent recent scholarship examines the period's complex notions of race,
dispelling ideas of the Middle Ages as preracial. This approach, however
valuable *eo ipso*, cannot reckon for the continuing hold of the medieval on
the white imaginary. It is insufficient of antiracist scholarship to respond
to the fantasy of a pure white premodern solely by correcting the record,
because it is attachment rather than accuracy that is at stake.

Thinking through the possibilities of a mode of reading based in
affective response and personal identification, Carolyn Dinshaw (1999)
offers a reading of John Mirk's *Instructions for Parish Priests*, a Middle
English religious manual written in the late fourteenth century. In the course
of a conventional discussion of "synne agynes kynde" (sin against nature),
Mirk advises that children older than seven should not sleep together "Leste
they by-twynne hem brede / the lykynge of that fowle dede" (quoted in Dinshaw 1999: 10; lest they between them breed / the liking of that foul deed).[2]
Dinshaw argues that the passage proscribes not just heterosexual fornica-
tion but also "that unnamable sin against nature," and that Mirk is advising

---

2. Unless otherwise stated, all translations are my own.

against letting children of the same gender share a bed (10). She meditates on these "boys and these girls, these men and these women" posited by Mirk as poised to discover unspeakable pleasures when they share a bed. "How can we know them?" Dinshaw asks. "And thinking we know them, what do we know?" (12).

The simplicity and directness of these questions attest to their emotional intensity. "How can we know them?" Dinshaw asks, meaning, I know them, or I know that moment, the adolescents in the dark room and the shared bed and the unnamable feeling that may or may not lead to sex. The conditions of possibility for these questions are fraught, premised on private, inchoate experience. This experience that Dinshaw gestures to is one that subsequently grants membership into a more recognizable and well-defined identity-based community: acts of sexual deviancy, or even the more nameless desires that precede deviant acts, are, in our contemporary formulations, a qualifier for queer identities. This speculative reading of Mirk functions to instantiate Dinshaw's larger theoretical project, which she describes as doing the work of queer history, a "contingent history" in the sense that "its forms are intelligible but do not emerge out of teleological necessity" (3). To read Mirk in this way, looking for queer resonance or even affective identification, is to engage in the project of historical community making. These identificatory impulses can become totalizing or simplistic, but Dinshaw models a style of incomplete, constantly shifting, affective moments of community formation.[3] For Dinshaw, identification is not precise recognition or reclamation, not a claiming of definite heritage but an acknowledgment of a surge of emotion, a data point that emphasizes a way of both knowing and not-knowing the past. She calls these unstable historical connections "the touch of the queer." The question for Dinshaw is not *whether* "we" can know "them," but *how*.

In distinguishing between what she calls alterist and continuist approaches to queer historiography, Valerie Traub (2015: 83) writes that continuist scholarship tends to "emphasize a similarity between past and

3. This approach follows from classic work in the history of sexuality, including Foucault's (1977) description of genealogical history in "Nietzsche, Genealogy, History," and David Halperin's (2002: 107) work in *How to Do the History of Homosexuality*, in which Halperin argues that the "incoherence at the core of the modern notion of homosexuality" is what "furnishes the most eloquent indication of the historical accumulation of discontinuous notions that shelter within its specious unity." Valerie Traub (2015: 63) argues that Halperin's work is "committed to the view that modern sexual categories provide not just an obstacle to the past but also a window on to it."

present concepts of sexual understanding," while work that highlights historical difference, or alterity, tends to "emphasize problems of anachronism, changing terminologies and typologies, and resistance to teleology." Dinshaw's concept of "the touch of the queer" and her insistence on the epistemological affordances of an affective relation to the medieval past put her work on the continuist side of the spectrum.[4] Traub (2015: 61) surveys the way this debate often turns on accusations of teleology: scholars working on queer time explicitly intend to disrupt linear temporality, and they accuse stricter historicists of a "lingering attachment to identity that unduly stabilizes sexuality and recruits earlier sexual regimes into a lockstep march toward the present."[5] The problem for theorists of queer temporality is the stability of contemporary identity, so that historical difference works to solidify modern identity. For Traub, however, the reflexive avoidance of telos has made scholars unable to explain "the endurance or recurrence of some of the very similarities that interested them" (64). Traub's solution is to study what she describes as "cycles of salience" (85) in the history of lesbianism to account for moments of uncanny transhistoric familiarity. Recurring moments of recognition indicate not a stable unchanging identity but the "presence of symptomatic preoccupations" that make various historical forms of female eroticism intelligible as lesbianism.

Dinshaw valorizes personal identification, turning the thrill of recognition on the part of the modern reader into an intellectual resource. Simultaneously, her emphasis on contingency is intended to avoid the pitfalls of writing a past solely in the terms of the present. While proposing a different approach, Traub also values assertions of similarity and identification, arguing that such moments surface not some essential truth about identities gifted the privilege of recognition across vast historical distance but rather the recurrence of "perennial logics" that organize women's erotic lives. The impulse to make identificatory claims on the past is not unique to queer theorists: in fact, the white supremacist claims to the medieval described at the beginning of this essay might be said to follow a parallel

---

4. Dinshaw's work, like the work of scholars including Elizabeth Freeman, Madhavi Menon, Carla Freccero, and Jonathan Goldberg, can be broadly characterized as queer temporality, necessitating what Goldberg and Menon (2005: 1616) describe as "a reconsideration of relations between past and present."

5. Traub (2015: 65) notes that medievalists including Glenn Burger and Steven F. Kruger were quick to utilize postcolonial critiques of chronological timelines, emphasizing the politics behind casting the Middle Ages as the abject primitive other of the modern. See Burger and Kruger 2001: xii.

track of emotional recognition. What queer theory offers is an assessment of the epistemological procedures of these moments of recognition. "And thinking we know them, what do we know?" Dinshaw (1999: 12) asks, and the question of knowledge assumes a double syntax, referring to a state of both knowledge and ignorance. The problem at hand is knowing both the medieval past and a collective affective condition in the present that makes such claims to knowledge possible and intelligible.

What methods might be capable of explaining the endurance of emotional identification? In his study of the idealization of deviance in queer studies, Kadji Amin (2017) offers an "attachment genealogy"[6] of a collective queer investment in Jean Genet, the twentieth-century French writer, activist, petty thief, and prostitute. Genet was a criminalized sexual deviant par excellence; in queer studies, he sometimes functions as paradigm of deviance, full stop. Amin investigates the relation between Genet's radical political activism and Genet's pederasty and racial fetishization. Any investment in Genet as a self-identified criminal whose sexuality led directly to solidarity activism must grapple with his professions of erotic desire that read today less as radical and more as backward. Genet's failure—as Amin (2017: 6) says, his failure "to behave in the ways that I hoped he would"—is a "failure endemic to the project of revalorizing deviance."[7] Genet's work with the Black Panthers and with Palestinians seems unavailable as a model for coalitional politics when read alongside his outmoded and embarrassing writing about racial fetishization as means of forming coalitions. In deidealizing Genet, and attending to the disappointment, anger, and loss such a project entails, Amin investigates the conditions that lead to such attachments. As Amin argues, "attachment's analytical purchase inheres in its capacity to mark all that is passive, needy, historically overdetermined, compulsive, phantasmatic, and nonvolitional about interpersonal relations" (13). Instead of simply pointing to the ways that Genet fails to be a perfect political model, fails to "consistently and routinely secrete political value" (6), Amin investigates the motivations behind Genet's conscription into an ideal-

6. Amin draws on Christopher Nealon's (2001: 14) work on affect genealogies.
7. Amin's fully conventional use of a first-person pronoun here marks his set of feelings about sexual deviancy and attendant personal expectations. Read alongside Dinshaw's more presumptive "we" in reference to a similar set of emotions, a shadow or gap emerges: What right does the queer scholar have to speak on behalf of an imagined community? And if the right is forfeited, and a singular "I" substituted for the collective, so that Amin's disappointment with Genet reads as personal and singular, to what extent does that first-person pronoun obscure a more communal investment?

ized version of deviancy and the discrepancies between past and present that threaten that idealization.

In his book on the melancholy historicism that haunts Black studies, Stephen Best (2018: 64) draws on queer futurity to ask, "Through what process has it become possible to claim the lives and efforts of history's defeated as ours either to redeem or to redress?" The question of desired connection in Black studies is one routed through the unredressed violence of slavery. The status of affective relation with the past in Black studies is rife with foreclosed possibilities, and Best calls for a clearer articulation of the process by which relationships to history come to depend on personal biography. Quoting David Lloyd (2005: 152–53), Best writes, "The figures in the past with whom we crave a connection possess their own 'specific and unreproducible orientation to the future,' and our present, rather than representing the fulfillment of that projection, is more likely 'the future imposed on the dead by past violence'" (Best 2018: 65). Amin's focus on erotic coalitions of the past disavowed in the present and Best's attention to the impossibility of being in solidarity with "history's defeated" share an attention to the thwarted but still fervent energies that motivate connection to the past.

In keeping with the deflationary impulse operative in the work of Amin and Best, and without eschewing the utility and epistemological leverage of historical identification, it is possible to think about what it is we know when we think we know "them." Heather Love (2021: 15), examining the disavowed but significant influence of sociological deviance studies on queer studies, argues that confronting these tarnished histories of thought is necessary to address the field's "false universalism." Love tracks the recurrence of the word *spoiled* across the scholarship of Erving Goffman, Eve Kosofsky Sedgwick, and Amin, a term that she says strikes a "recherché" note (13). The queer ideals that issue out of "a messy, damaged past" are "ripe for spoiling," Love argues, not in order to distance the current moment from the past it emerges from or to restore ideals to their former positions of authority but to offer a better account of the present (17). A spoiled history deidealizes cherished objects without displacing them in search of a new ideal.[8] Rather than posturing as the first-line defenders of accurate history from the interloping threat of white supremacists or locating the true starting point of race, colonialism, or the invention of the human in the Middle

---

8. I think here of Robyn Wiegman's work on the institutional substitution of "gender" for "women" as the sign of choice to denote the aspirational political promises of feminism. See "Doing Justice with Objects" in *Object Lessons* (Wiegman 2012: chap. 1).

Ages, medievalist scholars are uniquely positioned to produce attachment genealogies of a period whose special status *needs* spoiling.

Leprous Historiography

In the rhetoric of nineteenth-century imperial physicians, leprosy is always a storied disease. Alongside its highly visible symptoms, leprosy writes centuries of history on the surface of a living body. Leprosy's disfiguration, the capacity of the disease to cause exterior lesions that obliterate normative bodily boundaries, carries with it the whiff of the past, as though rents in the flesh of European lepers literalize the return of a repudiated heritage, routed through the margins and threatening to bloom in the center, necrotic fantasies that necessitate ever-stricter protocols of cleanliness and classification. Other skin disorders are visibly disfiguring, and other diseases are more contagious, but leprosy's distinguishing threatening characteristic is its historicity. The descriptions of leprosy by prominent nineteenth-century physicians like Erasmus Wilson links present-day symptoms to ancient case studies. To be a leper is to embody that which should have been left behind in the past, to suffer a disease that makes you anachronistic.

Lepers were consigned by ecumenical council to social exclusion in leprosariums, first in the 583 Council of Lyon, which forbade association between lepers and the healthy population, and then again in the Third Council of the Lateran in 1179, which detailed the separate spiritual and physical accommodations established for lepers.[9] Across medical tracts, theology, saints' lives, and poetry, medieval lepers assume a significance in outsize proportion to their historical presence.[10] The seeming disappearance of leprosy from Europe by the sixteenth century reinforces this impression: despite the dwindling number of lepers, leprosy lingers as metaphor and archetype. Based on the number of examinations on record, leprosy seems to have been on the decline in the fourteenth and fifteenth centuries, and the archaeological record confirms that cases of leprosy after 1550 are extremely rare (see Roberts 2021). The emptying out of leprosariums, the social houses of the socially dead, marks for Michel Foucault (2006: 5–6)

9. Christian leprosariums did not admit Jewish and Muslim lepers. See Shoham-Steiner 2014.
10. In framing her empirical study of leprosy in medieval England, Carole Rawcliffe (2006: 1) argues that leprosy was a disease that "played a notable part in the medieval imagination and was accorded significance far beyond the physical threat it actually posed to the population."

an epistemic shift in his genealogical study of the history of madness: "What lasted longer than leprosy, and persisted for years after the lazar houses had been emptied, were the values and images attached to the leper, and the importance for society of this insistent, fearsome figure. . . . Once leprosy had gone, and the figure of the leper was no more than a distant memory, these structures still remained." For Foucault, the practices associated with leprosy as a social contagion and threat to the body politic continues to structure contemporary arrangements, even as the leper as such functions as a discontinuity. Foucault's historiography traces the way the present is shaped by the almost compulsive solidity of institutional regimes and intellectual habits, but the figure that initially inspired these forms becomes the face of the defunct past. In Foucault's argument for continuity, the "great confinement" attends to the question of madness, not leprosy, and the figure of the leper becomes the means of marking distance between then and now.

In the nineteenth century, there was renewed interest in leprosy and in medieval medical and literary sources on lepers. It is this engagement that renders the leper synonymous with the cruel marginalization of society's most hated and feared. Reading physician disease models and medical journals that draw on medieval sources, Kathleen Vongsathorn and Magnus Vollset discuss how nineteenth-century popular interest in leprosy was related to the death of a missionary in Hawaii. This interest peaked because of fear that leprosy would return to Europe, an anxiety Vongsathorn and Vollset (2021: 348) relate to "a desire to distance 'civilised' Europe from its 'backward' colonies, and therefore also from Europe's medieval, diseased past." The relevance of medieval models for nineteenth-century medicine was challenged by Gerhard Armauer Hansen's laboratory techniques that identified associated bacteria under a microscope. The disease would come to be called Hansen's disease in 1931, in explicit hopes of mitigating the stigma associated with the term *leprosy*. Nineteenth-century medical monographs stoke fear of contagion of a backward, disfiguring disease and simultaneously emphasize the cruelty of medieval segregation models in the treatment of leprosy. One such publication, an acclaimed 1847 study of the disease by Norwegian physicians Daniel Cornelius Danielssen and Carl Wilhelm Boek, even includes an index entry for "cruel persecution."[11] Twenty years later Erasmus Wilson (1867: 231–44), an English doctor, produced eighteen case

11. See Daniel Cornelius Danielssen and Carl Wilhelm Boek's (1847: 99) *Om Spedalskhed*, quoted in Vongsathorn and Vollset 2021: 350. In his investigation of premodern medical discourses of leprosy, Luke Demaitre (2007) distinguishes his work from "stereotypes" about leprosy, arguing that contrary to popular belief, the stigma against lepers

studies of Europeans with leprosy who lived in the colonies of India, British Ceylon (present-day Sri Lanka), Mauritius, and the West Indies, and one case study of a native of India. Wilson's work links best treatment practices for contemporary cases of leprosy with the historical evidence for leprosy: the subheading for his essay on "The Nature and Treatment of Leprosy" (an English summary of Danielssen and Boek's earlier findings) is "Jewish Leprosy, Leprosy of the Middle Ages, Leprosy of the Crusades, Leprosy of the Arabians" (1856: 339). These case studies, which circulated widely, emphasize the role of the tropics in contracting the disease, while also noting analogous case studies from the Middle Ages.

European legislation on sanitary reform in the colonies in response to leprosy is inflected by this muddled association between past cruelty and present colonialism. Tropes of colonial fantasies, in which the metropole is threatened with the same violence it routinely visits upon the colonies, appear in these nineteenth-century discourses on leprosy. As Rod Edmond (2006: 35) argues, colonial sanitary reforms are driven by fears of leprosy escaping the colonies and returning to the colonial center, "turning the fortress of England into a doomed fever camp" (see also Robertson 2007). In the actual reality of colonial era infection, colonizers introduce new diseases to the colonized. Leprosy narratives invert this dynamic, such that the center of the metropole is threatened by a disease already known to it.

Diagnostically, leprosy in the Middle Ages focuses on the skin of the patient and functions as a catch-all term for disfiguration that discomfits onlookers: what is called "leprosy" in the Middle Ages thus encompasses a range of skin disorders that vary in their severity.[12] The early fourteenth-century French physician Bernard de Gordon describes leprosy as "a systemic disease that breaks down the appearance, shape, and composition of the member and ultimately dissolves the integrity" (Demaitre 2007: 110).[13]

---

was not so strong as to prevent doctors from physically examining patients. These stereotypes, against which Demaitre distinguishes his own careful archival analysis, calcify in the nineteenth century.

12. Andrzej Grzybowski and Małgorzata Nita (2016: 3) list "psoriasis, seborrheic dermatitis, favus, dermatophyte infections, nummular dermatitis, atopic dermatitis, pityriasis rosea, crusted scabies, syphilis, impetigo, sycosis barbae, alopecia areata, furuncles, scabies, neurodermatitis, scarlet fever, lupus erythematosus, lichen sclerosus et atrophicus, folliculitis decalvans, morphea, sarcoidosis, and lichen planopilaris." The list is not exclusive. See also Demaitre's (2007: chap. 3) "The Many Labels of Leprosy."

13. For a table listing the many different definitions of *lepra* in premodern medicine, see Demaitre 2007: 112–13.

This sort of medical definition understands leprosy as hypervisible, a stark and obvious disfiguration, and simultaneously makes leprosy's operations produce a sort of liquefication. To look at the face of a leper is to pay close attention to disintegration and to see not a person but the afterimage of where a person once was.

Crucially, lepers in the Middle Ages problematize issues of recognition because of leprosy's tendency to destroy, decompose, or blur the form and outline of the body it infects. This disfiguration leads to a unique dynamic in medieval literary treatments of the leper: on the one hand, the leper is unrecognizable, due to facial lesions and bodily decomposition; on the other, when faced with a leper there is never any confusion about what one is faced with. The leper is always identifiable as such, but the categorical sorting often stops there, so that the leper is rarely individuated. This dynamic is exemplified in saints' lives, where the figure of the leper often literally vanishes after interaction with the saint.[14] This vanishing sometimes retroactively makes the leper into an incarnation of Christ and thus dissolves the leper's individuality. Julie Orlemanski's treatment of the leprous kiss—a trope in which the saint encounters a disfigured leper, experiences a wave of disgust, and, ashamed of that initial reaction, subsequently leaps forward to kiss the abject leper's ruined face—crystallizes the stakes of recognition figured in the medieval leper. Orlemanski (2012: 146) argues that leprosy and the kiss share a tendency to "make strange the human face," leprosy because of the way it disfigures the human face, and the kiss because it necessitates bringing two faces closer and closer together until, as Orlemanksi puts it, "the space of recognition, the zone between bodies that we look across and speak across in meeting one another, is drawn down toward zero." That moment of fleshly interaction, disrupting ordinary modes of recognition in favor of more demanding and strange ones, is the special doubled provenance of the leprous kiss.

Horror lingers around the figure of the leper, a sense of dread connected to leprosy's association with transgression and immorality. Caroline Walker Bynum (1992: 276) argues that leprosy is frequently used as a metaphor for sin because of the disease's association with disintegration, because "parts broke off the leper's body, because it fragmented and putrefied and became insensate when alive, in other words because it was a liv-

---

14. Hagiographic treatments of interactions between lepers and saints are widespread. For a recent summary of the ambivalence in depictions of the medieval leper, see Welch and Brown 2016.

ing death."[15] The early church father John Chrysostom, in his commentary on Matthew, typifies this sort of associative thinking regarding defilement while musing on the prohibition of handling a corpse: "Do not touch a dead body, it is said. For such is the nature of sin, it is dead and rotten. The leper is unclean. For sin is a leprosy, various and multiform" (quoted in de Wet 2018: 482). In Chrysostom's treatment, the essential nature of sin, death, and leprosy is metastatic, multiplying pathogenic sites while assuming non-identical shapes. To be infected with the sin or the leprosy of another does not necessarily ensure that the infected person will resemble the person who infected them. Sin and leprosy both disfigure, but disfiguration takes unique forms.

In addition to living death, leprosy acquires a special association with sex. The fifth-century Byzantine physician Aetius assumed that leprosy was contracted via sexual intercourse, a view that seems to have been quoted with especial frequency by nineteenth-century medical authorities.[16] In the twelfth century, Hildegard of Bingen linked the disease to lust; writing contemporaneously, the theologian Adam Scotus typifies this characterization when he asks, "Nam quid est inhonestas leprae, nisi peccatum luxuriate?" (quoted in D'Arcy 2005: 102; For what else is the disgrace of leprosy but the sin of lust?). In the Bible, leprosy (Hebrew: צָרַעַת; Greek: λέπρα; Latin: *lepra*) is associated with purification rituals, as when Christ heals lepers. The most vivid biblical depiction is in Leviticus, where leprosy is described similiarly to a mold or fungal infestation, as raw white boils that can spread from living flesh to clothing to the walls of one's dwelling.[17] In Numbers, the prophet Miriam is punished with *tsara't* for speaking disparagingly of her brother Moses's marriage. Her skin affliction is compared to the condition of a stillborn baby who emerges from the womb with flesh half eaten away ("אֲשֶׁר בְּצֵאתוֹ מֵרֶחֶם אִמּוֹ וַיֵּאָכֵל חֲצִי בְשָׂרוֹ"; Num. 12:12; Who emerges from the womb of his mother and his flesh is half consumed). Miriam's punishment is caused by her slanderous speech: in his gloss on Leviticus, Rashi, the elev-

---

15. Another medieval figure treated as though dead while alive is the holy anchorite, whose distance from society is a pious choice.

16. See the work of the French doctor Pierre J. G. Cabanis (1823: 90) and the Scottish doctor and translator Adam Francis (1846: 10), who cites Aetius throughout his commentary on ancient medicine.

17. "Leprosy" is arguably a mistranslation of the Hebrew term *tsara't*, as the disease described in the New Testament is distinct from the one in the Old Testament. This vagueness attests to the semantic field leprosy covers, as an umbrella diagnostic of visible deformity associated with moral rot.

enth century rabbi whose comprehensive biblical exegesis would become the standard foundation for later commentaries, identifies the cause of leprosy as "לשון הרע" (slander, or evil speech), an analysis repeated for a later medieval Christian audience by Nicholas of Lyra.[18]

In medieval texts, the leper's hypervisibility and sexual unseemliness works in tandem with moralizing about social abjection, so that judgments about leprosy allow medieval thinkers to parse the contradictions that structure their ambivalence about topics like sin, desire, and sickness. As an anachronism, the figure of the leper from the perspective of the present is histrionically past. Nineteenth-century pronouncements about the cruelty of past treatment of lepers shape our contemporary historiography. The qualities of excessive signification attached to the leper in medieval texts appear to me from the vantage point of the present to enter into a recursive loop of their own, a circuit from abject overdetermination to cruel ostracization to anachronism. Epistemologically, this circuit sparked by the leper solidifies a comforting distance between past and present: the extreme emotions excited by leprosy in medieval treatments are proof positive of leprosy's incongruity and inappropriate lateness in the present.

Like the sodomite, the medieval leper organizes a vastly overdetermined range of affects. But the sodomite needs seeking out and is often implied without being named, a sinner against nature whose deviance resides in ephemeral acts. Lepers, by contrast, insistently present their deformities as surface to be read rather than depth to be plumbed. Where premodern sodomy has the quality of a secret, generative insofar as it is cryptic or indeterminate, leprosy is meaning made excessive, a super plurality of signification. Dinshaw's "touch of the queer," with its capacity to make affective historical community, necessitates identification on at least one end of the transhistoric connection. But who wants to be a leper?[19]

Leprous Recognition

In Robert Henryson's (2010) *Testament of Cresseid* the leper is an abject figure in a self-consciously ancillary text. The poem, in its content and in its material history, is framed in relation to Chaucer's *Troilus and Cri-*

18. For a reading on the relationship between slander, blasphemy, and leprosy in the *Testament*, see d'Arcy 2005.
19. I think here of Leo Bersani's (1995: 1) *Homos*, which opens with a characteristically flat polemical assertion: "No one wants to be called a homosexual."

seyde. William Thynne's 1532 print edition of Chaucer's works includes the *Testament* without authorial attribution, linking the two poems within Chaucer's oeuvre.[20] Henryson's narrator opens the poem setting aside "worthie" (line 41) Chaucer's poem in favor of "ane uther quair" (line 61; another book) that contains a new account of the tragic fate of Cresseid after she abandons her lover Troilus. The citations of Chaucer's *Troilus* within the *Testament* bluntly situate Henryson's poem in relation to an earlier authoritative treatment of the same subject. In a lovely moment of ironic self-awareness, the narrator asks "Quha wait gif all that Chauceir wrait was trew? / Nor I wait nocht gif this narratioun / Be authoreist" (lines 64–66; Who knows if all that Chaucer wrote was true? / Nor do I know if this narrative / Is authoritative). Henryson questions Chaucer's historical accuracy *without* preserving authority for his own poem: neither treatment of events should be received by readers as definitive historical truth.

The events in the book that Henryson's narrator discovers take place after Troilus learns of Cresseid's affair but before his death, depicted in book 5 of *Troilus and Criseyde*. The *Testament* is therefore more of an interpolation into the story of *Troilus and Criseyde* than it is a continuation or addendum.[21] Henryson's intervention is to punish Cresseid with leprosy. In the *Testament*, leprosy pries open settled plotlines, leveraging room for an original meditation on Cresseid's infamy. Henryson doesn't need to overwrite Chaucer's previous account, and the *Testament* is not a challenge to Chaucerian authority. Rather, the leprosy in the poem allows Henryson space to treat events already depicted in *Troilus and Cresseid* with different emphases. The disease in the *Testament* is depicted graphically, even grotesquely, and this crudeness displaces without fully erasing the majes-

---

20. In manuscript, the poem survives only in fragments: three stanzas in the Ruthven manuscript (University of Edinburgh Library MS Dc.I.43), and one in the Book of the Dean of Lismore (ascribed to "Bochas that wes full gud"). In "Changing Emotions in Troilus," David Wallace (2016: 164) describes Chaucer's and Henryson's poems as appearing in a "single conceptual package." Megan Cook's scholarship on Frances Thynne's annotations of his father's edition of Chaucer makes it clear that the lack of attribution of *The Testament* to Henryson did not mean readers assumed the poem was written by Chaucer. Cook (2012: 229) notes that Thynne "underlines the references to Chaucer in the text" and understood that the poem was not written by Chaucer himself.
21. Scholars have disagreed about the best way to characterize the connection between Chaucer and Henryson. George Edmondson (2008), in particular, objects to filial descriptors in favor of "neighborly" as a way of capturing the unconscious hostility he finds in Henryson's poem.

tic authoritative sweep of Chaucer's work. Leprosy is the means by which the poem negotiates an overdetermined relationship with its predecessor.

The poem relies on audience familiarity with the general contour of the plot. The poet "neidis nocht reheirs" (line 57; need not rehearse) Troilus' distress upon learning of Cresseid's infidelity; instead, the action begins with the aftermath. After abandoning Troilus and being abandoned in turn by her lover Diomedes, Cresseid returns to her father's house, seeking seclusion and privacy in the face of vicious rumors about her sexual promiscuity. These rumors are lavishly described: Cresseid is filthy, defiled, "giglotlike" (line 83; whorish). In the very next stanza the poet expresses a desire to excuse and defend Cresseid from the scorn of the world, the misogynistic disgust at her sexuality seesawing into moralistic pity. This bait and switch is characteristic of the poem's general treatment of Cresseid, in which a sadistic impulse to inflict suffering interchanges freely with care, even tenderness, without admitting of the slightest contradiction. Cresseid, as a character, is an excellent conductor of emotional intensities.

At her father's house, Cresseid rails against the gods of love, Venus and Cupid, accusing them of having capriciously transformed all of her experiences of love into woe. Swooning, she has a dream vision in which the gods, angered by her blasphemy, sentence her to "seiknes incurabill" (line 307; incurable sickness).[22] The poem lingers on her physical transformation from leprosy: her crystalline eyes mingled with blood, her sweet voice hoarsened, her beautiful face covered with black spots and morbid growths. From this point on the poem might be read as enacting a series of horrified partial recognitions. Waking, Cresseid immediately checks her visage in a mirror; finding it deformed by the disease, she calls her father, who looks at "hir uglye lipper face" (line 372; her ugly leper face) and wrings his hands in dismay; Cresseid begs her father to convey her to the leper hospital in secret so that she "wald not be kend" (line 380; would not be recognized); as for the local people who encounter her with begging cup and clapper, "Sum knew hir weill, and sum had na knowledge /

---

22. Cresseid's punishment is linked to blasphemy, though many of the poem's readers have been struck by the incongruity of its early emphasis on Cresseid's promiscuity and this later justification of her punishment. Gayle Margherita (2000: 272) notes the curious fact that Cresseid's punishment "has little to do with her betrayal of Troilus." Felicity Riddy (1997: 243) offers a string of possible sins including infidelity, blasphemy, and vanity, and observes that "all of these at some point or other in the poem, are brought to the fore as things for which she deserves to be punished."

Of hir becaus scho was sa deformait, / With bylis blak ovirspred in hir vis-age" (lines 393–95; Some knew her well, and some had no knowledge / Of her because she was so deformed, / With black boils spread over her vis-age). In sentencing Cresseid, the gods predict everyone will flee her pres-ence once she becomes a leper with a clapper. On the contrary, with these lines, the poem and the people around Cresseid lean in closer and closer, peering into her face, debating her identity. If leprosy determines scripts of emotional resonance and social behavior (revulsion, abjection, almsgiving), so too does Cresseid, in her capacity in the poem as either local celebrity or intertextual character, determine behavior (prurient curiosity). Leprosy might have offered Cresseid anonymity, some relief from the daily burden of her infamy. Instead her infamy seems to deanonymize leprosy—within the radius of her leprosarium every leper becomes a potential Cresseid.

All these moments of tortured partial recognition reach their apo-theosis toward the end of the poem, when Cresseid encounters Troilus on his way back to Troy after a battle. She turns her face toward him, perhaps blind from the advance of the leprosy, and he stares back, not recognizing her but thinking that "he sumtime hir face befoir had sene" (line 500; he had seen her face sometime before). Cresseid is so sick that Troilus does not know her; nevertheless, something about this leper's "luik" (look, visage) brings to his mind the amorous vision of "fair Cresseid, sumtyme his awin darling" (line 504). Overcome with emotion, Troilus breaks out in a fever, trembles, and almost faints. Without recognizing her, he casts all the gold he is carrying with him at Cresseid's feet and rides off. He doesn't offer money because he recognizes her; the poem stresses that neither Cresseid nor Troilus recognize each other. Instead, the poem explains:

> The idole of ane thing in cace may be
> Sa deip imprentit in the fantasy
> That it deludis the wittis outwardly,
> And sa appeiris in forme and lyke estait
> Within the mynd as it was figurait.
> (lines 507–11)

> The image of a thing in certain cases may be
> So deeply impressed in the imagination
> That it deludes the outward senses
> And so appears in similar form and state
> Within the mind as it was remembered.

It is not that Troilus looks on Cresseid's leprous face, half recognizes her, and, uneasy at the imperfect identification, offers her all the money he has with him. Troilus's love for Cresseid has so imprinted the fantasy of her face in his mind he could half glimpse her anywhere, in anything. Interposed in the line of sight between Troilus and Cresseid is the "idole" of his fantasy, her unblemished face. Moved by the memory of his former lover, overlaid and overwriting the leper before him, Troilus treats Cresseid as a leprous object of charity, throws down his gold, and rides away. As Kathryn Lynch (2010) argues, the poem indicates that Troilus' confused mistake is because "so pervasively does she dominate his imagination, he sees Cresseids everywhere." Similarly, Orlemanski (2013: 170–71) describes the poem's "double vision of Cresseid," which repeatedly conjures two versions of the same face, "one leprous and one lily pale." This failed anagnorisis is a moment of startled discovery that produces no knowledge, no recognition.

Cresseid's particularity, the narrative weight that accompanies her, her status as an intertextual character, the swirl of kinship ties and class status and love relations that surround her, render the failure of recognition particularly tragic. The leprosy that blurs Cresseid's recognizable profile ensures that while Troilus might see Cresseids everywhere, when he actually meets her his fantasy is interrupted by the lesions that index a prior but vanished person. Lynch puts the stress on Troilus's fantasy; Orlemanski on Cresseid's ruined face. Both readings note the way this misapprehension multiplies Cresseid. Between Troilus's gaze and Cresseid's face, there are a thousand Cresseids, and a thousand lepers. She resists being entirely subsumed under the obliterating header "leper." So too does leprosy exceed the personhood of Cresseid. On the tombstone Troilus commissions for Cresseid he inscribes an epitaph addressed to all women: "Lo, fair ladyis, Cresseid of Troy the toun, / Sumtyme countit the flour of womanheid, / Under this stane, lait lipper, lyis deid" (Henryson 2010, lines 607–9; Lo, fair ladies, Cresseid of Troy the town, / Sometimes counted the flower of womanhood, / Under this stone, late leper, lies dead). The tombstone frames Cresseid's fate as a warning for all women, which the poet develops in the next and final stanza as a misogynistic instruction not to mix love with deception. The parenthetical "lait lipper" delimits a temporal interruption of her identity. Once there was Cresseid, flower of womanhood, then in her place there was a leper, and now under this stone, lies Cresseid again, dead.

Characterizing the feminist imperative in relation to the *Testament*, Gayle Margherita (2000: 260) writes: "I would like to contemplate that which can be said to live on, to remain, after moral and aesthetic judgments have been passed, after all the bodies have been buried and consigned to silence. What remains, it seems to me, is precisely the question of the body, a question that encrypts yet another, more uncertain one: the question of justice." The leprous body that Henryson parades as spectacle through the poem is what brings the poem to an abrupt end when it is buried: the final line of the poem is "Sen scho is deid I speik of hir no moir" (Henryson 2010, line 616; Since she is dead I speak of her no more). But the very existence of the poem belies its sudden insistence on closure—Cresseid is as dead when the narrator begins as when he ends. It is possible to read this conclusion as of a piece with Henryson's style of irony: he inclines to be a poet who is knitting with one hand and unraveling with the other. The insistence that the end of the poem coincide with Cresseid's death contrasts distinctly with the famous ending of Chaucer's (2008: book 5, line 1808) *Troilus*, where the brief account of Troilus's death is followed by the astonishing image of Troilus's "lighte goost" floating above the carnage and laughing at earthly woe. Chaucer gifts his hero a moment to laugh at his formed benighted state; Henryson affords Cresseid no such extraterrestrial perspective. The testament she writes before her death consigns her corpse to worms, her possessions to lepers, and a ring to Troilus. Carnal to the very end, her story ends with her flesh.

Since she is dead I speak of her no more: it is possible to read this line as the final sally in the misogynistic barrage aimed at Cresseid. More generously, we might imagine Henryson's rhetorical overemphasis paradoxically surfacing those aspects of the poem that escape total closure. I think, however, it is equally possible to understand this line as a pronouncement about a failed and ever-failing emotional connection with the past, which persists in spite of better judgment. Cresseid is hard to recognize—leprosy has dissolved her face and interrupted the sequence of her personal history. Troilus, at the moment of their confrontation, is unable to identify her correctly and can't lay any sort of claim to her, cannot accuse or berate or reconcile with her. He's lost the capacity to interfere; he can only shiver with emotion and ride on. The generosity he extends toward her in the form of charity is a gesture that reasserts a social script. Troilus cannot relate to Cresseid anymore, but he can relate to a leper, if only as a giver of alms, a unidirectional form of relation that overwrites their previous complex and individuated connection. The late leper Cresseid embodies the erotics of thwarted emotional identification with the past. The poet aims his closing injunction at himself, an abrupt command to stop speaking that leaves in its wake a loud silence. This directive or promise—I will speak of Cresseid no more—is a retrospective diagnosis of a problem or intention gone awry. Something has been thwarted, something involuntary, excessive, a relation Amin might characterize as "needy"—an emotional attachment that needs to be cut off. Even within this effort to leave Cresseid in peace, unbothered by hordes of leering lovers squinting at her face and trying to draw lessons from her body, the attachment remains, an indigestible fact that must be dealt with.

It is impossible to redeem history or claim it fully. In their various deployments of medieval imagery, American white supremacists argue that the Middle Ages is white and also that there is something essential—stable, coherent—about whiteness. The stability of this white identity can only be maintained through violence. Lines of continuity, inheritance, and identification drawn between crusaders and Proud Boys speak to a thrill of recognition, an emotional connection made possible because of the perennial recurrence of ethnonationalist logics. Precisely because the Middle Ages has so frequently been made to assume the status of break in historiography, it offers us a way to examine the process by which we speak of the dead or claim them as our own.

References

Amin, Kadji. 2017. *Disturbing Attachments: Genet, Modern Pederasty, and Queer History.* Durham, NC: Duke University Press.

Bersani, Leo. 1995. *Homos.* Cambridge, MA: Harvard University Press.

Best, Stephen. 2018. *None Like Us: Blackness, Belonging, Aesthetic Life.* Durham, NC: Duke University Press.

Biddick, Kathleen. 1998. *The Shock of Medievalism.* Durham, NC: Duke University Press.

Burger, Glenn, and Stephen F. Kruger, eds. 2001. *Queering the Middle Ages.* Minneapolis: University of Minnesota Press.

Bynum, Caroline Walker. 1992. *Fragmentation and Redemption: Essays on Gender and the Human Body in Medieval Religion.* Brooklyn: Zone Books.

Cabanis, Pierre Jean Georges. 1823. *An Essay on the Certainty of Medicine.* Translated by R. La Roche. Philadelphia: Robert Desilver. https://wellcomecollection.org/works/gfcuegnu.

Chaucer, Geoffrey. 2008. *The Riverside Chaucer.* Edited by Larry D. Benson. Oxford: Oxford University Press.

Cook, Megan. 2012. "How Frances Thynne Read His Chaucer." *Journal of the Early Book Society for the Study of Manuscripts and Printing History,* no. 15: 215–43.

D'Arcy, Ann Marie. 2005. "'Into the Kirk Wald Not Hir Self Present': Leprosy, Blasphemy, and Heresy in Henryson's *The Testament of Cresseid*." In *Studies in Late Medieval and Early Renaissance Texts in Honour of John Scattergood*, edited by Ann Marie D'Arcy, Alan John Fletcher, and V. J. Scattergood, 100–20. Dublin: Four Courts.

Danielssen, Daniel Cornelius, and Carl Wilhelm Boek. 1847. *Om Spedalskhed*. Bergen: Christiania.

Demaitre, Luke. 2007. *Leprosy in Premodern Medicine: A Malady of the Whole Body*. Baltimore: Johns Hopkins University Press.

de Wet, Chris L. 2018. "The Leprous Body as Ethical-Theological Strategy: John Chrysostom's Interpretation of the Cleansing of the Leper in Matthew 8:1–4." *Neotestamentica* 52, no. 2: 471–88.

Dinshaw, Carolyn. 1999. *Getting Medieval: Sexualities and Communities, Pre- and Postmodern*. Durham, NC: Duke University Press.

Edmond, Rod. 2006. *Leprosy and Empire: A Medical and Cultural History*. Cambridge: Cambridge University Press.

Edmondson, George. 2008. "Henryson's Doubt: Neighbors and Negation in *The Testament of Cresseid*." *Exemplaria* 20, no. 2: 165–96.

Foucault, Michel. 1977. "Nietzsche, Genealogy, History." In *Language, Countermemory, Practice: Selected Essays and Interviews*, edited by Donald F. Bouchard, translated by Donald F. Bouchard and Sherry Simon, 139–64. Ithaca, NY: Cornell University Press.

Foucault, Michel. 2006. *History of Madness*. Edited by Jean Khalfa, translated by Jonathan Murphy and Jean Khalfa. New York: Routledge.

Francis, Adam. 1846. *The Seven Books of Paulus Aegineta*. 3 vols. London: Sydenham Society. https://wellcomecollection.org/works/qmwq5kuj.

Giles, Ryan D. 2018 "The Breath of Lazarus in the Mocedades de Rodrigo." In *Beyond Sight: Engaging the Senses in Iberian Literatures and Cultures, 1200–1750*, edited by Ryan D. Giles and Steven Wagschal, 17–30. Toronto: University of Toronto Press.

Goldberg, Jonathan, and Madhavi Menon. 2005. "Queering History." *PMLA* 120, no. 5: 1608–17.

Grzybowski, Andrzej, and Małgorzata Nita. 2016. "Leprosy in the Bible." *Clinics in Dermatology* 34, no. 1: 3–7.

Halperin, David. 2002. *How to Do the History of Homosexuality*. Chicago: University of Chicago Press.

Henryson, Robert. 2010. *The Complete Works*. Edited by David J. Parkinson. Kalamazoo, MI: Medieval Institute Publications.

Lloyd, David. 2005. "The Indigent Sublime: Specters of Irish Hunger." *Representations* 92, no. 1: 152–85.

Lomuto, Sierra. 2016. "White Nationalism and the Ethics of Medieval Studies." *In the Middle*, December 5. https://www.inthemedievalmiddle.com/2016/12/white -nationalism-and-ethics-of.html.

Love, Heather. 2021. *Underdogs: Social Deviance and Queer Theory*. Chicago: University of Chicago Press.

Lynch, Kathryn L. 2010. "Robert Henryson's 'Doolie Dreame' and the Late Medieval Dream Vision Tradition." *Journal of English and Germanic Philology* 109, no. 2: 177–97.

Margherita, Gayle. 2000. "Criseyde's Remains: Romance and the Question of Justice" *Exemplaria* 12, no. 2: 257–92.

Nealon, Christopher. 2001. *Foundlings: Lesbian and Gay Historical Emotion before Stonewall*. Durham, NC: Duke University Press.

Orlemanski, Julie. 2012. "How to Kiss a Leper." *postmedieval* 3, no. 2: 142–57.

Orlemanski, Julie. 2013. "Desire and Defacement in *The Testament of Cresseid*." In *Reading Skin in Medieval Literature and Culture*, edited by Katie L. Walker, 161–81. London: Palgrave Macmillan.

Rawcliffe, Carole. 2006. *Leprosy in Medieval England*. New York: Boydell.

Riddy, Felicity. 1997. "Abject Odious: Feminine and Masculine in Henryson's *Testament of Cresseid*." In *The Long Fifteenth Century: Essays for Douglas Gray*, edited by Helen Cooper and Sally Mapstone, 229–48. Oxford: Clarendon.

Roberts, Charlotte. 2021. "Reflections on the Bioarcheology of Leprosy and Identity." In *Leprosy and Identity in the Middle Ages: from England to the Mediterranean*, edited by Elma Brenner and François-Olivier Touati, 21–44. Manchester: Manchester University Press.

Robertson, Jo. 2007. "In Search of M. Leprae: Medicine, Public Debate, Politics and the Leprosy Commission to India." In *Economies of Representation, 1790–2000: Colonialism and Commerce*, edited by Dale Leigh and Helen Gilbert, 44–58. Farnham, UK: Taylor and Francis Ashgate.

Shoham-Steiner, Ephraim. 2014. *On the Margins of a Minority: Leprosy, Madness, and Disability among the Jews of Medieval Europe*. Detroit: Wayne State University Press.

Traub, Valerie. 2015. *Thinking Sex with the Early Moderns*. Philadelphia: University of Pennsylvania Press.

Vongsathorn, Kathleen, and Magnus Vollset. 2021 "'Our Loathsome Ancestors': Reinventing Medieval Leprosy, 1850–1950." In *Leprosy and Identity in the Middle Ages: from England to the Mediterranean*, edited by Elma Brenner and François-Olivier Touati, 347–82. Manchester: Manchester University Press.

Wallace, David. 2016. "Changing Emotions in Troilus: The Crucial Year." In *Love, History, and Emotion in Chaucer and Shakespeare: "Troilus and Criseyde" and "Troilus and Cressida,"* edited by Andrew James Johnston, Russell West-Pavlov, and Elisabeth Kempf, 157–71. Manchester: Manchester University Press.

Welch, Christina, and Rohan Brown. 2016. "From Villainous Letch and Sinful Outcast, to 'Especially Beloved of God.'" *Historical Reflections* 42, no. 1: 48–60.

Wiegman, Robyn. 2012. *Object Lessons*. Durham, NC: Duke University Press.

Wilson, Erasmus. 1856. "On the Nature and Treatment of Leprosy, Ancient and Modern." *Lancet*, no. 1690: 60–62.

Wilson, Erasmus. 1867. "Observations on the True Leprosy or Elephantiasis, with Cases." In *Report on Leprosy by the Royal College of Physicians Prepared for and Published by Her Majesty's Secretary of State for the Colonies*, printed by George Edward Eyre and William Spottiswood, 231–44. London: Royal College of Physicians of London. https://wellcomecollection.org/works /be76ek86.

Afterword: In and beyond the Boundaries of Medievalism

Elizabeth J. West

Reading and reflecting on Sierra Lomuto's (2023a) introduction to this special issue of *boundary 2*, I journeyed back in time to my early childhood, where in school and in cinema the Middle Ages and precontemporary civilizations seemed ubiquitously embodied as European and, hence, white. These stories were much like the cowboy and western frontier shows that I grew up watching on television with my parents. We absorbed these dramas without reflecting on how they propagated myths of a world expanding and advancing through the push of Anglo/Western civilization. For decades now, the academy has explored their impact on non-Western/nonwhite peoples and populations through intellectual frameworks such as postcolonialism, neocolonialism, identity studies, race studies, and a host of hyphenated-named disciplines. Among the conventional liberal arts disciplines of Western tradition, medieval studies is one of the last holdouts in denying its deep ties—if not its outright lead role—in the academy's legacy of intellectual racism. While much has been made of the amendment to the original name of the discipline, Lomuto argues that eradicating its entrenched racism will

boundary 2 50:3 (2023) DOI 10.1215/01903659-10472457 ©2023 by Duke University Press

require a heavier lift. Prefacing the centuries-old term *Middle Ages* with the term *global* will not erase the historical tie to white supremacist ideology and actions. Lomuto's reminder of the connection between the Charlottesville 2017 riot and Anglo-constructed symbolisms of the Middle Ages illustrates the discipline's service to some of the nation's deeply planted seeds of racism. Long-term and genuine change in Middle Ages/medieval studies might begin with name change, but impactful work requires greater depth in work and imagination. The essays in this special issue collectively explore how the field might advance in this regard. In general, the contributors suggest that to help forge a new direction in studies across the humanities, the global Middle Ages must reimagine human movement and migration in more meaningful ways across a deeper prism of time.

Mariah Min (2023) emphasizes the necessity of exploring the dynamic of time and human movement beyond boundaries of Western thinking. Min argues that to effect substantive change in its white supremacist origins, the so-called Middle Ages and any iteration of the field must grow beyond their self-constructed and self-serving borders. Foundational to the very idea of a Middle Ages, the confines of periodization and race have locked us into a stasis of time, place, and identity. Min maintains that working across disciplines can unloosen the white-centered bonds that have maintained the Middle Ages as a Western cosmology. A shift from this worldview allows for a more accurate understanding of the mobility and varied constructs of race across and within Western established time and space. Utilizing Patience Agbabi's "Prologue (Grime Mix)" as an example, Min demonstrates how a work like Agbabi's can circle back to the subtle racialized landscape of Chaucer's fourteenth-century General Prologue to highlight its deeply rooted white epistemology—one that imagines people exclusively within the framework of Christian and European. Michelle R. Warren's (2023) essay also insists that advancing scholarship to more accurately represent an early global humanity requires medievalists to disconnect from the grips of periodization. Warren calls us to think of the medieval in the context of the Clock of the Long Now, a clock that will measure time across longer stretches of years or centuries; we might reshift our concept of time in the dimensions of the now as well as the future and the past. This intellectual reset could then guide us to understand human populations, national identities, cultures, movements, and migrations beyond the restrictive and contrived paradigms of the West.

I engaged the essays in this collection with the aim of exploring how the challenges of representing human experience, movement, and identity in the era called the Middle Ages might offer insight for studies of this dynamic in later periods. On the road to this comparative pondering, I found these essays directing me to consider these questions through a more personal lens. From early childhood to my graduate studies, social and educational structures demanded or coerced my engagement with stories such as Robin Hood, knights of the Round Table, and Shakespeare's plays focusing on the British Middle Ages. I remember introductions to some of these stories in both the book versions for young readers as well as reruns of black-and-white and early color films that were regularly scheduled programming on the local television station of my Chicago childhood. In particular, *The Adventures of Robin Hood*, with actor Errol Flynn, was a popularized film adaptation of the medieval character that replayed for decades and generations on television beyond its 1938 debut. Similarly, the 1953 film *Knights of the Round Table*, directed by Richard Thorpe, and Laurence Olivier's *Richard III*, first released in theaters in 1955, were mainstay reruns on the local stations known for showing oldies. The trajectory of these kinds of popularized white recreations of the medieval world can be traced through decades to the present century. This cinematic collection includes box office successes such as Roman Polanski's *Macbeth* (1971), John Boorman's *Excalibur* (1981), and Mel Gibson's *Braveheart* (1995). In the twenty-first century, Peter Flinth's *Arn: The Knight Templar* (2007), Antoine Fuqua's resurrection of *King Arthur* (2004), and Ridley Scott's revival of *Robin Hood* (2010) demonstrate that even though modern films may integrate nonwhite characters and offer excursions into spaces beyond medieval Europe, the histories and literary works that the academy has sustained for centuries will continue to receive new life in the world of film—which operates in collaboration with the academic tradition. The overload of these stories and their imagery continues to perpetuate the myth of an "old world" dominated and shaped by white people, and they require that we ignore the mobility of race across time. They further inform an ethos and a history of whiteness in the twenty-first century that maintains its constancy as an identity—a biological and cultural one—that reaches back into the Middle Ages and prior.

In elementary school it did not occur to me to consider where Black people were or what they might be doing in this era. I do not recall thinking consciously that Black people did not exist or were not present in this arbitrarily constructed era, but I do recall thinking they were not in this part of the world or in contact with Europeans. It was not until later, as an adult with children, that I realized how I had been conditioned to perceive this era as the era of white people, a time when Black people were not living or traveling outside their locations on the African continent or in European spaces. The moment of this dissonance, of what seemed a paradigm collision, occurred when I was a graduate student studying literature and was well educated through an Afrocentric community in my teenage years. On an outing with my children one summer to an outdoor Renaissance festival just south of Atlanta, I was surprised to see two Black actors among those cast in reenactment scenes from the period. I remember thinking that this was a forced overture to racial diversity and being a little annoyed that their casting represented the typical racial tokenism that stood in for the real racial reckoning the country was dodging.

I usually corrected historical or cultural misrepresentations for my children as part of the debriefing that Black parents customarily have to do in the United States. I held off at that moment, however, as something in my psyche told me that perhaps I was not connecting the dots. I knew that by the period of the European Renaissance, Africa had seen the rise and fall of many great empires, and that many were still in existence in the sixteenth century. I realized that it was the "forcing" of the impression of contact between Europeans and Africans in this era that I found disturbing. This, of course, sent me back to the history books and even to the Bible. This reimmersion reminded me that, dating well into antiquity, Black people had traveled the world and that first encounters with others predated the so-called era of exploration by centuries. I recalled the texts I had read that indicated this history, and the art found throughout European museums that clearly illustrates this as well. So, why had I been so annoyed at seeing a couple of Black faces in a festival reenactment of Renaissance Europe? I mused over this for years. It was not until I was well into my graduate studies in English that I began to understand what had thrown me so off-balance at that festival. It was a combination of things: to start, it was simply the matter of encountering a visual image that the dominant Western culture rarely presents—an image that suggested a pre-emancipation Black-white encounter in which the Black person was represented as unapologetically Black and the European not the power player in the encounter.

In post–Civil Rights Era America, critics of racial equity initiatives regularly brand this kind of representation as "affirmative action" play or "politically correct" revisitations to "real" history. This white normative perspective rests in the supposition that a Black presence in the long history of civilization represents a kind of fabricated historical choreography. Remarkably, though well aware that Black history permeates the history of human civilization, Black people themselves often take on the defensive posture of weeding out intellectualism or fact-based history that rests in a simple mission of racial inclusivity. My reaction at the Renaissance festival was dangerous, or faulty, to this extreme. Because I was sensitive to—even defensive of—charges that Afrocentric histories were mere desires to be in company with Western history, the visual of that insertion of a Black body into the white space of time and history raised a flag. I realized that this is how Euro-American constructions of a racialized white dominant history continue to stand. When you always make others feel the obligation to prove their story and their presence, then your stories remain the default truth or absolute or universal metric. I did not want to see those Black faces in that space because I had not been allowed the opportunity to vet that version of history that was being conveyed for all onlookers. I knew that in the Georgia, where I lived, white people walking through the festival were sneering and commenting under their breaths that this is what diversity brings—this dilution of "real" history—of white-constructed history.

I knew what *I knew*, and that is that Black people inhabited and traveled the globe pre–Middle Passage, but what constrained me at that moment was the conditioned feeling that I was always responsible for "proving" this as a fact. And at that festival, I was simply anticipating an afternoon outing, not another reminder of white-imposed ontologies that linger like intellectual malignancies. In essence, I could stomach the misrepresentation of the white-constructed historical moment of the Renaissance festival in white face much more easily than with the insertion of Black faces. The Black faces reminded me, I suppose, of the presumptiveness of whiteness that prevails in Western studies of early and ancient civilizations. When reenactments only have white faces, I feel oddly less agitated—only because I do not then feel the obligation to explain why it is white when only white faces represent it. I regularly debriefed my children on the histories and images that their school education and their everyday world presented to them. It was easier, for instance, to tour a plantation with them and explain why the all-white images and narratives clearly misrepresent history. With the addition of Black faces to reenactments and narratives, an alarm set off that called me to action—in defense of Blackness in history because the record has shown that white histories of others rarely represent them well or accurately, and thus, they cannot be trusted. I had to then critique how and where Black people were included in these new white but "liberal" histories. The critique became a necessity, sometimes on the spot, without the luxury of waiting for debriefing after the fact.

In teaching literature, we encounter and engage history because history is so intertwined with the literary. This interrelatedness includes both the immersion of history in literary works as well as the influence of history in the development and evolution of literary periods and traditions. Together, in the Western academy these disciplines have operated to fabricate a sense of time and place and measurements of human and social worthiness that, no matter how scrambled or rescrambled, bring us back to the paradigm of white and Western as the polar locale of our grander and worthier humanity. The compilation of essays in "The 'Medieval' Undone: Imagining a New Global Past" brings this point to the forefront with a collective lucidity. These works examine the difficulty of reframing the long-standing field of the "Middle Ages/medieval studies" as the global Middle Ages. The global Middle Ages calls on us to see the world during the Western-designated dates of 500–1500 CE as inhabited by populations of Brown, Black, and non-European people who have developed, complex societies. It asks that we stretch our imaginations to see the non-European world as "civilized," and as Shoshana Adler (2023) reminds us in the essay "Spoiled History," engaging global in the new era of medieval studies challenges us to consider early globalism beyond heteronormative constructs of being. The name shift alone will not dismantle intersectional levels of exclusion that have dominated the field from its inception. While global medieval studies acknowledges that the worlds worth knowing before the so-called Age of Exploration were not all white, it remains a discipline unable to break from a Western-constructed ethos that normalizes and situates whiteness as the model from which we are to gauge the merit of all others. And it further continues to impose an ethos of time whose axis moves around a presumption of time that emerges out of white historiography. As conveyed in Rafii's essay in this collection, the damaging racist intellectualism inherent in medieval studies has long flowed over into Western society. This spillover continues to feed a version of history and place that privileges a white supremacist worldview. Invention and interpretation of a white superior humanity encapsulated within and fueled by medievalism survives through the academy's concomitant adherence to Western arrangements of time that follow and center certain Western-valued moments in history.

Even if the academy changes directions, a white population that is served by this mythical version of history and time is unlikely to turn away from it. Long-term change will occur in the social landscape, but it will be a fractured landscape much like the one unveiled in the aftermath of January 6, 2021. We cannot separate the project of Western intellectual imperialism from the seeming innocuous application of numerical divisions of time—that is, periodization—to organize studies of humanity. Time is connected to ethos, to ideology, to experience, and the creation of time and chronology emerge out of particular beliefs about existence and being. The invention called the Middle Ages exemplifies this dependent relationship of time to human cognition. Marked by events in narratives of Western historiography, in concept and effect, the Middle Ages marks time through glorification and validation of Western ideals, experiences, and actions. Non-Westerners/nonwhites are ancillary to the story, and their roles will be bent, broken, and reconfigured to adhere to the larger and looming interconnected narrative of Western time, Western progress, and Western people. Breaking these artificially constructed time walls will not only deliver us from a stasis of white imaginary called the medieval but will also allow us to navigate places and spaces on both sides. Dismantling Western imagined lines of time that separate the Middle Ages from the Age of Exploration, the colonial period, and the modern age, can open up an expanse of possibilities for a more comprehensive understanding of the world at large and a more humane coexistence of global populations.

Throughout the years that I have taught American, African American, Africana, and world literatures, I have found it necessary to revisit literary and historical periods prior to the settler and colonial periods to understand the people and traditions that emerge at the dawn of the exploration age and into modernity. What I find continuously is that while students can envision a transition of white/Europeanism from Old English to Middle/medieval to Renaissance into modernity, they typically do not understand Black people and populations and their histories similarly. They continue to see Black people through the Western-constructed image of tabula rasa—the empty slate that came into being only after Black contact with Europeans. This disconnect has changed my teaching of literature as well as my own research. While in my early career I framed my focus in early Black Atlantic literatures by beginning with the eighteenth century, I could not sustain this fixed point. As I tried to encourage students to understand the fluidity of culture, history, and time that literature captures, I had to seek out ways of knowing and representing human experience through this lens. If African American literature begins in the eighteenth century with figures such as Phillis Wheatley, Prince Hall, and Job ben Solomon, how do we understand the DNA of their imagination if we only start at the shores of America? If they are representative of the great numbers of Africans captured and forced into enslavement in the Americas, then they make the clear case for exploring the continental African histories that brought them to the Americas and informed the world they shaped there.

It was out of research on a current biography project that I became acutely aware of the relevance of the current debates in medieval studies over race and history. These debates again surface as reminders of their implications that reach beyond the discipline of medieval studies itself and the academy as well. In this biography project, I became aware of the necessity of looking back to the pre-1500 period of Western exploration to understand the cultural DNA of the post-1500 African and African descended populations in the Americas. While we readily understand the concept of biological DNA, it is less intuitive to consider that biology is often reflected in human experience. Much like the anatomy of our present human bodies are the embodiment of physical building blocks from centuries of biological reformations and handoffs, present-day cultures or societies are no less the products of lineages that stretch back through ongoing and "mutated"/altered linkages to previous eras. Centuries may separate a generation from a certain traumatic event, but the waves of effect do not halt with the birth of a new generation. This is strikingly evident in the twenty-first century as we look back at the seismic impact that centuries of enslavement still have on Black people, as well as society in general, a century and a half past emancipation.

In the case of my research that has been focusing on a line of descent of two post–Civil War freedwomen in Mississippi, DNA tests showed that the matriarchal haplogroup of one points to the present-day Temne people of West Africa. The recollection of nineteenth-century Black Episcopal priest and activist Alexander Crummell immediately raised my curiosity over this finding. Crummell, whose writings and life were the focus of my dissertation, was a Temne descendant. Crummell's father, Boston Crummell, was captured as a young man and sold into slavery in New York. According to the son Crummell, at some point in Boston Crummell's young adult life, he declared himself free and assumed the status of a free Black citizen of New York (Moses 1989: 12). The son Crummell was born in 1809, and his father, Boston, was likely born sometime in the 1760s or early 1770s. Alexander Crummell reported his family's lineage as having originated from the Temne people in West Africa, and speculation is that Boston was captured around 1780 (11). During Crummell's near-twenty-year span as a missionary for the Episcopal Church in Liberia, he wrote despairingly about the influence of Islam in Liberia and his frustration that this presence negatively impacted the ability of missionaries like himself to make inroads with "the natives," who were either more likely to maintain their own indigenous religions or to practice the Islamic faith. When I wrote my dissertation on Crummell more than two decades ago, I did not consider that his agitation with Islam might have been informed by anything more than his zeal for Christianity. It was only after I looked at the matriarchal DNA that connected descendants of Louisa Dent of Mississippi to the Temne of West Africa that I reconsidered the source of Crummell's frustration and animosity toward Islam.

The Temne people's history is connected to the entrance and spread of Islam during the period known in the Western academy as the Middle Ages (500–1500 AD). In the late 1700s, when Crummell's father was captured, the Sierra Leone or Liberian region from where he may have been captured was then a mix of Islamic, Christian, and Indigenous African faiths. The Temne migrated to coastal Sierra Leone "from Futa Jallon sometime in the late fourteenth or early fifteenth century" (Gomez 1998: 89). The intermingled presence of religious faiths in eighteenth-century Sierra Leone was the result of incursions of Islamic forces from the east and European Christian forces from the Atlantic north. Like his son, Boston Crummell appears to have been a practicing Christian in his life in America. The practicing faith of his family and community in Africa is not clear, but as a Temne, he would have known the history of his ancestors' forced migration from the interior to their pre-eighteenth-century homelands. He would, as well, have known the history of the further push of Temne people toward the coastlines during intensified Muslim takeovers of inland populations during the eighteenth-century period of his life and that of his parents and recent ancestors.

As I pondered how the fourteenth-century migration and resettlement might have impacted the fate of eighteenth-century Temne, I wondered whether the foremother or ancestors of the nineteenth-century matriarch of my study had reached the shores of America by historical circumstances similar to those that informed Boston Crummell's arrival. Just as generations into the future will continue to be impacted by the nation's legacy of enslavement—whether it is consciously acknowledged or silenced—the impact of their forced migration lived on in the cultural DNA of the Temne. While I cannot confirm that Boston Crummell shared the story of his native peoples' removal from their homeland at the hands of Muslim invaders, Alexander Crummell's disdain for Islam could very well have been informed by his father's account. This memory may have served as the impetus for Crummell's determination to be recognized in the Episcopal Church—so much so that when denied entry into the Episcopal priesthood of America, he traveled to England to be granted this opportunity. Crummell claimed that his father had been a Temne prince, but as happened frequently during the period of transatlantic slaving, if captured, African royalty or elites were not spared the forced voyage to the Americas. Crummell's claim of his father's royal status, however, would explain his knowledge of the story and his recollection of the specific nation affiliation. As a prince, his father would have known the history of the Temne and their migration story: he was probably acutely aware of the eighteenth-century jihads that, between the earlier 1700–1749 incursion and the 1750–99 jihad, resulted in a nearly six-to-one increase of African captives (Gomez 1998: 91). Again, Boston Crummell would have remembered the history of his homeland, the part that Islam had played in the migrations of his people, and the wars that resulted in the capture of many who were then remanded into the Atlantic slave trade. Reportedly captured and delivered to the Boston port around 1780, Boston was probably abducted during one of the many conflicts of this warring era.

The conscious memory of migration that had been imparted to Crummell from his father led me to consider the Temne ancestor of Louisa Dent and her descendants. When she arrived at the shores of America and was remanded to enslavement, was this Temne matriarch conscious of the migration history of her continental forebears? Was she a war captive from one of the Temne's resistance to Islamic invasions or other ethnic groups in conflict with the Temne? Did she arrive in the Americas already a Muslim convert? That is, did she live among the population of Temne already converted to Islam? If Louisa's Temne ancestor arrived in the New World already a product of generational migration trauma, already living under the fear of forced removal, how might this have informed her Middle Passage and enslavement experience? How would this have influenced the ethos of migration, geography, and movement that she would have passed down to her children? Would this ethos inform a generational ethos of the inevitability of movement, of migration? Would it create generations of migration anxiety, of longing for security of place? These questions came to mind because, as a descendant of Louisa Dent, I could recall migration stories passed down about my Mississippi ancestors, and I saw throughout my early childhood the anxieties of movement and migration that were negotiated by those family members and close friends who either stayed or left. While it may seem quite a stretch to look at twentieth-century and contemporary African American migration as an extension of the pre–Middle Passage— that is, African migration and movement experiences and philosophies from the Middle Ages—it is clearly worth considering.

Rather than a stretch, exploration of these connections might well be an illustration of global medieval studies done well. This work is not simply an overture to inclusion; instead, with its disengagement from white periodization, it brings to light a more global understanding of Africa and its populations. This assertion is not negligent of Lomuto's reminder that working within medieval studies to undo its Anglocentric imposed lens could easily bring us back to the perplexity of Belle da Costa Greene's legacy at the Morgan Library. Though of African descent, Belle da Costa Greene's mission to help build an American likeness to the legacy of European curations does not appear to have diverted her from the emulation of a Eurocentric tradition. Even as she expanded the library's holdings to include works from non-Western civilizations, there was no overt interrogation of how these works call for rethinking Europe as the metropole of civilization. My point is not to interrogate the motives or character of Belle da Costa Greene but rather to look to her as an example of how working within both the physical and intellectual confines of the academy we might easily slip into a reaffirmation of the very racist paradigms that we call into question. Audre Lorde (1984: 112) issued this warning decades ago with her assertion that "the master's tools will never dismantle the master's house. They may allow us to temporarily beat him at his own game, but they will never enable us to bring about genuine change." With the reminder of Belle da Costa Greene's legacy, Lorde's question looms large. If the quest is to facilitate meaningful and long-lasting change, can those who have been historically and systematically castigated by and exiled from the academy—and its presumptive position as gatekeeper of "worthwhile" art and intellectualism—make the "reuse" of this machinery into something more to the benefit of all?

I live within the academy guided by a will to affect the genuine change that is needed for the benefit of the collective, but I also accept that the structure was built out of the alloys of white interests and white ways of knowing and weighing the world (and people). That alloy is oxidizing, but whether it simply needs a coat of paint or a partial or complete replacement remains unclear. In the meantime, I find myself journeying into the world of global medieval studies. As its specialists revisit who they are and where the field is heading, I cross over their intellectual borderlines—interloping perhaps—in search of knowledge and resources to fill out more clearly the more probable reality that Africans arrived *tabula inscripta* to the shores of the Americas from their forced voyages across the Atlantic. Their forced journeys were not the consequence of an inevitable march to progress powered by destined forces of whiteness through the unfolding of time, as Western anthropocentric narrations suggest. African captives in the Americas had come from population groups that were varied in the degree to which they were in contact with or impacted by other nations—on and beyond the continent of

Africa. They came from centuries-old cultures and nations that had their own worldviews and traditions, and they held these as they arrived in the Americas. The circumstances of their abduction and enslavement in the Americas were tied to the state of affairs of their nations at the time of their capture, but as my reflection on Alexander Crummell illustrates, their moment of capture was connected to times and histories that preceded the Middle Passage.

The analysis of Alexander Crummell as a product of more than the nearly nine decades of his lifetime took me into deeper time, into the so-called medieval period more than four centuries prior to Atlantic slaving. Essays in this *boundary 2* special issue that focused on the matter of interpreting Islam within the construct of the Middle Ages were especially thought-provoking for my reflections on Crummell and the historical scope of his views on Islam. In particular, with the reminder that medieval Christianity gave birth to the Western academy, Christopher Livanos and Mohammad Salama (2023) traced the arc of Islamophobia from the Middle Ages to the present. Their article led me to consider more closely how Crummell's nineteenth-century anti-Islamic rhetoric might have been shaped by both his formal theological training and the history of his forebears impacted by West African jihads centuries earlier. Having crossed over briefly into the battleground of the global Middle Ages, it will become increasingly difficult for me to operate within the silos of periodization and time that have long confined my scholarly work and perspective. I traverse these boundaries keeping in mind Audre Lorde's profound assertion on the paradox of employing the master's tool as a means to liberation. In fact, I hear echoes of Lorde's warning in Julie Orlemanski's (2023) essay, which warns against belief in the power of postmedievalism to move us past the originating ethos of white, Eurocentric medievalism. She argues that prefixing medievalism with "post-" will not stave off the systemic racist propensity built into the originating language and ethos of its antecedent. As the new iteration of the field circles back to its origins, Europe remains the prototype for understanding the world through a globalist lens.

In contrast to Orlemanski, Anne Le and Adam Miyashiro suggest that perhaps medieval studies can reconcile its Eurocentric roots to engage studies in world populations and cosmologies. Both Le and Miyashiro rest their arguments in what they see as academia's already improving trajectory in addressing its history of racial exclusionism. Le's (2023) essay argues for employing postcolonial frameworks as a pathway to steer studies in medieval French literature out of restrictive Western epistemologies. Extolling the contributions of works such as Edward Said's *Orientalism*, Conklin Akbari's *Idols in the East*, and Sharon Kinoshita's *Medieval Boundaries* as examples, Le sees the potential of academia to combat its own historical racism. Similarly, Miyashiro (2023) points to comparative literature as example of how medieval studies can effectively address the racism embedded in the field. Miyashiro points out that comparative literature still struggles to disengage itself from its Eurocentric origins but that scholarship in this field has offered inroads and insight from which medievalists might benefit. In particular, Miyashiro underscores the paradigm of "tributary empires" as a pathway from the limiting and Western-imposed ideals of periodization, nation, and identity. Le and Miyashiro offer promising looks at methodologies and works that show pathways to the needed racial reckoning in medieval studies. The challenge remains, however, for a reckoning or conceding of power from within: medieval studies is a house built on the premise that the poles of civilization and humanity point to whiteness. Socially, politically, and economically this has been a lucrative paradigm for those who identify as white—both in and outside the academy. The question, then, is whether individual works contesting this history can amount to a systematic paradigm shift. Can the discriminated as well as the master herself employ the master's tools to reboot the master machinery?

A turn to Raha Rafii's (2023) essay brings us back to Audre Lorde's emphatic "no" to such speculation. With the conclusion that Western academic institutions are simply part of a machinery that reinscribes and reimposes Eurocentric knowledge and epistemologies, Rafii's essay echoes Lorde's warning. I am guided in the academy by hearing the arguments on both sides. Perhaps as a wish or desire to believe in the work that I do and its potential for meaningful change, I proceed within the academy armed with Lorde's wisdom but convinced that it is imperative to work both within and beyond. I adopt this approach mindful of what Shokoofeh Rajabzadeh divulges as the structural inequity of intellectual query in academia. Rajabzadeh's article explains that one of the more harrowing realities of Eurocentrism in medieval studies is its regenerative force—that is, that graduate students and newly minted PhDs are some of the most staunch proponents of long-standing practices and ideologies of exclusion. In general, nontraditionalists in medieval studies agree that to dismantle the field's white supremacist anchoring, those committed must themselves make a concerted effort to avoid practices and ideologies that replicate colonialist epistemologies. However, if the example of her own graduate education experience portends the future, Rajabzadeh suggests that trying to intervene is nearly impossible. Whether it will ever be possible to dismantle the embedded racist epistemology that is the master tool of Western intellectualism, part of the struggle is to not leave it uncontested. There is certainly danger in attempting repair with the tool that has inflicted injury; however, entering the belly of the beast is often a necessity, if only to map out more clearly its operations. With the conclusion that the academy's foundation will not allow for a remodeling that would reverse its undergirding Eurocentrism, Rafii maintains that to realize long-lasting impact, the work must be done beyond the halls of the academy. Again, I concur that the machine operates for its own interests, but to leave it to itself, unchallenged from within, is to grant it wider spaces for regeneration. It is in the dual space of within and beyond the academy that tools of resistance will be cultivated to affect genuine change within and beyond academia.

References

Adler, Shoshana. 2023. "Spoiled History: Leprosy and the Lessons of Queer Medieval Historiography." In Lomuto 2023: 211–32.

Gomez, Michael. 1998. *Exchanging Our Country's Marks: The Transformation of African Identities in the Colonial and Antebellum South*. Chapel Hill: University of North Carolina Press.

Le, Anne. 2023. "Different and Familiar: *Les enfances Renier* and the Question of Medieval Orientalism." In Lomuto 2023: 189–209.

Livanos, Christopher, and Mohammad Salama. 2023. "A Bridge Too Far? Ludovico Marracci's Translation of the Qur'an and the Persistence of Medieval Biblicism." In Lomuto 2023: 145–69.

Lomuto, Sierra. 2023a. "Belle da Costa Greene and the Undoing of 'Medieval' Studies." In Lomuto 2023: 1–30.

Lomuto, Sierra, ed. 2023b. "The 'Medieval' Undone: Imagining a New Global Past." Special issue, *boundary 2* 50, no. 3.

Lorde, Audre. 1984. "The Master's Tools Will Never Dismantle the Master's House." In *Sister Outsider: Essays and Speeches*, 110–13. Berkeley, CA: Crossing.

Min, Mariah. 2023. "Undoing Medieval Race Studies." In Lomuto 2023: 173–88.

Miyashiro, Adam. 2023. "Race, Medieval Studies, and Disciplinary Boundaries." In Lomuto 2023: 107–21.

Moses, Wilson Jeremiah. 1989. *Alexander Crummell: A Study of Civilization and Discontent*. New York: Oxford University Press.

Orlemanski, Julie. 2023. "What Is 'Postmedieval'? Embedded Reflections." In Lomuto 2023: 57–81.

Rafii, Raha. 2023. "Making Islam (Coherent): Academic Discourse and the Politics of Language." In Lomuto 2023: 33–55.

Rajabzadeh, Shokoofeh. 2023. "Fighting for the Middle: Medieval Studies Programs and Degrees within Higher Education." In Lomuto 2023: 123–44.

Warren, Michelle R. 2023. "The Medieval of the Long Now." In Lomuto 2023: 83–103.

Contributors

Shoshana Adler is assistant professor of English at Vanderbilt University, specializing in medieval English literature, cultural histories of race, and queer theory. Her work is forthcoming in *Exemplaria* and *The Routledge Companion to Global Chaucer*.

Anne Le holds a PhD in French and Francophone Studies from the University of California, Los Angeles, and is the Public Humanities Postdoctoral Fellow at the University of Notre Dame's Medieval Institute. She specializes in romances and chansons de geste from the twelfth and thirteenth centuries. Her research interests include representations of interfaith contact across the medieval Mediterranean, conversion narratives, and genealogy.

Christopher Livanos is professor of comparative literature at the University of Wisconsin–Madison. He has published on medieval Latin literature and theology and relations between Eastern and Western Christianity in the medieval and early modern periods. His work also examines the intersections of classical and Middle Eastern influences on medieval Latin and Greek literature.

Sierra Lomuto (she/her) is assistant professor of English and global medieval literatures at Rowan University. She holds a PhD from the University of Pennsylvania and an MA and BA from Mills College. Her research focuses on the relations between Latin Europe and the Mongol Empire, and the racialization of Asians in medieval England's literature and culture.

Mariah Min is a postdoctoral fellow in medieval studies and race at Brown University. She received her PhD in English from the University of Pennsylvania in 2019. Her book manuscript, "Figure Writing: Technologies of Character in Medieval Literature," examines medieval literary characters in order to disentangle the long-standing conflation of character and human subjectivity within both critical and popular discourse.

boundary 2 50:3 (2023)   DOI 10.1215/01903659-10799221   ©2023 by Duke University Press

Adam Miyashiro is associate professor of literature at Stockton University in New Jersey. He completed a PhD in comparative literature at Penn State, is on the advisory board of the journal *Early Middle English*, and has published articles and reviews in *Literature Compass*, *postmedieval*, *Comparative Literature Studies*, the *Journal of Law and Religion*, *Notes and Queries*, and *Neophilologus*.

Julie Orlemanski is associate professor of English at the University of Chicago and author of *Symptomatic Subjects: Bodies, Medicine, and Causation in the Literature of Late Medieval England* (2019). She is coeditor of *postmedieval: a journal of medieval cultural studies* and of *The Middle Ages*, volume A of *The Norton Anthology of English Literature*, 11th ed. (forthcoming in 2023).

Raha Rafii is an honorary fellow at the Institute of Arab and Islamic Studies at the University of Exeter. She received her PhD from the Department of Near Eastern Languages and Civilizations at the University of Pennsylvania in 2019, MSt degrees in Oriental Studies and Jewish Studies from the University of Oxford, and a BS in International Politics from Georgetown University.

Shokoofeh Rajabzadeh holds a PhD in English and medieval studies from the University of California, Berkeley, and an MPhil from Oxford University. Her dissertation, "The Muslim Prism: Reflections and Refractions of the Racialized Premodern Muslim Body," theorizes the racialization of Muslims. She is a 2020 Ford Foundation Fellow. Her scholarly articles have been published in *Literature Compass*, an MLA Teaching Volume, and *postmedieval*.

Mohammad Salama is professor and chair of the Department of Modern and Classical Languages at George Mason University. His recent work includes *The Qur'an and Modern Arabic Literary Criticism* (2018) and *Islam and the Culture of Modern Egypt* (2018). His current book project, *God's Other Book*, interrogates recent trends in Euro-American scholarship and turns to literary significations in pre-Islamic poetry as more appropriate tools for approaching the Qur'an.

Michelle R. Warren (she/they) is professor of comparative literature at Dartmouth College. Their most recent book is *Holy Digital Grail: A Medieval Book on the Internet* (2022). They also lead the collaborative digital research project *Remix the Manuscript: A Chronicle of Digital Experiments* (https://sites.dartmouth.edu/RemixBrut). Their motto is The Middle Ages Aren't Old.

Elizabeth J. West is professor of English and the John B. and Elena Diaz-Verson Amos Distinguished Chair in English Letters at Georgia State University. She serves as director of academics for the Center for Studies on Africa and Its Diaspora (CSAD). She is the author of *Finding Francis: One Family's Journey from Slavery to Freedom* (2022).